HUMOROUS HITS

AND

How to Hold an Audience

Printing Statement:

Due to the very old age and scarcity of this book,
many of the pages may be hard to read due to the
blurring of the original text, possible missing pages,
missing text and other issues beyond our control.

Because this is such an important and rare work, we
believe it is best to reproduce this book regardless of
its original condition.

Thank you for your understanding.

HUMOROUS HITS

AND

How to Hold an Audience

A COLLECTION OF SHORT
SELECTIONS, STORIES AND
SKETCHES FOR ALL OCCASIONS

By

GRENVILLE KLEISER

Author of "How to Speak in Public"

FIFTH EDITION

FUNK & WAGNALLS COMPANY

NEW YORK AND LONDON

1912

INTRODUCTORY

In preparing this volume the author has been guided by his own platform experience extending over twelve years. During that time he has given hundreds of public recitals before audiences of almost every description, and in all parts of the country. It may not be considered presumptuous, therefore, for him to offer some practical suggestions on the art of entertaining and holding an audience, and to indicate certain selections which he has found have in themselves the elements of success.

The "encore fiend," as he is sometimes called, is so ubiquitous and insistent that no speaker or reader can afford to ignore him, and, indeed, must prepare for him in advance. To find material that will satisfy him in one or in a dozen of the ordinary books of selections is an almost impossible task. It is only too obvious that many compilations of the kind are put together by persons who have had little or no practical platform experience. In an attempt to remedy this defect this volume has been prepared.

It is believed that the book will be valuable not only to the amateur and the professional reader, speaker, elocutionist, and entertainer, but also to the after-dinner and impromptu speaker, the politician who wants to make a "hit," the business man who wishes to tell a good story and tell it effectively, the school-teacher in arranging her "Friday Afternoon" programs, as well as for reading aloud in the family circle, and for many other occasions.

Providing, as this work does, helpful hints on how to hold an audience, it is hoped that the additional suggestions offered regarding the use of the voice and its modulation, the art of pausing, the development of feeling and energy, the use of gesture and action, the cultivation of the imagination, the committing of selections to memory, and the standing before an audience, while not as elaborate and detailed as found in a regular manual of elocution, will be of practical benefit to those who can not conveniently command the services of a personal instructor.

The author has been greatly assisted in this undertaking not only by the kind permission of publishers and authors to use their copyrighted work, but also by the hearty co-operation of many distinguished platform speakers and readers who have generously contributed successful selections not hitherto published.

The author gratefully acknowledges the special permission granted him by the publishers to print the following copyright selections: "Keep A-goin'!" the Bobbs-Merrill Company; "A Modern Romance," the Publishers of *The Smart Set;* "The Fool's Prayer," Houghton, Mifflin & Company; "Mammy's Li'l' Boy," and " 'Späcially Jim," the Century Company; "Counting One Hundred," the Lothrop, Lee & Shepard Company; "At Five O'clock Tea," the Publishers of *Lippincott's Magazine.*

GRENVILLE KLEISER.

New York City,
  February, 1908.

CONTENTS

PAGE

PART III—SERIOUS HITS

CONTENTS xiii

PART I

HOW TO HOLD AN AUDIENCE

HOW TO HOLD AN AUDIENCE

To hold the interest of an audience and to successfully entertain it—whether from public platform, in fraternal organization, by after-dinner speech, or in the home circle—is a worthy accomplishment. Moreover, the memorizing of selections and rendering them before an audience is one of the best preparations for the larger and more important work of public speaking. Many of our most successful after-dinner speakers depend almost entirely upon their ability to tell a good story.

The art of reciting and story-telling has become so popular in recent years that a wide-spread demand has arisen for books of selections and suggestions for rendering them. Material suitable for encores has been particularly difficult to find. It is thought, therefore, that the present volume, containing as it does a great variety of short numbers, will meet with approval.

There is, perhaps, no talent that is more entertaining and more instructive than that of reciting aloud specimens of prose and poetry, both humorous and serious, from our best writers. Channing says:

"Is there not an amusement, having an affinity with the drama, which might be usefully introduced among us? I mean, Recitation.

"A work of genius, recited by a man of fine taste, enthusiasm, and powers of elocution, is a very pure and high gratification.

"Were this art cultivated and encouraged, great numbers, now insensible to the most beautiful compositions, might be waked up to their excellence and power.

"It is not easy to conceive of a more effectual way of spreading a refined taste through a community. The drama undoubtedly appeals more strongly to the passions than recitation; but the latter brings out the meaning of the author more. Shakespeare, worthily recited, would be better understood than on the stage.

"Recitation, sufficiently varied, so as to include pieces of chaste wit, as well as of pathos, beauty, and sublimity, is adapted to our present intellectual progress."

To recite well, and to be able to hold an audience, one should be trained in the proper use of the voice and body in expression. This requires painstaking study and preparation. It is a mistake to suppose that much can be safely left to impulse and the inspiration of the occasion. With all great artists everything is premeditated, studied, and rehearsed beforehand.

Salvini, the great Italian tragedian, said to the pupils in his art: "Above all, study,—*study,*—STUDY. All the genius in the world will not help you along with any art, unless you become a hard student. It has taken me years to master a single part."

THE VOICE

The voice can be rapidly and even wonderfully developed by practising for a few minutes daily exercises prescribed in any good manual of elocution.[1] Learn to speak

---

[1] See "How to Speak in Public," a complete manual of elocution, by Grenville Kleiser. Published by Funk & Wagnalls Company. Price, $1.25 net.

in the natural voice. If it is high-pitched, nasal, thin, or unmusical, these defects can be overcome by patient and judicious practise. Do not assume an artificial voice, except in impersonation. Remember that intelligent audiences demand intelligent expression, and will not tolerate the ranting, bombast, and unnatural style of declamation of former days.

Many people speak with half-shut teeth and mouth. Open the mouth and throat freely; liberate all the muscles around the vocal apparatus. Aim to speak with ease, and endeavor to improve the voice in depth, purity, roundness, and flexibility. Daily conversation offers the best opportunity for this practise.

A writer recently said: "Only a very, very few of us Americans speak English as the English do. We have our own 'accent,' as it is called. We are a nervous, eager, strident people. We know it, tho we do not relish having foreigners tell us about it. We speak not mellowly, not with lax tongues and palates, but sharply, shrilly, with hardened mouth and with tones forced back upon the palate. We strangulate two-thirds of our vowels and swallow half the other third. Pure, round, sonorous tones are almost never heard in our daily speech."

Speak from the abdomen. All the effort, all the motive power, should come from the waist and abdominal muscles. These are made to stand the strain that is so often incorrectly put upon the muscles of the throat. Aim at a forward tone; that is, send your voice out to some distant object, imaginary or otherwise, without unduly elevating the pitch. The voice should strike against the hard palate, the hard bony arch just above the upper teeth. Most of the practising should be done on the low pitches.

If there is any serious physical defect of the throat or nose, consult a reliable physician.

Do not overtax the voice. Three periods of ten minutes each are better than an hour's practise at one time. Stop at the first sign of weariness. Do not practise within an hour after eating. Avoid the habitual use of lozenges. There is nothing better for the throat than a gargle of salt and water, used night and morning. Dash cold water on the outside of the throat and rub it vigorously with a coarse towel.

THE BREATH

The proper management of the breath is an important part of good speaking. Some teachers say the air should be inhaled on all occasions exclusively through the nose. This is practically impossible while in the act of speaking. The aim should be to speak on full lungs as much as possible; therefore a breath must be taken at every opportunity. This is done during the pauses, but often the time is so short that the speaker will find it necessary to use both mouth and nose to get a full supply of air. The breathing should be inaudible.

Practise deep breathing until it becomes an unconscious habit. *In taking in the breath the abdomen and chest both expand, and in giving out the breath the abdomen and chest both contract.* By this method of respiration the abdomen is used as a kind of "bellows," and the strain is taken entirely off the throat. The breathing should be done without noticeable effort and without raising the shoulders. Whenever possible the breathing should be long and deep. While speaking, endeavor to hold back in the lungs, or reservoir, the supply of air, "feeding" it very gradually to the vocal cords in just the quantity required for a given tone. Reciting aloud, when properly done, is a healthful exercise, and the voice should grow and improve through use; but to speak on half-filled lungs, or from the throat, is distressing and often injurious.

Keep your shoulders well thrown back, head erect, chin level, arms loosely at the sides, and in walking throw the leg out from the hip with easy, confident movement. The weight of the body should be on the ball of the foot, altho the whole foot touches the floor. The breathing should be deep, smooth, and deliberate.

When the breath is not being used in speech, breathe exclusively through the nose. This is particularly desirable during the hours of sleep. As someone has said, if you awake at night and find your mouth open, get up and shut it. A well-known English authority on elocution says that as a golden rule for the preservation of the health, he considers the habit of breathing through the nose invaluable if not imperative. Air, which is the breath of life, has always floating in it also the seeds of death. The nose is a filter and deodorizer, in passing through which the air is cleansed and sent pure into the lungs. The nose warms the air as well as purifies it, and thus prevents it from being breathed in that raw, damp state which is so injurious to those whose lungs are delicate.

Speak immediately upon opening your mouth. Try to turn into pure-toned voice every particle of breath you give out. Replenish the lungs every time you pause. Light gymnastics, brisk walking, running, horseback riding, and other exercise will improve your breathing capacity.

MODULATION

Modulation simply means change of voice. These changes, however, must be intelligent and appropriate to the thought. Monotony—speaking in one tone—must be avoided. The speaker should have the ability to raise or lower the pitch of his voice at will, as well as to vary it in force, intensity, inflection, etc.

Do not confuse "pitch" with "force." Pitch refers to the *key* of the speaking voice, while force relates to the *loudness* of the voice. The movement or rate of speaking should be varied to suit the particular thought. It would be ridiculous to describe a horse-race in the slow, measured tones of a funeral procession.

Most of your speaking should be done in the middle and lower registers; but the higher pitches, altho not so often required, must be trained so as to be ready for use. These higher tones are frequently thin and unmusical, but they can be made full and firm through practise.

It is not necessary to study many rules for inflection. The speaker should know in a general way that when the sense is suspended the voice follows this tendency and runs up, and when the sense is completed the voice runs down. In other words, the voice should simply be in agreement with the tendency of the thought, whether it opens up or closes down. The lengths of inflection vary according to the thought and the required emphasis.

For most occasions **the speaking should be clear-cut and deliberate.** The larger the room or hall, the slower should be the speech, to give the vocal vibrations time to travel. Dwelling on words too long, drawling, or over precision in articulation, is tedious to an audience. The other extreme, undue haste, suggests lack of self-control, and is fatal to successful effort. Of course this does not apply to special selections demanding rapid speech.

There are numerous words in English that represent or at least suggest their meaning in their sound. One who aims to read or recite well should study these effects so as to use them skilfully and with judgment.

The most complete and concise treatment on the subject of expression is perhaps that given in *Hamlet's* advice to the players when he says:

"Speak the speech, I pray you, as I pronounced it to you—*trippingly* on the tongue; but if you mouth it, as many of your players do, I had as lief the town crier spoke my lines. Nor do not saw the air too much with your hand, thus; but use all gently: for in the very torrent, tempest, and as I may say whirlwind of your passion, you must acquire and beget a temperance that may give it smoothness. O! it offends me to the soul, to hear a robustious periwig-pated fellow tear a passion to tatters, to very rags, to split the ears of the groundlings; who, for the most part, are capable of nothing but inexplicable dumb-shows, and noise. I would have such a fellow whipped for o'erdoing Termagant; it out-herods Herod: pray you, avoid it. . . .

"Be not too tame neither, but let your own discretion be your tutor: suit the action to the word, the word to the action, with this special observance, that you o'erstep not the modesty of nature; for anything so overdone is from the purpose of playing, whose end, both at the first, and now, was, and is, to hold, as 't were, the mirror up to nature; to show virtue her own feature, scorn her own image, and the very age and body of the time, his form and pressure. Now, this overdone, or come tardy off, tho it make

the unskilful laugh, can not but make the judicious grieve;
the censure of the which one must, in your allowance,
o'erweigh a whole theater of others. O! there be players,
that I have seen play—and heard others praise, and that
highly—not to speak it profanely, that, neither having
the accent of Christians, nor the gait of Christian, pagan,
nor man, have so strutted and bellowed, that I have thought
some of nature's journeymen had made men, and not made
them well, they imitated humanity so abominably.''

PAUSING

Words naturally divide themselves into groups according to their meaning. Grammatical pauses indicate the
construction of language, while rhetorical pauses mark
more particularly the natural divisions in the sense. To
jumble words together, or to rattle them off in "rapid-
fire" style, is not an entertaining performance. Proper
pausing secures economy of the listener's attention, and
is as desirable in spoken as in written language.

Pauses should vary in frequency and duration. It
should be remembered that words are only symbols, and
that the speaker should concern himself seriously about
the thought which these symbols represent. The concept
behind the sign is the important thing. The fine art of
pausing can be acquired only after long and faithful study.
Then it may become an unconscious habit. An old rime
on this subject is worth repeating:

> "In pausing, ever let this rule take place,
> Never to separate words in any case
> That are less separable than those you join;
> And, which imports the same, not to combine
> Such words together, as do not relate
> So closely as the words you separate."

FEELING AND ENERGY

Before you can properly *feel* what you say you must *understand* it. Artificial and imitative methods do not produce enduring results. In studying a passage or selection for recitation, the imagination must be kindled, the feelings stimulated, and the mind trained to concentrate upon the thought until it is *experienced*. This subjective work should always precede the attempt at objective expression. Everything must first be conceived, pictured, and experienced in the mind. When this is done with intelligence, sincerity, and earnestness, there should be little difficulty in giving true and adequate expression to thought.

In all speaking that is worth the while there must be energy, force, and life. The speaker should be wide-awake, alert, palpitating. A speaker—and this applies to the reciter and elocutionist—should be, as someone has said, "an animal galvanic battery on two legs."[1] He must know what he is about. He must *be in earnest.*

Make a distinction between loudness and intensity. Often the best effects are produced by suggesting power in reserve rather than giving the fullest outward expression. Intensity in reading or reciting is secured chiefly through concentration and a thorough grasp of the thought. Endeavor to put yourself into your voice. Do not forget that deep, concentrated feeling is never loud. Avoid shouting, ranting, and "tearing a passion to tatters." Go to nature for models. Ask what one would do in real life in uttering the thoughts under consideration.

---

[1] See "Before an Audience," by Nathan Sheppard. Published by Funk & Wagnalls Company. Price, 75 cents.

The emotions must be brought under control by frequent practise. Joy, sorrow, anger, fear, surprize, terror, and other feelings are as colors to the artist and must be made ready for instant use. To quote Richard Mansfield:

"When you are enacting a part, think of your voice as a color, and, as you paint your picture (the character you are painting, the scene you are portraying), mix your colors. You have on your palate a white voice, *la voix blanche;* a heavenly, ethereal or blue voice, the voice of prayer; a disagreeable, jealous, or yellow voice; a steel-gray voice, for quiet sarcasm; a brown voice of hopelessness; a lurid, red voice of hot rage; a deep, thunderous voice of black; a cheery voice, the color of the green sea that a brisk breeze is crisping; and then there is a pretty little pink voice, and shades of violet—but the subject is endless."

GESTURE AND ACTION

No better advice can be given upon this subject than to "Suit the action to the word; the word to the action." Unless a gesture in some way helps in the expression and understanding of a thought, it should be omitted. Gesture is not a mere ornament, but a natural and necessary part of true expression. The arms and hands should be trained to perform their work gracefully, promptly, and effectively. If too many gestures are used they lose their force and meaning. Furthermore, too many gestures confuse and annoy the auditor.

Gesture should be practised, preferably before a looking-glass, so thoroughly *beforehand* as to make it an unconscious act when the speaker comes before his audience.

The correct standing position is to have one foot slightly in advance of the other. The taller the person, the broader should be the base or width between the feet. The body should be erect but not rigid. In repose the arms should drop naturally at the sides. Except in the act of gesticulating do not try to put the hands anywhere, and above all, if a man, not in the pockets.

IMPERSONATION

The aim here should be to lose one's self in the part. To subordinate one's tones, gestures, and manners, and to live the character for the time being, requires no mean ability. Impersonation calls for imagination, insight, concentration, and adaptability. The impersonator must be all at it, and at it all, during the whole time he is impersonating the character.

"To fathom the depths of character," said Macready, the distinguished English actor, "to trace its latent motives, to feel its finest quiverings of emotion, to comprehend the thoughts that are hidden under words, and thus possess one's self of the actual mind of the individual man, is the highest reach of the player's art, and is an achievement that I have discerned but in few. Kean—when under the impulse of his genius he seemed to *clutch* the whole idea of the man—was an extraordinary instance among those possessing the faculty of impersonation."

Where dialect is used it should be closely studied from life. Stage representations of foreign character are not always trustworthy models.

ARTICULATION AND PRONUNCIATION

Articulate and pronounce correctly and distinctly without being pedantic. The organs of articulation—teeth, tongue, lips, and palate—should be trained to rapidly and accurately repeat various sets of elements, until any combination of sounds, no matter how difficult, can be uttered with facility, accuracy, and precision.

A standard dictionary should be consulted whenever there is a doubt either about the meaning or the pronunciation of a word. As to the standard of pronunciation, the speaker should consider at least these three things: (1) authority, (2) custom, and (3) personal taste.

There are many words commonly mispronounced, but only a few can be referred to here: Do not say *Toos*-day or *Chews*-day for Tuesday; *ur*-ride for ride; i-*ron* for i-*urn;* w*us* for w*as*; th*un* for th*an*; subj*i*ct for subj*e*ct; a*wf*-fiss for *off*-fiss; fig-*ger* for figure; to-*wards* for tords; *dook* for d*uke*; k*etch* for c*atch*; *day*-po for *de*-po; ab'domen for abdo'men; advertise'ment for adver'tisement; ly'ceum for lyce'um; oc'cult for occult'; of*ten* for of'n; s*e*nce for s*i*nce; su*j*gest for su*gg*est; *wow*nd for w*oo*nd; w*eth*er for wh*eth*er; sen'ile for se'nile; a*d*'dress for ad*dress*'; il'lustrate for illus'trate; k*er*-own for crown; wind*er* for wind*ow;* s*or* for s*aw;* wick*ud* for wick*ed;* *i*ngine for *e*ngine; *o*ntil for *u*ntil.

Words should drop from the mouth like newly-made coins from the mint. Practising on words of several syllables is helpful. Some such as these will serve as examples: ''particularly,'' ''unconstitutional,'' ''incompatibility,'' ''unnecessarily,'' ''voluminous,'' ''overwhelmingly,'' ''sesquipedalian,'' etc.

IMAGINATION

The ability to make vivid mental pictures of what one recites is of great value to both reader and hearer. Everyone has this faculty to some degree, but few develop it as it should be developed for use in speaking. The clearer the mental picture the speaker has in mind the more vivid will it be to the hearer. Practise making mental images with pictures that appeal strongly to you. **Try to see everything in detail.** If at first the impressions are obscure, persevere in your practise and substantial results will surely come. Dr. Silas Neff gives a splendid illustration of this kind that can be effectively used for practise:

"A woodman once lived with his family near a shallow stream which flowed between high banks and in the middle of which, opposite his house, was an island. Half a mile up the stream was a dam which supplied water for a sawmill a hundred yards below. One morning after the father had gone to the mill to work, leaving his wife in the back yard washing some little garments, their two little boys clambered down the bank and waded through the water to the island where they had spent many happy hours in play. About the middle of the forenoon, from some unknown cause, the wall of the dam suddenly gave way, the water plunging through and nearly filling the banks of the stream. The father in the mill heard the noise and looking out saw what had happened. Immediately thinking of his boys he dashed out, hat and coat off, on an awful race down the creek to save their lives. The water after leaving the dam flowed rather slowly for some time and he was soon quite a distance ahead, but he knew that unless he gained very rapidly here, the descent being much greater farther down, the water would overtake his boys before he could reach them. His wife suddenly looked up as the agonizing cries of her husband fell upon her ear. She rushed to the front yard. In quick succession she distinguished the words, 'Get the boys!' The father was a few hundred yards from his home. The water had reached the rapid part of the stream but some distance behind the man. The wife on hearing the words, tho not knowing what was wrong, jumped down the bank and ran through the water, shrieking to the boys. Just as she reached the island they ran to her and, without uttering a word, she took one under each arm and started back as wildly as she came. When half way over she saw her husband dashing out from the edge of the woods and the water not twenty feet behind him. They met at the top of the bank, the father grasped wife and children in his arms and the water passed harmlessly by.''[1]

HOW TO MEMORIZE A SELECTION

Do not learn a selection simply by rote—that is, by repeating it parrot-like over and over again—but fix it in the mind by a careful and detailed analysis of the thought. As you practise aloud, train your eye to take in as many words as possible, then look away from the book as you recite them aloud. This will give the memory immediate practise and will tend to make it self-reliant.

Having chosen a selection, read it over first in a general way to secure an impression of it in its entirety. Then read it a second time, giving particular attention to each part. Consult a dictionary for the correct meaning and pronunciation of every word about which you are in doubt. Next underline the emphatic words—those which you think best express the most important thoughts. Underscoring one line for emphatic words and two lines for the most emphatic will do for this purpose. Now indicate the various pauses, both grammatical and rhetorical, by drawing short perpen-

"Talks on Education and Oratory," by Silas S. Neff, Neff College of Oratory, Philadelphia, Pa.

dicular lines between the words where they occur. In a
general way use one line for a short pause, two lines for a
medium pause, and three lines for a long pause. On the
margin of the selection you may make other notes, such as
the dominant feeling, transitions, changes of rate, force
and pitch, special effects, gestures, facial expression, etc.

There is, of course, nothing arbitrary about this work of
analysis. Its purpose is to make the student *think*, to an-
alyze, to be painstaking. The following annotated selection
should be carefully considered. Words on which chief emphasis is to be placed are printed in small capitals; those on
which less emphasis is to be placed, in italics. It is not intended to be mechanical, but suggestive. After a few selections have been analyzed in this way, pausing and emphasis,
and many other elements of expression, will largely take
care of themselves.

"To BE || or NOT | to be, || *that* | is the question :—|||
Whether | 't is *nobler* | in the mind, || to *suffer*
The *slings* | and *arrows* || of *outrageous* fortune; ||
Or | to take *arms* | against a *sea* | of troubles, ||
And by *opposing* || *end* them? |||—To DIE,—|| to SLEEP, |||
No *more;*—||| and, by a *sleep*, || to say we end
The *heart-ache,* | and the *thousand* natural shocks ||
That flesh is *heir* to,—||| 't is a consummation ||
Devoutly | to be *wish'd.* ||| To DIE,—||| to SLEEP :—|||
To SLEEP ||| perchance to DREAM : || ay, | *there's* the *rub;* ||
For in that sleep | of *death* || what *dreams* | MAY | come, ||
When we have shuffled off | this mortal coil, ||
Must give us *pause.* ||| *There's* the *respect,* |
That makes *calamity* | of *so long life:* |||
For who would bear | the *whips* and *scorns* | of *time,* ||

The oppressor's *wrong,* || the proud man's *contumely,* ||
The pangs | of *despis'd* love, || the law's *delay,* ||
The *insolence* | of office, || and the *spurns* |
That patient *merit* | of the *unworthy* takes, ||
When he *himself* | might his *quietus* make ||
With a bare *bodkin?* || who'd these *fardels* bear, ||
To *grunt* and *sweat* | under a weary life, ||
But that the *dread* | of SOMETHING | *after* death—||
The *undiscover'd* country, || from whose bourn |
No traveler returns,—|| puzzles the *will,* ||
And makes us rather bear | those ills we *have,* ||
Than fly | to *others* || that we know not of? ||||
Thus CONSCIENCE || does make COWARDS | of us all ; ||
And thus | the native hue | of *resolution* ||
Is sicklied o'er | with the *pale cast* | of *thought;* ||
And enterprises | of great *pith* and *moment* ||
With *this* regard | their currents turn awry, ||
And *lose* | the *name* || of ACTION.''

BEFORE THE AUDIENCE

As you present yourself to your audience, bow slightly and graciously from the waist. Be courteous, but not servile. Avoid haste and familiarity. Be punctilious in dress and deportment, and be prompt in keeping your appointments.

Be sure you have everything ready in advance. If you have to use any properties, such as a table, chair, eye-glass, books, reading-stand, coat, hat, gloves, letters, etc., see that everything is provided and in its place before the time set for your appearance.

Success often depends upon the judicious choice of selections for the occasion. What will be acceptable to one audience may not please another. The sentiment and the length of selections depend upon the time and place where they are to be given. When an audience expects to be entertained with humorous recitations, to announce in a sepulchral voice that you will give them a poem of your own composition, entitled "The Three Corpses," of melancholy character, is likely to send a chill of disappointment through them.

Never keep your audience waiting. If an encore is demanded, return and bow, or if the demand is insistent, give another number, preferably a short one. Do not be too eager to give encores; if the applause is not insistent, a bow will suffice.

PART II

HUMOROUS HITS

THE TRAIN-MISSER

BY JAMES WHITCOMB RILEY

'Ll where in the world my eyes has bin—
Ef I haint missed that train agin!
Chuff! and whistle! and toot! and ring!
But blast and blister the dasted train!—
How it does it I can't explain!
Git here thirty-five minutes before
The dern thing's due!—and, drat the thing!
It'll manage to git past—shore!

The more I travel around, the more
I got no sense!— To stand right here
And let it beat me! 'Ll ding my melts!
I got no gumption, ner nothin' else!
Ticket-agent's a dad-burned bore!—
Sell you a ticket's all they keer!—
Ticket-agents ort to all be
Prosecuted—and that's jes' what!—
How'd I know which train's fer me?
And how'd I know which train was not?—
Goern and comin' and gone astray,
And backin' and switchin' ever'-which-way!

Ef I could jes' sneak round behind
Myse'f, where I could git full swing,
I'd lift my coat, and kick, by jing!
Till I jes' got jerked up and fined!—
Fer here I stood, as a dern fool's apt
To, and let that train jes' chuff and choo
Right apast me—and mouth jes' gapped
Like a blamed old sandwitch warped in two!

THE ELOCUTIONIST'S CURFEW

BY W. D. NESBIT

England's sun was slowly setting—(Raise your right hand to
    your brow),
Filling all the land with beauty—(Wear a gaze of rapture now);
And the last rays kissed the forehead of a man and maiden fair
(With a movement slow and graceful you may now push back
    your hair);
He with sad, bowed head—(A drooping of your head will be all
    right,
Till you hoarsely, sadly whisper)—"Curfew must not ring
    to-night."

"Sexton," Bessie's white lips faltered—(Try here to resemble
    Bess,
Tho of course you know she'd never worn quite such a charming
    dress),
"I've a lover in that prison"—(Don't forget to roll your r's
And to shiver as tho gazing through the iron prison bars),
"Cromwell will not come till sunset"—(Speak each word as
    tho you'd bite
Every syllable to pieces)—"Curfew must not ring to-night."

"Bessie," calmly spoke the sexton—(Here extend your velvet
    palm,
Let it tremble like the sexton's as tho striving to be calm),
"Long, long y'ars I've rung the curfew"—(Don't forget to make
    it y'ars
With a pitiful inflection that a world of sorrow bears),
"I have done my duty ever"—(Draw yourself up to your height,
For you're speaking as the sexton)—"Gyurl, the curfew rings
    to-night!"

Out she swung, far out—(Now here is where you've got to do
    your best;
Let your head be twisted backward, let great sobs heave up your
    chest,
Swing your right foot through an arc of ninety lineal degrees,
Then come down and swing your left foot, and be sure don't
    bend your knees;
Keep this up for fifteen minutes till your face is worn and white,
Then gaze at your mangled fingers)—"Curfew shall not ring
    to-night!"

O'er the distant hills came Cromwell—(Right hand to the brow
    once more;
Let your eyes look down the distance, say above the entrance
    door)—
At his foot she told her story—(Lift your hands as tho they
    hurt)—
And her sweet young face so haggard—(Now your pathos you
    assert,
Then you straighten up as Cromwell, and be sure you get it right;
Don't say "Go, your liver loves!")—well: "Curfew shall not ring
    to-night!"

Reprinted from *Harper's Magazine*, by permission of Harper and Brothers.

MELPOMENUS JONES

BY STEPHEN LEACOCK

    Some people find great difficulty in saying good-by when making
a call or spending the evening. As the moment draws near when
the visitor feels that he is fairly entitled to go away, he rises and
says abruptly, "Well, I think——" Then the people say, "Oh,
must you go now? Surely it's early yet!" and a pitiful struggle
ensues.

    I think the saddest case of this kind of thing that I ever knew
was that of my poor friend Melpomenus Jones, a curate—such
a dear young man and only twenty-three! He simply couldn't get
away from people. He was too modest to tell a lie, and too relig-

ious to wish to appear rude. Now it happened that he went to call on some friends of his on the very first afternoon of his summer vacation. The next six weeks were entirely his own—absolutely nothing to do. He chatted a while, drank two cups of tea, then braced himself for the effort and said suddenly:

"Well, I think I——"

But the lady of the house said, "Oh, no, Mr. Jones, can't you really stay a little longer?"

Jones was always truthful—"Oh, yes, of course, I—er—can."

"Then please don't go."

He stayed. He drank eleven cups of tea. Night was falling. He rose again.

"Well, now, I think I really——"

"You must go? I thought perhaps you could have stayed to dinner——"

"Oh, well, so I could, you know, if——"

"Then please stay; I'm sure my husband will be delighted."

"All right, I'll stay"; and he sank back into his chair, just full of tea, and miserable.

Father came home. They had dinner. All through the meal Jones sat planning to leave at eight-thirty. All the family wondered whether Mr. Jones was stupid and sulky, or only stupid.

After dinner mother undertook to "draw him out" and showed him photographs. She showed him all the family museum, several gross of them—photos of father's uncle and his wife, and mother's brother and his little boy, and awfully interesting photos of father's uncle's friend in his Bengal uniform, an awfully well-taken photo of father's grandfather's partner's dog, and an awfully wicked one of father as the devil for a fancy-dress ball.

At eight-thirty Jones had examined seventy-one photographs. There were about sixty-nine more that he hadn't. Jones rose.

"I must say good-night now," he pleaded.

"Say good-night! why it's only half-past eight! Have you anything to do?"

"Nothing," he admitted, and muttered something about staying six weeks, and then laughed miserably.

Just then it turned out that the favorite child of the family, such a dear little romp, had hidden Mr. Jones' hat; so father said that he *must* stay, and invited him to a pipe and a chat. Father had the pipe and gave Jones the chat, and still he stayed. Every moment he meant to take the plunge, but couldn't. Then father began to get very tired of Jones, and fidgeted and finally said, with jocular irony, that Jones had better stay all night— they could give him a shake-down. Jones mistook his meaning and thanked him with tears in his eyes, and father put Jones to bed in the spare-room and curst him heartily.

After breakfast next day, father went off to his work in the city and left Jones playing with the baby, broken-hearted. His nerve was utterly gone. He was meaning to leave all day, but the thing had got on his mind and he simply couldn't. When father came home in the evening he was surprized and chagrined to find Jones still there. He thought to jockey him out with a jest, and said he thought he'd have to charge him for his board, he! he! The unhappy young man stared wildly for a moment, then wrung father's hand, paid him a month's board in advance, and broke down and sobbed like a child.

In the days that followed he was moody and unapproachable. He lived, of course, entirely in the drawing-room, and the lack of air and exercise began to tell sadly on his health. He passed his time in drinking tea and looking at photographs. He would stand for hours together gazing at the photograph of father's uncle's friend in his Bengal uniform—talking to it, sometimes swearing bitterly at it. His mind was visibly failing.

At length the crash came. They carried him up-stairs in a raging delirium of fever. The illness that followed was terrible. He recognized no one, not even father's uncle's friend in his Bengal uniform. At times he would start up from his bed and shriek: "Well, I think I——" and then fall back upon the pillow with a horrible laugh. Then, again, he would leap up and cry: "Another cup of tea and more photographs! More photographs! Hear! Hear!"

At length, after a month of agony, on the last day of his vacation he passed away. They say that when the last moment came, he sat up in bed with a beautiful smile of confidence playing upon his face, and said: "Well—the angels are calling me; I'm afraid I really must go now. Good afternoon."

HER FIFTEEN MINUTES

BY TOM MASSON

At exactly fifteen minutes to eight
His step was heard at the garden gate.

And then, with heart that was light and gay,
He laughed to himself in a jubilant way,

And rang the bell for the maiden trim
Who'd promised to go to the play with him;

And told the servant, with joyous air,
To say there were fifteen minutes to spare.

And then for fifteen minutes he sat
In the parlor dim, and he held his hat,

And waited and sighed for the maiden trim
Who'd promised to go to the play with him,

Until, as the clock overhead struck eight,
He muttered: "Great Scott! it is getting late";

And took a turn on the parlor floor,
And waited for fifteen minutes more;

And thought of those seats in the front parquet.
And midnight came, and the break of day;

That day and the next, and the next one, too,
He sat and waited the long hours through.

Then time flew on and the years sped by,
And still he sat, with expectant eye

And lengthening beard, for the maiden trim
Who'd promised to go to the play with him;

Until one night, as with palsied hand
He sat in the chair, for he couldn't stand,

And drummed in an aimless way, she came
And opened the door with her withered frame.

The moon's bright rays touched the silvered hair
Of her who had fifteen minutes to spare.

And then in tones that he strained to hear,
She spoke, and she said: "Are you ready, dear?"

Reprinted by permission of *Life* Publishing Company.

MY FUNNY EXPERIENCE WITH A WHISTLER[1]

BY G. H. SNAZELLE

The little yarn I am about to spin is connected with a visit I paid to Switzerland some five years ago. Of course, I presume that many of my audience have been to Switzerland, and they will bear me out that it is a very beautiful country to take a holiday in; and, for the information of those among my audience who have never been there, I would inform them that it is not only beautiful, but it is a country where you can choose your own climate. I mean in this way: If you want it warm, all you've got to do is to stay in the valleys; if you want it cooler, all you've got to do is to go higher up the mountains. Of course, it's a scientific fact that the higher you go the colder you get—if you want it colder you go higher, and so on—but don't go too high, for it's so cold at the top of some of those Swiss mountains that you can't tell the truth. Well, I was taking a holiday there

---

[1] When the whistle is to be long it is printed so _____
When the whistle is to be short _____.

When it goes from a low to a high note

When it goes from high to low

some time ago, and I got as far as Lucerne, and everybody kept telling me that I ought to climb the Rigi. As you know, the Rigi is only 8,000 feet high, a mere mole-hill as far as Swiss mountains go; but, personally, I found it quite enough. At last I got to the top, and I found that there was a very commodious hotel there. I discovered there was very beautiful scenery to be seen, and I also discovered that I appeared to be the only idiot staying there at that time of year—this was in October—and after being there about three days, and not seeing a soul about, I thought I had had about enough of it, so I sent for the hotel proprietor and asked for my bill, saying I thought I'd get back to the valley again—that is to say, to Lucerne.

The landlord said, "You not comfortable here, sare?"

"Yes," I said, "I'm very comfortable, but I feel dull; I like society, and there appears to be nobody staying here except myself."

"Vell, sare," he said, "of course you come to Switzerland in October, nobody here, but if you come in July you not able to get a bed."

I made a note that I would never go in July, because I like a bed to sleep on sometimes. "However," I said, "if you have anybody staying at the hotel besides myself I'll put in a day or two."

"Vell, sare," he said, "I have von gentleman he stop here."

I remarked that one would be enough if he were good company and sociable.

"Ah, sare," says the landlord, "he not very good company; *he nevare speak.*"

"Never speak!" I said; "good heavens!" Then it struck me that he might be deaf and dumb. So I asked if that were the case.

"No, sare, he not a deaf, he not a dumb; poor gentleman, he nevare speak, but he *whistle a good deal.*"

"Whistle a good deal. I don't understand you."

"Vell, sare, he try to speak and toujours he finish up mit a vhistle."

"I still fail to follow you—how long has he been here?"

"About four months."

"Has he whistled all the time?"

"Vell, sare, ze poor gentleman, he——"

"Excuse the apparent rudeness of the remark, but has he paid his bill?"

"No, sare, he not pay his bill yet."

"Well, what does he do when you show him his bill?"

"Oh! mostly he *vhistle.*"

"If there's no charge for seeing this curiosity, I'd like to have a look at him if he is on show this morning."

"The poor gentleman is in the schmoke-room this morning."

So I adjourned to the smoke-room, and there I saw a young man sitting at a table, wearing a light tourist suit and reading an old copy of the *Referee;* he looked a gentleman, but looked particularly wretched, so I thought I would not commit myself by commencing the conversation. I thought if he'd got anything to say, he'd better begin—and I went and gazed out at the beautiful scenery one sees from the Rigi Kulm. Well, he'd got a good deal to say, and he did begin; he came up and touched me on the shoulder behind, and he said, "   ," and then he touched me on the other shoulder, and he said, "   ."

Then I faced round, and I said, "My friend, I don't somehow seem to grasp your meaning."

He remarked, after making all manner of facial contortions, "   ."

"Yes," I said, "that's all very pretty as far as it goes, but it doesn't go far, a lot of it might become monotonous and not *being a canary* I don't understand you."

"Y—you d—don't under   stand me?"

"No," I said, "can't say I do." Probably I was a little bit handicapped. I hadn't been brought up in an aviary to start with. I've kept birds. Canaries I've had and bullfinches, and, of course, we understand that it's a bird's mission to come here and build a nest and whistle and so on, but when a man is sprung upon one on the top of a mountain who can't talk, and merely whistles, it is a bit of a staggerer. "But," I said, "I hear you can talk, my friend. There's my card (*handing it to him*). What is your name?"

He said, "G—G—G——————," said he.

"Oh, indeed! How do you spell it?" says I. "Where do you come from?"

"I—I—I c—come from ~~~~~~ ."

"Yes," I said, "that's where I should imagine you would come from."

"No—n—no," he added, "I c—c—come from New ⟋ York."

"Oh," I said, "I know New ⟍ York very well; a very nice city it is—but," I asked, "might I respectfully inquire why you are located up the mountains, and looking so wretched, and whistling, and going on in that peculiar manner?"

Then he buttonholed me, and he gave me this right in my ear:

"I—I—I was ⟋ engaged ⟍ to a ⟋ ."

"Oh, indeed," I said; "nice girl?"

" ~~~~~~ " he answered, "and sh—sh—she wouldn't ~~~~~~ because I ⟍ stuttered."

"Well," I remarked, "you certainly have got it very bad. Are you taking anything for it?"

"Y—y—yes. Th—th—the ⟋ doc ⟍ tor, he ~~~~~~ said th—th—that if I—I—I—was to ⟋ whistle every t—t—time before I ~~~~~~ spoke, I sh—sh—should g—g—get cured a—a—and th—th— that's wh—why I ~~~~~~ whistle, sir."

THE DEAD KITTEN

ANONYMOUS

You's as stiff an' cold as a stone, little cat;
Dey's done frowed out an' left you all alone, little cat;
I's a-strokin' you's fur
    But you don't never purr,
    Nor hump up anywhere—
    Little cat, why is dat?
Is you's purrin' an' humpin' up done?

An' why is you's little foot tied, little cat?
Did dey pisen you's tummick inside, little cat?
Did dey pound you wif bricks
    Or wif big nasty sticks
    Or abuse you wif kicks?
    Little cat, tell me dat.
Did dey laff whenever you cried?

Did it hurt werry bad when you died, little cat?
Oh, why didn't you wun off and hide, little cat?
Dey is tears in my eyes,
    'Cause I most always cries
    When a pussy-cat dies,
    Little cat, tink of dat,
An' I am awfully solly, besides.

Des lay still, down in de sof' groun', little cat,
While I tucks the green grass awound, little cat,
Dey can't hurt you no more,
    W'en you's tired and so sore;
    Des' sleep quiet, you pore
    Little cat, wif a pat,
And forget all the kicks of the town.

THE WEATHER FIEND

ANONYMOUS

One hot day last summer, a young man dressed in thin clothes, entered a Broadway car, and seating himself opposite a stout old gentleman, said, pleasantly:

"Pretty warm, isn't it?"

"What's pretty warm?"

"Why, the weather."

"What weather?"

"Why, this weather."

"Well, how's this different from any other weather?"

"Well, it is warmer."

"How do you know it is?"

"I suppose it is."

"Isn't the weather the same everywhere?"

"Why, no,—no; it's warmer in some places and it's colder in others."

"What makes it warmer in some places than it's colder in others?"

"Why, the sun,—the effect of the sun's heat."

"Makes it colder in some places than it's warmer in others? Never heard of such a thing."

"No, no, no. I didn't mean that. The sun makes it warmer."

"Then what makes it colder?"

"I believe it's the ice."

"What ice?"

"Why, the ice,—the ice,—the ice that was frozen by—by—by the frost."

"Have you ever seen any ice that wasn't frozen?"

"No,—that is, I believe I haven't."

"Then what are you talking about?"

"I was just trying to talk about the weather."

"And what do you know about it,—what do you know about the weather?"

"Well, I thought I knew something, but I see I don't and that's a fact."

"No, sir, I should say you didn't! Yet you come into this car and force yourself upon the attention of a stranger and begin to talk about the weather as tho you owned it, and I find you don't know a solitary thing about the matter you yourself selected for a topic of conversation. You don't know one thing about meteorological conditions, principles, or phenomena; you can't tell me why it is warm in August and cold in December; you don't know why icicles form faster in the sunlight than they do in the shade; you don't know why the earth grows colder as it comes nearer the sun; you can't tell why a man can be sunstruck in the shade; you can't tell me how a cyclone is formed nor how the trade-winds blow; you couldn't find the calm-center of a storm if your life depended on it; you don't know what a sirocco is nor where the southwest monsoon blows; you don't know the average rainfall in the United States for the past and current year; you don't know why the wind dries up the ground more quickly than a hot sun; you don't know why the dew falls at night and dries up in the day; you can't explain the formation of fog; you don't know one solitary thing about the weather and you are just like a thousand and one other people who always begin talking about the weather because they don't know anything else, when, by the Aurora Borealis, they know less about the weather than they do about anything else in the world, sir!"

THE RACE QUESTION

BY PAUL LAURENCE DUNBAR

SCENE: *Race-track. Enter old colored man, seating himself.*

"Oomph, oomph. De work of de devil sho' do p'ospah. How 'do, suh? Des tol'able, thankee, suh. How you come on? Oh, I was des asayin' how de wo'k of de ol' boy do p'ospah. Doesn't I frequent the race-track? No, suh; no, suh. I's Baptis' myse'f an' I 'low hit's all devil's doin's. Wouldn't 'a' be'n hyeah to-day, but I got a boy named Jim dat's long gone in sin an' he gwine ride one dem hosses. Oomph, dat boy! I sut'ny has talked to him and labohed wid him night an' day, but it was allers in vain, an' I's feahed dat de day of his reckonin' is at han'.

"Ain't I nevah been intrusted in racin'? Humph, you don't s'pose I been dead all my life, does you? What you laffin at? Oh, scuse me, scuse me, you unnerstan' what I means. You don' give a ol' man time to splain hisse'f. What I means is dat dey has been days when I walked in de counsels of de ongawdly and set in de seats of sinnahs; and long erbout dem times I did tek most ovahly strong to racin'.

"How long dat been? Oh, dat's way long back, 'fo I got religion, mo'n thuty years ago, dough I got to own I has fell from grace several times sense.

"Yes, suh, I ust to ride. Ki-yi! I nevah furgit de day dat my ol' Mas' Jack put me on 'June Boy,' his black geldin', an' say to me, 'Si,' says he, 'if you don' ride de tail offen Cunnel Scott's mare, "No Quit," I's gwine to larrup you twell you cain't set in de saddle no mo'.' Hyah, hyah. My ol' Mas' was a mighty han' fu' a joke. I knowed he wan't gwine to do nuffin' to me.

"Did I win? Why, whut you spec' I's doin' hyeah ef I hadn' winned? W'y, ef I'd 'a' let dat Scott maih beat my 'June Boy' I'd 'a' drowned myse'f in Bull Skin Crick.

"Yes, suh, I winned; w'y, at de finish I come down dat track lak hit was de Jedgment Day an' I was de las' one up! 'f I didn't race dat maih's tail clean off. I 'low I made hit do a lot o' switchin'. An' aftah dat my wife Mandy she ma'ed me. Hyah, hyah, I ain't bin much on hol'in' de reins sence.

"Sh! dey comin' in to wa'm up. Dat Jim, dat Jim, dat my boy; you nasty, putrid little raskil. Des a hundred an' eight, suh, des a hundred an' eight. Yas, suh, dat's my Jim; I don' know whaih he gits his dev'ment at.

"What's de mattah wid dat boy? Whyn't he hunch hisse'f up on dat saddle right? Jim, Jim, whyn't you limber up, boy; hunch yo'sef up on dat hoss lak you belonged to him and knowed you was dah. What I done showed you? De black raskil, goin' out dah tryin' to disgrace his own daddy. Hyeah he come back. Dat's bettah, you scoun'ril.

"Dat's a right smaht-lookin' hoss he's a-ridin', but I ain't a-trustin' dat bay wid de white feet—dat is, not altogethah. She's a favourwright, too; but dey's sumpin' else in dis worl' sides playin' favourwrights. Jim battah had win dis race. His hoss ain't a five to one shot, but I spec's to go way fum hyeah wid money ernuff to mek a donation on de pa'sonage.

"Does I bet? Well, I don' des call hit bettin'; but I resks a little w'en I t'inks I kin he'p de cause. 'Tain't gamblin', o' co'se; I wouldn't gamble fu nothin', dough my ol' Mastah did ust to say dat a hones' gamblah was ez good ez a hones' preachah an' mos' nigh ez skace.

"Look out dah, man, dey's off, dat nasty bay maih wid de white feet leadin' right f'um de pos'. I knowed it! I knowed it! I had my eye on huh all de time. O Jim, Jim, why didn't you git in bettah, way back dah fouf? Dah go de gong! I knowed dat wasn't no staht. Troop back dah, you raskils, hyah, hyah.

"I wush day boy wouldn't do so much jummyin erroun' wid day hoss. Fust t'ing he know he ain't gwine to know whaih he's at.

"Dah, dah dey go ag'in. Hit's a sho' t'ing dis time. Bettah, Jim, bettah. Dey didn't leave you dis time. Hug dat bay maih, hug her close, boy. Don't press dat hoss yit. He holdin' back a lot o' t'ings.

"He's gainin'! doggone my cats, he's gainin'! an' dat hoss o' his'n gwine des ez stiddy ez a rockin'-chair. Jim allus was a good boy.

"Counfound these spec's, I cain't see 'em skacely; huh, you say dey's neck an' neck; now I see 'em! and Jimmy's a-ridin' like—— Huh, huh, I laik to said sumpin'.

"De bay maih's done huh bes', she's done huh bes'! Dey's turned into the stretch an' still see-sawin'. Let him out, Jimmy, let him out! Dat boy done th'owed de reins away. Come on, Jimmy, come on! He's leadin' by a nose. Come on, I tell you, you black rapscallion, come on! Give 'em hell, Jimmy! give 'em hell! Under de wire an' a len'th ahead. Doggone my cats! wake me up w'en dat othah hoss comes in.

"No, suh, I ain't gwine stay no longah—I don't app'ove o' racin'; I's gwine 'roun' an' see dis hyeah bookmakah an' den I's

gwine dreckly home, suh, dreckly home. I's Baptis' myse'f, an'
I don't app'ove o' no sich doin's!"

Reprinted by permission from " The Heart of Happy Hollow," Dodd, Mead &
Company, New York.

WHEN THE WOODBINE TURNS RED

ANONYMOUS

They sat in a garden of springing flowers,
   In a tangle of woodland ways;
And theirs was the sweetest of summer bowers,
   Where they passed long summer days.
But, alas, when the sunbeams faded away,
   And those brightest of days had fled
'Neath the old trysting trees they parted for aye,
   When the woodbine leaves turned red.

When the woodbine leaves turned red,
And their last farewell was said,
   They swore to be true, as all lovers do,
When the woodbine leaves turn red.
She gave him a flower sweet;
They vowed they would surely meet
   In a year and a day; tho they parted for aye
When the woodbine leaves turned red.

They met in the garden again next year,
   And their ways had been far apart.
He grasped both hands with a sigh and a tear,
   And murmured, "My old sweetheart,
I have to confess it, I can't marry you,
   For already have I been wed."
And she answered, blushing, "So have I, too."
   And the woodbine turned red.

CUPID'S CASUISTRY

BY W. J. LAMPTON

We were sitting in the moonlight
Of a radiant, rosy June night,
When I whispered: "Kitty, don't you
Wish I'd kiss you? Let me, won't you ?"

Kitty was a rustic maiden,
And I thought not heavy laden
With the wisdom of the ages
Writ on cultured cupid's pages.

Kitty answered: "No, I mustn't
Let you kiss me: my ma doesn't
Think it proper that her Kitty
Be like maidens in the city."

"Oh!" I stammered. Then did Kitty
Whisper in a tone of pity:
"I might kiss *you* and be true, sir,
To my mother; would that do, sir?"

WHEN MAH LADY YAWNS

BY CHARLES T. GRILLEY

When mah Cah'line yawns, ah'm 'spicious
Dat she tinks de time po'pitious
  Fo' me to tu'n mah 'tention to de clock upon de wall.
Dat's de cue to quit mah talkin',
An' a gentle hint dat walkin'
  Would flicitate de briefness of mah call.

Th' fus' gal that ah coh'ted
Ouah ma'idge it was thwa'ted
   Because ah was so green ah didn' know.
When she yawns it was behoovin'
Dat dis dahkey should be movin',
   Twell at las' she says, "Fo Lawd's sake, niggah, go!"

Den ah took mah hat an' stah'ted,
An f'om dat hour we pah'ted,
   An ah nevah seen dat cullud gal no mo'.
But it taught me dis yer lesson
Dat a yawn am de expression
   Dat invites yo' to be movin' to'ards de do'.

So take dis friendly wah'nin',—
Should yo' lady love stah't yawnin'
   Altho de sudden pah'ting cost yo' pain,
If she's one you'd like t' marry,
Aftah one good yawn don' tarry,
   Den yo sho'ly will be welcome da again.

WATCHIN' THE SPARKIN'

BY FRED EMERSON BROOKS

Say, Jim, ye wanter see the fun?
Jemimy's sparkin's jess begun!
Git deown—this box won't hold but one
   Fer peekin' through the winder!
Yeou stay down thar jess whar ye be;
I'll tell ye all thar is to see;
Then you'll enjoy it well as me;
   An' deon't yeou try to hinder!

That teacher is the dumbdest goose
That Cupid ever turned eout loose;
His learnin' hain't no sort o' use
   In sparkin' our Jemimy!
Tho peekin's 'ginst the golden reule,
He told us t'other day in scheool
To watch him close; so git a steool
   An' stand up here close by me.

Neow he's got suthin' in his head
That somehow ruther's gotter be said;
Keeps hitchin' up, an' blushin' red,
   With one leg over t'other.
He wants to do the thing up breown.
Wall, he's the biggest gawk in teown:
Showin' her pictur's upside deown;
   An' she don't know it nuther!

He's got his arm areound her chair,
And wonders if she'll leave it there.
But she looks like she didn't care!
   I'll bet he's goin' to kiss 'er;
He's gittin' closer to her face,
An' pickin' out the softest place,
An' sort o' measurin' off the space,
   Jess so as not to miss 'er.

If she'd git mad, an' box his ear,
'Twould knock his plans clean out o' gear,
An' set him back another year;
   But she ain't goin' to do it:
She thinks the teacher's jess tip-top,
An' she won't let no chances drop;
If ever he sets in to pop,
   She's goin' to pull him through it!

I gum! an' if he ain't the wust!
Waitin' fer her to kiss him fust!
He's goin' to do it neow er bu'st:
    He's makin' preparation!
Neow watch him steppin' on her toes—
That's jess to keep her down, I s'pose.
Wall, thar, he's kissed her on the nose!
    So much fer edecation!

By permission of Messrs. Forbes & Co., Chicago.

THE WAY OF A WOMAN

BY BYRON W. KING

It was the last night before leap-year; it was the last hour before leap-year; in fact, the minute-hand had moved round the dial
face of the clock until it registered fifteen minutes of twelve,—
fifteen minutes of leap-year. John and Mary were seated in
Mary's father's parlor. There was plenty of furniture there but
they were using only a limited portion of it. John watched the
minute-hand move round the dial face of the clock until, like the
finger of destiny, it registered fifteen minutes of twelve,—fifteen
minutes of leap-year, when he gasped hard, clutched his coat
collar, and said,—

"Mary, in just fifteen minutes, Mary,—fifteen minutes by that
clock, Mary,—another year, Mary,—like the six thousand years
that have gone before it, Mary,—will have gone into the great
Past and be forgotten in oblivion, Mary,—and I want to ask you,
Mary,—to-night, Mary,—on this sofa, Mary,—if for the next six
thousand years,—Mary!!!——"

"John," she said with a winning smile, "you seem very much
excited, John,—can I do anything to help you, John?"

"Just sit still, Mary,—just sit still. In just twelve minutes,
Mary,—twelve minutes by this clock, Mary,—like the six thou-
sand clocks that have gone before it, Mary,—will be forgotten,
Mary,—and I want to ask this clock, Mary,—to-night, on this

sofa, Mary,—if when we've been forgotten six thousand times, Mary,—in oblivion, Mary,—and six thousand sofas, Mary!!——"

"John," she said, more smilingly than ever, "you seem quite nervous; would you like to see father?"

"Not for the world, Mary, not for the world! In just eight minutes, Mary,—eight minutes by that awful clock, we'll be forgotten, Mary,—and I want to ask six thousand fathers, Mary,—if when this sofa, Mary,—has been forgotten six thousand times, Mary,—in six thousand oblivions,—I want to ask six thousand Marys six thousand times, Mary!!!!——"

"John," she said, "you don't seem very well. Would you like a glass of water?"

"Mary,—in just three minutes, Mary,—three minutes by that dreadful clock, Mary,—we'll be forgotten, Mary,—six thousand times,—and I want to ask six thousand sofas, Mary,—if when six thousand oblivions have forgotten six thousand fathers in six thousand years, I want to ask six thousand Marys, six thousand times, Mary!!!!——"

Bang! the clock struck. It was leap-year. The clock struck twelve and Mary turning to John, sweetly said:

"John, it's leap-year; will you marry me?"

"Yes!!!"

Gentlemen, there is no use talking, the way of a woman beats you all.

THE YACHT CLUB SPEECH

ANONYMOUS

Mr. Chairman—a—a—a—Mr. Commodore—beg pardon—I assure you that until this moment I had not the remotest expectation that I should be called upon to reply to this toast. (*Pauses, turns round, pulls MS. out of pocket and looks at it.*) Therefore I must beg of you, Mr. Captain—a—a—Mr. Commatain—a—a— Mr.—Mr. Cappadore—that you will pardon the confused nature of these remarks, being as they must necessarily be altogether impromptu and extempore. (*Pauses, turns round and looks at MS.*) But Mr. Bos'an—a—a—Mr. Bosadore—I feel—I feel even in these few confused expromptu and intempore—intomptu and exprempore—extemptu and imprempore—exprompore remarks —I feel that I can say in the words of the poet, words of the poet—poet—I feel that I can say in the words of the poet—of the poet—poet, and in these few confused remarks—in the words of the poet—(*turns round, looks at MS.*)—I feel that I can say in the words of the poet that I feel my heart swell within me. Now Mr. Capasun, Mr. Commasun, why does my heart swell within me—in the few confused—why does my heart swell within me—swell within me—swell within me—what makes my heart swell within me—why does it swell—swell within me? (*Turns round and looks at MS.*) Why, Mr. Cappadore—look at George Washington—what did he do?—in the few confused——(*Strikes dramatic attitude with swelled chest and outstretched arm, preparing for burst of eloquence which will not come.*) He—huh—he—huh —he—huh—(*turns round and looks at MS.*)—he took his stand upon the ship of state—he stood upon the maintopgallant-jib-boomsail and reefed the quivering sail—and when the storms were waging rildly round to wreck his fragile bark, through all the howling tempest he guided her in safety into the harbor of perdition—a—a—a—into the haven of safety. And what did he do then? What did he do then? What did he do then? He—he—he —(*looks at MS.*)—there he stood. And then his grateful countrymen gathered round him—they gathered round George Washington—they placed him on the summit of the cipadel—their capadol —they held him up before the eyes of the assembled world— around his brow they placed a never-dying wreath—and then in thunder tones which all the world might hear——(*Flourishes MS. before his face, notices it and sits down in great confusion.*)

MAMMY'S LI'L' BOY

BY H. S. EDWARDS

Who all time dodgin' en de cott'n en de corn?
    Mammy's li'l' boy, mammy's li'l' boy!
Who all time stealin' ole massa's dinner-horn?
    Mammy's li'l' baby boy.

Byo baby boy, oh bye,
By-o li'l' boy!
Oh, run ter es mammy
En she tek 'im in 'er arms,
Mammy's li'l' baby boy.

Who all time runnin' ole gobble roun' de yard?
   Mammy's li'l' boy, mammy's li'l' boy!
Who tek 'e stick 'n hit ole possum dog so hard?
   Mammy's li'l' baby boy.

Byo baby boy, oh bye,
By-o li'l' boy!
Oh, run ter es mammy
En climb up en 'er lap,
Mammy's li'l' baby boy.

Who all time stumpin' es toe ergin er rock?
   Mammy's li'l' boy, mammy's li'l' boy!
Who all time er-rippin' big hole en es frock?
   Mammy's li'l' baby boy.

Byo baby boy, oh bye,
By-o li'l' boy!
Oh, run ter es mammy
En she wipe es li'l' eyes,
Mammy's li'l' baby boy.

Who all time er-losin' de shovel en de rake?
   Mammy's li'l' boy, mammy's li'l' boy!
Who all time tryin' ter ride 'e lazy drake?
   Mammy's li'l' baby boy.

Byo baby boy, oh bye,
By-o li'l' boy!
Oh, scoot fer yer mammy
En she hide yer f'om yer ma,
Mammy's li'l' baby boy.

Who all time er-trottin' ter de kitchen fer er bite?
　　Mammy's li'l' boy, mammy's li'l' boy!
Who mess 'esef wi' taters twell his clothes dey look er sight?
　　Mammy's li'l' baby boy.

　　　　　Byo baby boy, oh bye,
　　　　　By-o, li'l boy!
　　　　　En 'e run ter es mammy
　　　　　Fer ter git 'im out er trouble,
　　　　　Mammy's li'l' baby boy.

Who all time er-frettin' en de middle er de day?
　　Mammy's li'l' boy, mammy's li'l' boy!
Who all time er-gettin' so sleepy 'e can't play?
　　Mammy's li'l' baby boy.

　　　　　Byo baby boy, oh bye,
　　　　　By-o li'l' boy!
　　　　　En 'e come ter es mammy
　　　　　Ter rock 'im en 'er arms,
　　　　　Mammy's li'l' baby boy.
　　　　　Shoo, shoo, shoo-shoo-shoo,
　　　　　Shoo, shoo, shoo!

　　　　　Shoo, shoo, shoo-shoo-shoo,
　　　　　Shoo, li'l' baby, shoo!
　　　　　Shoo, shoo, shoo-shoo-shoo,
　　　　　Shoo, shoo, shoo,
　　　　　Shoo　　.　　.　　.

Deir now, lay right down on mammy's bed en go 'long back
　　ter sleep,—shoo-shoo!

CORYDON

BY THOMAS BAILEY ALDRICH

Shepherd

Good sir, have you seen pass this way
A mischief straight from market-day?
You'd know her at a glance, I think;
Her eyes are blue, her lips are pink;
She has a way of looking back
Over her shoulder, and, alack!
Who gets that look one time, good sir,
Has naught to do but follow her.

Pilgrim

I have not seen this maid, methinks,
Tho she that passed had lips like pinks.

Shepherd

Or like two strawberries made one
By some sly trick of dew and sun.

Pilgrim

A poet!

Shepherd

Nay, a simple swain
That tends his flock on yonder plain,
Naught else, I swear by book and bell.
But she that passed—you marked her well.
Was she not smooth as any be
That dwell herein in Arcady?

Pilgrim

Her skin was as the satin bark
Of birches.

Shepherd

Light or dark?

Pilgrim

Quite dark.

Shepherd

Then 't was not she.

Pilgrim

    The peach's side
That gets the sun is not so dyed
As was her cheek. Her hair hung down
Like summer twilight falling brown;
And when the breeze swept by, I wist
Her face was in a somber mist.

Shepherd

No, that is not the maid I seek,—
Her hair lies gold against the cheek;
Her yellow tresses take the morn
Like silken tassels of the corn.
And yet—brown locks are far from bad.

Pilgrim

Now I bethink me, this one had
A figure like the willow tree
Which, slight and supple, wondrously
Inclines to droop with pensive grace,
And still retains its proper place;
A foot so arched and very small
The marvel was she walked at all;
Her hand—in sooth I lack the words—
Her hand, five slender snow-white birds;
Her voice—tho she but said "Godspeed"—
Was melody blown through a reed;
The girl Pan changed into a pipe
Had not a note so full and ripe.

And her eye—my lad, her eye!
Discreet, inviting, candid, shy,
An outward ice, an inward fire,
And lashes to the heart's desire—
Soft fringes blacker than the sloe.

Shepherd—thoughtfully
Good sir, which way did *this* one go?

.   .   .   .

Pilgrim—solus
So, he is off! the silly youth
Knoweth not Love in sober sooth.
He loves—thus lads at first are blind—
No woman, only womankind.

From the Poems of Thomas Bailey Aldrich, Household Edition, by permission of
Messrs. Houghton, Mifflin & Co.

GIB HIM ONE UB MINE

BY DANIEL WEBSTER DAVIS

A little urchin, ragged, black,
  An old cigar "stump" found,
And visions of a jolly smoke,
  Began to hover 'round.
But finding that he had no match,
  A big store he espied,
And straightway for it made a dash
  To have his wants supplied.

"I have no match!" the owner said,
  "And, even if I do,
I have no match, you understand,
  For such a thing as you!"

Down in the ragged pantaloons,
  The little black hand went,
And forth it came, now holding fast
  A big old-fashioned cent.

"Gib me a box," the urchin said,
  His bosom filled with joy;
And calmly lighted his "cigar,"
  A radiant happy boy.
Then handing back the box, he said,
  As his face with pride did shine:
"Nex' time a gent'mun wants a match,
  Jes' gib him one ub mine!"

A LESSON WITH THE FAN

ANONYMOUS

If you want to learn a lesson with the fan,
I'm quite prepared to teach you all I can.
So ladies, everyone, pray observe how it is done,
This simple little lesson with the fan!

If you chance to be invited to a ball,
To meet someone you don't expect at all,
And you want him close beside you, while a dozen friends divide
    you,
Well, of course—it's most unladylike to call.

So you look at him a minute, nothing more,
And you cast your eyes demurely on the floor,
Then you wave your fan, just so, well—toward you, don't you
    know,—
It's a delicate suggestion,—nothing more!

When you see him coming to you (simple you),
Oh! be very, very careful what you do;
With your fan just idly play, and look down, as if to say
It's a matter of indifference to you!

Then you flutter and you fidget with it, so!
And you hide your little nose behind it low,
Till, when he begins to speak, you just lay it on your cheek,
In that fascinating manner that you know!

And when he tells the old tale o'er and o'er,
And vows that he will love you evermore,—
Gather up your little fan, and secure him while you can,—
It's a delicate suggestion,—nothing more!

THE UNDERTOW

BY CARRIE BLAKE MORGAN

You hadn't ought to blame a man fer things he hasn't done
Fer books he hasn't written or fer fights he hasn't won;
The waters may look placid on the surface all aroun',
Yet there may be an undertow a-keepin' of him down.

Since the days of Eve and Adam, when the fight of life begar,
It aint been safe, my brethren, fer to lightly judge a man;
He may be tryin' faithful fer to make his life a go,
And yet his feet git tangled in the treacherous undertow.

He may not lack in learnin' and he may not want fer brains;
He may be always workin' with the patientest of pains,
And yet go unrewarded, an', my friends, how can we know
What heights he might have climbed to but fer the undertow?

You've heard the Yankee story of the hen's nest with a hole,
An' how the hen kept layin' eggs with all her might an' soul,
Yet never got a settin', not a single egg, I trow;
That hen was simply kickin' 'gainst a hidden undertow.

There's holes in lots of hen's nests, an' you've got to peep below
To see the eggs a-rollin' where they hadn't ought to go.
Don't blame a man fer failin' to achieve a laurel crown
Until you're sure the undertow aint draggin' of him down.

MARKETING

ANONYMOUS

A little girl goes to market for her mother.
Butcher.—"Well, little girl, what can I do for you?"
Little Girl.—"How much is chops this morning, mister?"
B.—"Chops, 20 cents a pound, little girl."
L. G.—"Oh! 20 cents a pound for chops; that's awful expensive. How much is steak?"
B.—"Steak is 22 cents a pound."
L. G.—"That's too much! How much is chicken?"
B.—"Chicken is 25 cents a pound" (*impatiently*).
L. G.—"Oh! 25 cents for chicken. Well my ma don't want any of them!"
B.—"Well, little girl, what *do* you want?"
L. G.—"Oh, I want an automobile, but my ma wants 5 cents' worth of liver!"

A SPRING IDYL ON "GRASS"

BY NIXON WATERMAN

Oh, the gentle grass is growing
    In the vale and on the hill;
We can not hear it growing,
    Still 'tis growing very still:

And in the spring it springs to life,
  With gladness and delight;
I see it growing day by day,—
  It also grows by night.
And, now, once more as mowers whisk
  The whiskers from the lawn,
They'll rouse us from our slumbers,—
  At the dawning of the dawn:
It saddens my poor heart to think
  What we should do for hay,
If grass instead of growing up
  Would grow the other way.
It's present rate of growing,
  Makes it safe to say that soon,
'Twill cover all the hills at morn
  And in the afternoon.
And I have often noticed
  As I watched it o'er and o'er,
It grows, and grows, and grows, awhile.
  And then it grows some more,—
If it keeps growing right along
  It shortly will be tall;
It humps itself thro' strikes,
  And legal holidays and all;
It's growing up down all the streets;
  And clean around the square;
One end is growing in the ground,
  The other in the air:
If the earth possest no grass
  Methinks its beauty would be dead;
We'd have to make the best of it,
  And use baled hay instead.

From "A Book of Verses," by permission of Forbes & Co., Chicago.

INTRODUCIN' THE SPEECHER

BY EDWIN L. BARKER

INTRODUCTORY REMARKS. This selection is a little caricature,
introducing two characters. "The Speecher" is one of those young
men who has passed through college in one year,—passed *through*,
—and has increasing difficulty in finding a hat large enough to fit
his head. His oratorical powers have been praised by his friends,
and he never misses an opportunity to exhibit his "great natural
talent." "The Chairman" is frequently met in the smaller towns.
He has lived there a long time, is acquainted with everybody,
makes it a point to form the acquaintance of all newcomers, takes
an interest in public affairs, and is often called upon to introduce
the speakers who visit the town. His principal weakness is that
in the course of his introductory remarks he usually says more
than the speaker himself.

THE CHAIRMAN. (*Comes forward to table at center, stands at
right, looks nervously at audience, goes to left of table, does not
know what to do with hands, returns to right of table, begins in
high, nervous voice.*) "Gentlemen an' ladies—an' the rest on ye—
(*goes left of table*) I s'pose ye all knowed afore, as per'aps ye
do now, that I did not come out to make a speech; but to—to
'nounce the speecher. Now, the speecher has jes come, an' is
right in there. (*Points with thumb over shoulder to L. and goes
R. of table.*) I don't know why 'twas they called on me to 'nounce
the speecher, unless it is that I've lived here in your midst fer a
long while, an' am 'quainted with very nigh every one fer four
or five miles about, an' I s'pose that's why they called on me to—
to 'nounce the speecher. Now, the speecher is—right in there.
(*Points L. and goes L.*) I s'pose I'm as well calc'lated to 'nounce
the speecher as any on ye, an' I s'pose that's why I'm here to—
to 'nounce the speecher. Now, the speecher is—right in there.
(*Points L. and goes R.*) You know I've lived here in your midst a
long time, an' have allus tuk an active part in all public affairs,
an' I s'pose that's why they called on me to—to 'nounce the
speecher. Now, the speecher is right in there. (*Points L. and

goes L.) As I said once afore, I've lived here in your midst fer a long time, an' have allus tuk active part in all public affairs, an' public doin's ginerally. Ye know I was 'pinted tax collector once, an' was road-overseer fer a little while, an' run fer constable of this here township—but I—I didn't git it. (*Quickly.*) Now, the speecher is—right there. (*Points L. and goes R. Wipes forehead with handkerchief.*) I jes want to say a word to the young men this evenin'—as I see quite a sprinklin' of 'em here—an' that is that I'd like fer all the young men to grow up an' hold high and honorable offices like I've done. But there, I can't stop any longer, 'cause the speecher is—right in there. (*Starts to go, but returns.*) Now, I don't want you to think I don't want to talk to ye, fer I do. I do so like to talk to the young men, an' the old men, an' them that are not men. (*Smiles.*) I love to talk to ye. But, of course, I can't talk to you now, 'cause the speecher is—right in there. (*Points L.*) But some other time when the speecher's not here—I think there'll be a time afore long—why, I'll talk to you. (*Grows confused.*) Of course, you know, I'd talk to you now; but—uh—that is—I think there'll be a time afore long—at some other—you know—I—you—the—(*desperately*) the speecher is right in there. (*Rushes to L., stops, and with back to audience, concludes.*) I will now interdoose to ye Charles William Albright, of Snigger's Crossroads, a very promisin' young attorney of that place, who will talk to ye. As I said afore, the speecher is right in here. Now, the speecher is right out there."
(*While standing with back to audience, run fingers through hair to give it a long, scholarly appearance, put on glasses, and take from chair roll of paper and place under arm. To be effective, this paper should be about one foot wide and ten feet long, folded in about five or six-inch folds. At conclusion of chairman's speech, turn and walk to table as the speecher.*)

THE SPEECHER. (*Walks to table with a strut. Face should have a wise, solemn, self-satisfied expression. Stops at table, surveys the audience with solemn dignity, clears the throat, lays roll of paper on table, takes out handkerchief, clears throat, wipes mouth, smacks lips, lays handkerchief on table, surveys audience again, slowly unrolls paper and lays on table, surveys audience again, clears throat, wipes mouth, smacks lips, poses with one hand on table.*) "Ladies—and—gentlemen—and fellow citizens. (*Rises on toes and comes back on heels, as practised by some public speakers.*) I have fully realized the magnitude of this auspicious occasion, and have brought from out the archives of wisdom one of those bright, extemporaneous subjects, to which, you know, I always do (*rising inflection*) ample justice. (*Rises on toes, clears throat, applies handkerchief to forehead.*) The subject for this evening's discussion (*very solemn*) is coal oil. (*Clears throat and looks wise.*) Now, the first question that arises is: How do they get it? (*In measured tone, on toes, tapping words off on fingers of left hand with forefinger of right hand.*) How—do—they—get —it? (*Soaringly.*) My dear friends, some get it by the pint, and some by the quart. (*Clears throat, wipes perspiration from forehead.*) But, you say, how do they get it in the first place? (*Tragically.*) Ah, my dear friends, as Horace Greeley has so fittingly exprest it—that is the question. (*Quickly.*) But I will explain. When they want to get it they take a great, mammoth auger (*imitates*) and they bore, and they bore, and they bore, and—(*looks at paper quickly*)—and they bore! And when they strike the oil it just squirts up. That's how they get it! (*Rises on toes, smacks lips and looks wise.*) Now, you all know, coal oil is used for a great many things. It is used for medicine, to burn in the lamp, to blow up servant girls when they make a fire with it, and—many other useful things. (*Wipes mouth and puts handkerchief in pocket.*) The gentlemen in charge will now pass the hat, being careful to lock the door back there so that none of those boys from Squeedunk can get out before they chip in. (*Takes paper and rolls it up.*) I will say that I expect to deliver another lecture here two weeks from to-night—two weeks from to-night—upon which occasion I would like to see all the children present, as the subject will be of special interest to (*rises on toes, closes eyes*) the little ones. The subject on that occasion will be 'Will We Bust the Trusts, or Will the Trusts Bust Us?' " (*Puts roll of paper under arm and stalks off as if having captured the world.*)

As recited by Edwin L. Barker and used by permission.

COUNTING ONE HUNDRED

BY JAMES M. BAILEY

A Danbury man named Reubens, recently saw a statement that counting one hundred when tempted to speak an angry word would save a man a great deal of trouble. This statement sounded a little singular at first, but the more he read it over the more favorably he became imprest with it, and finally concluded to adopt it.

Next door to Reubens lives a man who made five distinct attempts in a fortnight to secure a dinner of green peas by the first of July, but has been retarded by Reubens' hens. The next morning after Reubens made his resolution, this man found his fifth attempt had been destroyed. Then he called on Reubens. He said:

"What in thunder do you mean by letting your hens tear up my garden?"

Reubens was prompted to call him various names, but he remembered his resolution, put down his rage, and meekly said:

"One, two, three, four, five, six, seven, eight——"

The mad neighbor, who had been eyeing this answer with suspicion, broke in again:

"Why don't you answer my question, you rascal?"

But still Reubens maintained his equanimity, and went on with the test.

"Nine, ten, eleven, twelve, thirteen, fourteen, fifteen, sixteen ——"

The mad neighbor stared harder than ever.

"Seventeen, eighteen, nineteen, twenty, twenty-one——"

"You're a mean thief!" said the mad neighbor, backing toward the fence.

Reubens' face flushed at this charge, but he only said:

"Twenty-two, twenty-three, twenty-four, twenty-five, twenty-six——"

At this figure the neighbor got up on the fence in some haste, but suddenly thinking of his peas, he said:

"You mean, contemptible, old rascal! I could knock your head against my barn and I'll——"

"Twenty-seven, twenty-eight, twenty-nine, thirty, thirty-one, thirty-two, thirty-three——"

Here the neighbor ran for the house, and entering it, violently slammed the door behind him. Reubens did not let up on the enumeration, but stood out there alone in his own yard, and kept on counting, while his burning cheeks and flashing eyes eloquently affirmed his judgment. When he got up into the eighties his wife came out to him in some alarm.

"Why, Reubens, man, what is the matter with you? Do come into the house."

But he didn't stop.

"Eighty-seven, eighty-eight, eighty-nine, ninety, ninety-one, ninety-two——"

Then she came to him, and clung tremblingly to him, but he only turned, looked into her eyes, and said:

"Ninety-three, ninety-four, ninety-five, ninety-six, ninety-seven, ninety-eight, ninety-nine, one hundred! Go into the house, old woman, or I'll bust you!"

THEY NEVER QUARRELED

ANONYMOUS

They had been married about three weeks, and had just gone to housekeeping. He was starting down town one morning, and she followed him to the door. They had their arms wrapt around each other, and she was saying:

"O Clarence, do you think it possible that the day can ever come when we will part in anger?"

"Why, no, little girl, of course not. What put that foolish idea into my little birdie's head, eh?"

"Oh, nothing, dearest. I was only thinking how perfectly dreadful it would be if one of us should speak harshly to the other."

"Well, don't think of such wicked, utterly impossible things any more. We can never, never, never quarrel."

"I know it, darling. Good-by, you dear old precious, good-by, and—oh, wait a second, Clarence; I've written a note to mamma; can't you run around to the house and leave it for her some time to-day?"

"Why, yes, dearie; if I have time."

"If you have time? O Clarence!"

"What is it, little girlie?"

"Oh, to say 'if you have time' to do almost the very first errand your little wife asks you to do."

"Well, well, I expect to be very busy to-day."

"Too busy to please me? O Clarence, you hurt my feelings so."

"Why, child, I——"

"I'm not a child, I'm a married woman, and I——"

"There, there, my pet. I——"

"No, no, Clarence, if I were your p—p—pet you'd——"

"But, Mabel, do be reasonable."

"O Clarence! don't speak to me so."

"Mable, be sensible, and——"

"Go on, Clarence, go on; break my heart."

"Stuff and nonsense."

"Oh! o—o—o—o—oh!"

"What have I said or done?"

"As if you need ask! But go—hate me if you will, Clarence, I——"

"This is rank nonsense!"

"I'll go back to mamma if you want me to. She loves me, if you don't."

"You must have a brain-storm!"

"Oh! yes, sneer at me, ridicule me, break my poor heart. Perhaps you had better strike me!"

He bangs the door, goes down the steps on the jump, and races off, muttering something about women being the "queerest creatures."

Of course, they'll make it up when he comes home, and they'll have many a little tiff in the years to come, and when they grow old they'll say:

"We've lived together forty-five years, and in all that time have never spoken a cross word to each other!"

SONG OF THE "L"

BY GRENVILLE KLEISER

NOTE—*The New York elevated cars were so overcrowded at the rush hours of the day that passengers were obliged to ride on engines.*

Jam them in, ram them in,
  People still a-coming,
Slam them in, cram them in,
  Keep the thing a-humming!
Millionaires and carpenters,
Office boys, stenographers,
Workingmen and fakirs,
Doctors, undertakers,
Brokers and musicians,
Writers, politicians,
Clergymen and plumbers,
Entry clerks and drummers,
Pack them in, whack them in,
  People still a-coming!

Mash them in, crash them in,
  Still there's more to follow,
Shoot them in, boot them in,
  Don't take time to swallow!
Pretty maid and tailor-made,
Stylish maid and home-made,
Jersey maid and ready-made
House maid and old maid!
Billionaire and haughty air,
Bald head and golden hair,
Always there, never there,
Ah there and get there!
Squeeze them in, tease them in,
  Still there's more to follow.

Bump them in, thump them in,
  Why do people worry?
Throw them in, blow them in,
  Everyone must hurry.
Take a place behind the gate,
Get your clothes prest while you wait.
Grab a seat, don't give a rap
For the lady at the strap.
If your life is spared till night
You can tell your wife all right:

How the gateman shoved them in,
Slammed them in, jammed them in,
Crammed them in, damned them in,
Blew them in, cuffed them in,
Fired them in, kicked them in,
Bumped them in, thumped them in,
Beat them in, knocked them in,
Rapped them in, squashed them in,
Rammed them in, whipped them in,
Pushed them in, banged them in,
Crusht them in, rushed them in,
Dashed them in, slashed them in,
Flung them in, jerked them in,
Tossed them in, shied them in,
Hauled them in, forced them in,
Whacked them in, crowded them in,
Prodded them in, pulled them in,
Dumped them in, drove them in,
Hammered them in, battered them in,
Pitched them in, urged them in,
Hustled them in, bustled them in,
Hurried them in, worried them in,
As if their heads were hollow!

THE VILLAGE ORACLE

BY J. L. HARBOUR

"Why, Mis' Farley, is it really you? It's been so long sence I saw you that I hardly knowed you. Come in an' set down. I was jest a-wishin' some one would come in. I've felt so kind of downsy all mornin'. I reckon like enough it is my stummick. I thought some of goin' to see old Doctor Ball about it, but, la, I know jest what he'd say. He'd look at my tongue an' say, 'Coffee,' an' look cross. He lays half the mis'ry o' the world to coffee. Says it is a rank pizen to most folks, an' that lots o' the folks now wearin' glasses wouldn't need 'em if they'd let coffee alone. Says it works on the ocular nerves an' all that, but I reckon folks here in Granby will go on drinkin' coffee jest the same.

"You won't mind if I keep right on with my work, will you, seein' that it ain't nothin' but sewin' carpet-rags? I've got to send my rags to the weaver this week, or she can't weave my carpet until after she comes home from a visit she 'lows on makin' to her sister over in Zoar. It's just a hit-er-miss strip o' carpet I'm makin' for my small south chamber. I set out to make somethin' kind o' fancy with a twisted strip an' the chain in five colors, but I found I hadn't the right kind of rags to carry it through as I wanted to; so I jest decided on a plain hit-er-miss. I don't use the south chamber no great nohow. It's the room my first husband and his first wife and sev'ral of his kin all died in; so the 'sociations ain't none too cheerin', an' I—I—s'pose you know about Lyddy Baxter losin' her husband last week? No? Well, he's went the way o' the airth, an' Lyddy wore my mournin'-veil an' gloves to the funeral. They're as good as they were the day I follered my two husbands to the grave in 'em. When a body pays two dollars an' sixty-eight cents for a mournin'-veil, it behooves 'em to take keer of it, an' not switch it out wearin' it common as Sally Dodd did hern. If a body happens to marry a second time, as I did, a mournin'-veil may come in handy, jest as mine did.

"Yes, Liddy's husband did go off real sudden. It was this new-fashioned trouble, the appendysheetus, that tuk him off. They was jest gittin' ready to op'rate on him when he went off jest as easy as a glove. There's three thousand life-insurance; so Lyddy ain't as bereft as some would be. Now, if she'll only have good jedgement when she gits the money, an' not fool it away as Mis' Mack did her husband's life-insurance. He had only a thousand dollars, an' she put haif of it on her back before three months, an' put three hundred into a pianny she couldn't play. She said a pianny give a house sech an air. I up an' told her that money would soon be all 'air' if she didn't stop foolin' it away.

"I wouldn't want it told as comin' from me, but I've heerd that it was her that put that advertisement in the paper about a widder with some means wishin' to correspond with a gentleman similarly situated with a view to matrimony. I reckon she had about fifty dollars left at that time. I tried to worm something about it out of the postmaster; for of course he'd know about her mail, but he was as close as a clam-shell. I reckon one has to be kind of discreet if one is postmaster, but he might of known that anything he told me wouldn't go no farther if he didn't want it to. I know when to speak an' when to hold my tongue if anybody in this town does.

"Did you know that Myra Dart was goin' to marry that Rylan chap? It's so. I got it from the best authority. An' she's nine years an' three months an' five days older than him. I looked it up in the town hist'ry. It's a good deal of a reesk for a man to marry a woman that's much older than he is.

"But, my land, it's a good deal of a reesk to git married at all nowadays. You never know what you're gittin' ontil it's too late to undo the matter. Seems to me there must be a screw loose somewhere, or matrimony wouldn't be the fizzle it is in so many instances. An' it's about six o' one an' half a dozen o' the other when it comes to dividin' the blame. You know my first husband was jestice o' the peace five years, an' he had considdable marryin' to do, an' I saw a good deal o' what loose idees some people had about matrimony.

"I recollect of one couple comin' in to git married one evenin'. They was both in middle life, an' them kind usually acts the silliest with the exception of a real old pair. They are the beaterees for silly act'n'. Well, my husband never married any couple without maki'' sure that there was no onlawful hindrances in the way o' pa..t husbands and wives, an' so he says to the woman, 'Have you ever been married before?' An' she says jest as flippant, 'Yes, but he didn't live but three weeks; so it ain't wuth speakin' of.' Now wa'n't that scand'lous? It jest showed how lightly some folks look on the solemn ord'nance o' matrimony.

"I reckon you know that the Porters have a boy at their house? No? Well, they have. He was born at twenty minutes to one las' night, or this mornin' ruther, an' old Susan Puffer is to do the nussin'. I heard a wagon drive by here lickety-split at most midnight las' night an' I sez to myself, sez I, 'I'll bet that's Hi Porter tearin' off for old Susan Puffer', an' I got up, an' wrapped a blanket around me, an' waited for the wagon to come back; an' when it did, I called out, 'That you, Hi an' Susan?' It gives 'em a good deal of a start, but Susan called out that it was her, an' I went back to bed. Some folks would of been curious-minded enough to of went right over to the Porters', but I ain't that pryin' an' I didn't go over till after breakfast this mornin'.

"It's a real nice baby, an' it's goin' to be the livin' spit o' Hi exceptin' for its nose, which is its mother's all over; an' its mouth is the livin' counterpart o' its grandfather Porter's an' it's got the Davis ears. You know its mother was a Davis. I hope it won't have to be a bottle-riz baby. I don't care how good these infant foods may be; I don't think that a bottle-riz baby is ever the equal of one that ain't bottle-riz. The Lord must of intended mothers to nuss their babies, or He wouldn't of made 'em so they could. So I—must you be goin'? What's your hurry? I'd love to have you set all afternoon. It's so long sense you have been here, an' I do so enjoy havin' the neighbors drop in an' tell me all that's goin' on. I never go no place to hear the news. I wish you'd come in real often an' talk to me.

"Looks some like rain. I hope it'll be fair to-morrow, for I 'low on goin' over to Lucindy Baxter's to spend the day. Me an' her went over to Ware Monday, an' had a real nice all-day visit with Lucindy's married daughter. She's real nicely fixt, an' she had three kinds of cake besides cookies for tea. Seems to me one kind an' the cookies would o' been plenty. Mebbe she wanted to let us see that her husband was a good pervider.

I went over to Zion Tuesday, an' Wednesday me an' Nancy Dodd went over to Becky Means's, and helped her quilt her album quilt; an' she had a chicken-pie for dinner that went a little ahead of anything I ever et in the way of chicken-pie. Nancy's a good cook anyhow. She gives a kind of a taste to things that only a born cook can give. I'm goin' over to the fair in Greenfield Friday; so I—do come over again soon. I git real lonesome stayin' to home close as I do, an' it's nice to have some one come in an' talk to me as you have. Good-by.

"Yes, I'll come over soon. But don't you wait for me. Come when you kin. I'm allus to home. Good-by. See my little chicks? I put a hen on thirteen eggs, an' she hatched out every blessed one of 'em. Wa'n't she smart? An she laid all the eggs herself, too. I got another hen comin' off on the tenth. Didn't the minister preach beautifully Sunday? I dunno as I ever heard a more upliftin' sermon. I see that his wife has her black silk made up that the Ladies' Society gave her on her birthday. Didn't seem to me it fit real well under the arms. Well, good-by, good-by."

By permission of the author and the *Christian Endeavor World*.

IF I CAN BE BY HER

BY BENJAMIN FRANKLIN KING

I d-d-don't c-c-care how the r-r-robin sings,
Er how the r-r-rooster f-f-flaps his wings,
Er whether 't sh-sh-shines, er whether 't pours,
Er how high up the eagle s-s-soars,
    If I can b-b-b-be by her.

I don't care if the p-p-p-people s-say
'At I'm weak-minded every w-way,
An' n-n-never had no cuh-common sense,
I'd c-c-c-cuh-climb the highest p-picket fence.
    If I could b-b-b-be by her.

If I can be by h-h-her, I'll s-s-swim
The r-r-r-est of life thro' th-th-thick an' thin;
I'll throw my overcoat away,
An' s-s-s-stand out on the c-c-c-oldest day,
    If I can b-b-b-be by her.

You s-s-see sh-sh-she weighs an awful pile,
B-b-b-but I d-d-d-don't care—sh-she's just my style,
An' any f-f-fool could p-p-p-lainly see
She'd look well b-b-b-by the side of me,
    If I could b-b-b-be by her.

I b-b-b-braced right up, and had the s-s-s-and
To ask 'er f-f-f-father f-f-fer 'er hand;
He said: "Wh-wh-what p-p-prospects have you got?"
I said: "I gu-gu-guess I've got a lot,
    If I can b-b-b-be by her."

It's all arranged f-f-fer Christmas Day,
Fer then we're goin' to r-r-r-run away,
An' then s-s-some th-th-thing that cu-cu-couldn't be
At all b-b-efore will then, you s-s-see,
    B-b-b-because I'll b-b-b-be by her.

From "Ben King's Verse," by permission of Forbes & Co., Chicago.

McCARTHY AND McMANUS

ANONYMOUS

An Irishman named Patrick McCarthy, having received an invitation to visit some friends who were stopping at one of the prominent hotels, suddenly realized that his best suit needed pressing. He sent the suit to his friend Michael McManus, the tailor, with instructions to put it in proper shape and to return it with all haste.

After waiting an hour or more, he became very impatient, and asked his wife to go for the clothes, telling her to be sure to bring them back with her. When she returned he was surprized to find she had not brought back his suit, and he said:

"Well, where are my clothes?"

"Don't ask me, don't ask me. I'm thot mad I'm almost afther killin' thot McManus!"

"Pfhot's thot? Pfhot's McManus done with thim?"

"He's done nothin' with thim, and he barely took notice of me."

"Shure woman, dear, pfhot's that you be tellin' me? Did Mac insult you,—for the love of hivins tell me quick?"

"Well, I will tell you. Whin I wint into the shop, there was McManus; instid of sittin' on the table as usual, he was sittin' forninst it, with a long shate of paper spread out, and he was a-writin' and a-writin' and a-writin'. Says I, 'Mr. McManus.' No answer. Again I says, 'Mr. McManus.' Still no answer. Says I, 'Look here, Mr. McManus, pfhot do you mean by kapin' my husband waitin' for his clothes?—have you got thim done?' Without raisin' his head he says, 'No, I haven't,' and wint on writin' and writin'. Says I, 'He's waitin' for thim.' Says he, 'Let him wait.' Says I, 'He won't.' Says he, 'He'll have to.' Says I, 'Pfhot do you mean by writin' thot long document, knowin' well thot my husband is waitin' for his clothes?' Says he, 'Well, if you must know, it's important business. Do you see thot list?' pointin' to a long list of names. 'Well,' says he, 'thot's a list of all the min *thot I can lick* in this neighborhood.' Says I, 'Is thot so?' Says he, 'Yes, thot is so.' Says I, 'Mr. McManus, have you got my husband's name on thot list?' Says he, takin' up the list and holdin' it near my face, 'Look at thot,—the *very first* name on the list!' and I was thot mad I couldn't talk."

"Do you mean to tell me thot he had *my name* on thot list?"

"I do, and the *very first one,*—on the *very top.*"

"Well, wait till I go over and see McManus."

A few minutes later Mr. McCarthy entered the shop of Mr. McManus, and said,

"Is McManus here?"

McManus replied, "He is and he's *very busy.*"

"Is thot so?"

"Yes, thot is so."

"Look here, McManus, pfhot makes you so busy?"

"Oh, I'm just doin' a little writin'."

"Well, what is it you're writin'?"

"Well, I'll tell you. I'm makin' out a list of all the min thot I can lick in this neighborhood, and a moighty big list it is. Just look at thot."

"Say Mac, is *my name* on thot list?"

"Is Pat McCarthy's name on this list? Well, you can just bet your life it is, and it's the *very first one!*"

"Is thot so, McManus?"

"Yes, thot's so."

McCarthy, taking off his coat and rolling up his sleeves, said: "Look here, McManus, *I can lick you.*"

"Did you say you *thought* you could lick me?"

"I said I *can* lick you."

"You say you *can* lick me?"

"Yes, thot's what I said."

"All right. *Off goes your name from the list.*"

AND SHE CRIED

BY MINNA IRVING

Miss Muriel Million was sitting alone,
    With a very disconsolate air;
Her fluffy blue tea-gown was fastened awry,
    And frowsy and rumpled her hair.
"Oh, what is the matter?" I said in alarm,
    "I beg you in me to confide."
But she buried her face in her 'kerchief of lace,
    And she cried, and she cried, and she cried.

"Come out for a spin in the automobile,
    The motor-boat waits at the pier;
Or let's take a drive in the sunshiny park,
    Or a canter on horseback, my dear."
T'was thus that I coaxed her in lover-like tones,
    As I tenderly knelt at her side,
But refusing all comfort she pushed me aside,
    While she cried, and she cried, and she cried.

"Pray whisper, my darling, this terrible wo,
    You know I would love you the same,
If the millions of papa vanish in smoke
    And you hadn't a cent to your name,

By permission of the author and of the *New York Herald.*

If you came to the church in a garment of rags
　I would wed you with rapturous pride."
She nestled her cheek to my shoulder at this,
　Tho she cried, and she cried, and she cried.

"You know," she exclaimed in a piteous wail,
　"That love of a hat that I wore?—
The one with pink roses and chiffon behind,
　And a fluffy pink feather before?—
I paid Madame Modeste a hundred for that,
　And our parlor-maid, Flora McBride,
Has got one just like it for three twenty-five!"
　And she cried, and she cried, and she cried.

DOT LEEDLE BOY

BY JAMES WHITCOMB RILEY

Ot's a leedle Gristmas story
　Dot I told der leedle folks—
Und I vant you stop dot laughin'
　·Und grackin' funny jokes!—
So help me Peter-Moses!
　Ot's no time for monkeyshine,
Ober I vas told you somedings
　Of dot leedle boy of mine!

Ot vas von cold vinter vedder,
　Ven the snow was all about—
Dot you have to chop der hatchet
　Eef you got der sauerkraut!
Und der cheekens on der hind leg
　Vas standin' in der shine,
Der sun shmile out dot morning
　On dot leedle boy of mine.

He vas yoost a leedle baby,
  Not bigger as a doll
Dot time I got acquaintet—
  Ach! you ought to heard 'im squall!—
I grackys! dot's der moosic
  Ot make me feel so fine
Ven first I vas been marriet—
  Oh, dot leedle boy of mine!

He look' yoost like his fader!—
  So, ven der vimmen said,
"Vot a purty leedle baby!"
  Katrina shake her head—
I dink she must 'a' notice
  Dot der baby vas a-gryin',
Und she cover up der blankets
  Of dot leedle boy of mine.

Vell, ven he vas got bigger,
  Dot he grawl und bump his nose,
Und make der table over,
  Und molasses on his glothes—
Dot make 'im all der sweeter,—
  So I say to my Katrina:
"Better you vas quit a-sphankin'
  Dot leedle boy of mine!"

I vish you could 'a' seen id—
  Ven he glimb up on der chair
Und semash der lookin'-glasses
  Ven he try to comb his hair
Mit a hammer!—Und Katrina
  Say, "Dot's an ugly sign!"
But I laugh und vink my fingers
  At dot leedle boy of mine.

But vonce, dot vinter morning,
  He shlip out in der snow
Mitout no stockin's on 'im—
  He say he "vant to go
Und fly some mit der birdies!"
  Und ve give 'im medi-cine
Ven he catch der "parrygoric"—
  Dot leedle boy of mine!

Und so I set und nurse 'im,
  Vile der Gristmas vas come roun',
Und I told 'im 'bout "Kriss Kringle,"
  How he come der chimbly down;
Und I ask 'im if he love 'im
  Eef he bring 'im someding fine?
"Nicht besser as mein fader,"
  Say dot leedle boy of mine.

Und he put his arms aroun' me
  Und hug so close und tight,
I hear der glock a-tickin'
  All der balance of der night!—
Someding make me feel so funny
  Ven I say to my Katrina,
"Let us go und fill der stockin's
  Of dot leedle boy of mine."

Vell—ve buyed a leedle horses
  Dot you pull 'im mit a shtring,
Und a little fancy jay-bird—
  Eef you vant to hear 'im sing
You took 'im by der topknot
  Und yoost blow in behine—
Und dot make much *spectahkle*
  For dot leedle boy of mine.

Und gandies, nuts und raisins—
  Und I buy a leedle drum
Dot I vant to hear 'im rattle
  Ven der Gristmas morning come!
Und a leedle shmall tin rooster
  Dot vould crow so loud und fine
Ven he squeeze 'im in der morning,
  Dot leedle boy of mine.

Und—vile ve vas a-fixin'—
  Dot leedle boy vake out!
I t'ought he been a-dreamin'
  "Kriss Kringle" vas about,—
For he say—*"Dot's him!—I see 'im*
  Mit der shtars dot make der shine!"
Und he yoost keep on a-cryin'—
  Dot leedle boy of mine,—

Und gettin' vorse und vorser—
  Und tumble on der bed!
So—ven der doctor seen id,
  He kindo shake his head,
Und veel his pulse—und visper:
  "Der boy is a-dyin'."
You dink I could *believe* id?
  Dot leedle boy of mine?

I told you, friends—dot's someding,
  Der last time dot he spheak
Und say, *"Goot-by, Kriss Kringle!"*
  —Dot make me feel so veak
I yoost kneel down und drimble,
  Und bur-sed out a-cryin',
"Mein Gott, Mein Gott in Himmel!—
  Dot leedle boy of mine!"

Der sun don't shine *dot* Gristmas!
 . . . Eef dot leedle boy vould liff'd—
No deefer-en'! for *heaven* vas
 His leedle Gristmas gift! . . .
Und der *rooster,* und der *gandy,*
 Und me—und my Katrina—
Und der jay-bird—is a-vatin'
 For dot leedle boy of mine.

MR. DOOLEY ON THE GRIP

BY FINLAY PETER DUNNE

Mr. Dooley was discovered making a seasonable beverage, consisting of one part syrup, two parts quinine, and fifteen parts strong waters.

"What's the matter?" asked Mr. McKenna.

"I have th' lah gr-rip," said Mr. Dooley, blowing his nose and wiping his eyes. "Bad cess to it! Oh, me poor back! I feels as if a dhray had run over it. Did ye iver have it? Ye did not? Well, ye're lucky. Ye're a lucky man.

"I wint to McGuire's wake las' week. They gave him a dacint sind-off. No porther. An' himself looked natural, as fine a corpse as iver Gavin layed out. Gavin tould me so himsilf. He was as proud iv McGuire as if he owned him. Fetched half th' town in to look at him, an' give ivry wan iv thim cards. He near frightened ol' man Dugan into a faint. 'Misther Dugan, how old a-are ye?' 'Sivinity-five, thanks be,' says Dugan. 'Thin,' says Gavin, 'take wan iv me cards,' he says. 'I hope ye'll not forget me,' he says.

" 'Twas there I got th' lah grip. Lastewise, it is me own opinion iv it, tho th' docthor said I swallowed a bug. It don't seem right, Jawn, f'r th' McGuires is a clane fam'ly; but th'

docthor said a bug got into me system. 'What sort if bug?' says
I. 'A lah grip bug,' he says. 'Ye have Mickrobes in ye're lungs,'
he says. 'What's thim?' says I. 'Thim's th' lah grip bugs,' says
he. 'Ye took wan in, an' warmed it,' he says, 'an' it has growed
an' multiplied till ye're system does be full if thim,' he says, 'millions iv thim,' he says, 'marchin' an' counter-marchin' through ye.'
'Glory be to the saints!' says I. 'Had I better swallow some in-
sect powdher?' I says. 'Some iv thim in me head has a fallin'
out, an' is throwin' bricks.' 'Foolish man,' says he. 'Go to bed,'
he says, 'an' lave thim alone,' he says; 'whin they find who they're
in,' he says, 'they'll quit ye.'

"So I wint to bed, an' waited while th' Mickrobes had fun with
me. Mondah all iv thim was quiet but thim in me stummick.
They stayed up late dhrinkin' an' carousin' an' dancin' jigs till
wurruds come up between th' Kerry Mickrobes an' thim fr'm
Wexford; an' th' whole party wint over to me left lung, where
they cud get th' air, an' had it out. Th' nex' day th' little Mickrobes made a tobaggan slide iv me spine; an' manetime some
Mickrobes that was wurkin' f' th' tilliphone comp'ny got it in
their heads that me legs was poles, an' put on their spikes an'
climbed all night long.

"They was tired out th' nex' day till about five o'clock, whin
thim that was in me head begin flushin' out th' rooms; an' I knew
there was goin' to be doin's in th' top flat. What did thim Mickrobes do but invite all th' other Mickrobes in f'r th' ev'nin'. They
all come. Oh, by gar, they was not wan iv thim stayed away.
At six o'clock they begin to move fr'm me shins to me throat.
They come in platoons an' squads an' dhroves. Some iv thim
brought along brass bands, an' more thin wan hundred thousand
iv thim dhruv through me pipes on dhrays. A trolley line was
started up me back, an iv'ry car run into a wagon-load if scrap-
iron at th' base if me skull.

"Th' Mickrobes in me head must 've done thimselves proud.
They tipped over th' chairs an' tables; an' in less time thin it
takes to tell, th' whole party was at it. They'd been a hurlin'
game in th' back iv me skull, an' th' young folks was dancin'
breakdowns an' havin' leppin matches in me forehead; but they
all stopt, to mix in. Oh, 'twas a grand shindig—tin millions

iv men, women, an childher rowlin' on th' flure, hands an' feet
goin', ice-picks an' hurlin' sticks, clubs, brick-bats, flyin' in th'
air! How many iv thim was kilt I niver knew; f'r I wint as daft
as a hen, an' dhreamt iv organizin' a Mickrobe Campaign Club
that'd sweep th' prim'ries, an' maybe go acrost an' free Ireland.
Whin I woke up, me legs was as weak as a day-old baby's, an'
me poor head impty as a cobbler's purse. I want no more iv thim.
Give me anny bug fr'm a cockroach to an aygle, save an' excipt
thim West if Ireland Fenians, th' Mickrobes.''

By permission of Small, Maynard & Company.

A RAINY DAY EPISODE

ANONYMOUS

One morning recently as I was about to start from my home,
I noticed that it was raining very hard outside, and as I turned
to the rack to get an umbrella I was surprized to find that out of
five umbrellas there was not one in the lot I could use. On the
impulse of the moment I decided to take the whole five down town
to the umbrella hospital and have them all repaired at once.

Just as I started from the door my wife asked me to be sure
and bring her umbrella back as she wanted to use it that evening.
This imprest the subject of umbrellas very vividly on my mind,
so I did not fail to leave the five umbrellas to be repaired, stating
I would call for them on my way home in the evening.

When I went to lunch at noon it was still raining very hard,
but as I had no umbrella this simply imprest the subject on my
mind. I went to a nearby restaurant, sat down at a table, and
had been there only a few minutes when a young lady came in
and sat down at the same table with me. I was first to finish,
however, and getting up I absent-mindedly picked up her umbrella and started for the door. She called out to me and reminded me that I had her umbrella, whereupon I returned it to
her with much embarrassment and many apologies.

This incident served to impress the subject more deeply on
my mind, so on my way home in the evening I called for my

umbrellas, bought a newspaper, and boarded a street-car. I was deeply engrossed in my newspaper, having placed the five umbrellas alongside of me in the car, but all at once I had a peculiar feeling of someone staring at me. Suddenly I looked up from my paper, and was surprized to see sitting directly opposite me the same young woman I had met in the restaurant! She had a broad smile on her face, and looking straight into my eyes she said knowingly: "You've had a successful day, to-day, haven't you?"

I KNEW HE WOULD COME IF I WAITED

BY HORACE G. WILLIAMSON

I knew he would come if I waited,
  Tho waiting, it caused me despair;
And I sat by the window and listened
  To hear his first step on the stair:
For I knew he would come if I waited,
  But anxiously I paced 'round the floor;
Oh, to see his own form on the threshold
  As I hastened to open the door.
Would he come? But how dare I question
  His faithfulness to his own word;
Would he dare not come at my calling?
  Or was that his dear step that I heard?
Oh, I rush to the door for to meet him,
  For to welcome him here after all,
For I knew he would come if I waited,
  He would come to answer my call.
Yes, yes, it is he on the pavement,
  He's coming, he's ringing the bell,
And my heart beats wild with rapture
  Of a joy which I never can tell,
For I knew he would come if I waited,
  Yes, he'd come at my call; joy, O joy,
What happiness it is to welcome
  Just to welcome: "the messenger boy."

LOVE'S MOODS AND SENSES

ANONYMOUS

Sally Salter, she was a young lady who taught,
And her friend Charley Church was a preacher who praught!
Tho his enemies called him a screecher who scraught.

His heart when he saw her kept sinking, and sunk,
And his eye, meeting hers, began winking, and wunk;
While she in her turn fell to thinking, and thunk.

He hastened to woo her, and sweetly he wooed,
For his love grew until to a mountain it grewed,
And what he was longing to do then he doed.

In secret he wanted to speak, and he spoke,
To seek with his lips what his heart long had soke;
So he managed to let the truth leak, and it loke.

He asked her to ride to the church, and they rode,
They so sweetly did glide, that they both thought they glode,
And they came to the place to be tied, and were tode.

Then, "homeward," he said, "let us drive," and they drove,
And soon as they wished to arrive, they arrove;
For whatever he couldn't contrive she controve.

The kiss he was dying to steal, then he stole:
At the feet where he wanted to kneel, then he knole,
And said, "I feel better than ever I fole."

So they to each other kept clinging and clung;
While time his swift circuit was winging, and wung;
And this was the thing he was bringing, and brung:

The man Sally wanted to catch, and had caught—
That she wanted from others to snatch, and had snaught—
Was the one that she now liked to scratch, and she scranght.

And Charley's warm love began freezing, and froze,
While he took to teasing, and cruelly toze
The girl he had wished to be squeezing, and squoze.

"Wretch!" he cried, when she threatened to leave him, and left,
"How could you deceive me, as you have deceft?"
And she answered, "I promised to cleave, and I've cleft!"

A NOCTURNAL SKETCH

BY THOMAS HOOD

Even is come; and from the dark park, hark,
The signal of the setting sun—one gun!
And six is sounding from the chime, prime time
To go and see the Drury-Lane Dane slain,—
Or hear Othello's jealous doubt spout out,—
Or Macbeth raving at that shade-made blade,
Denying to his frantic clutch much touch;
Or else to see Ducrow with wide stride ride
Four horses as no other man can span;
Or in the small Olympic Pit, sit split
Laughing at Liston, while you quiz his phiz.
Anon Night comes, and with her wings brings things
Such as, with his poetic tongue, Young sung;
The gas up-blazes with its bright, white light,
And paralytic watchmen prowl, howl, growl,
About the streets and take up Pall-Mall Sal,
Who, hasting to her nightly jobs, robs fobs.

Now thieves to enter for your cash, smash, crash,
Past drowsy Charley, in a deep sleep, creep,
But frightened by Policeman B 3, flee,
And while they're going, whisper low, "No go!"
Now puss, while folks are in their beds, treads leads.
And sleepers waking, grumble: "Drat that cat!"
Who in the gutter caterwauls, squalls, mauls
Some feline foe, and screams in shrill ill will.

Now Bulls of Bashan, of a prize size, rise
In childish dreams, and with a roar gore poor
Georgy, or Charley, or Billy, willy-nilly;—
But Nursemaid, in a nightmare rest, chest-prest,
Dreameth of one of her old flames, James Games,
And that she hears—what faith is man's!—Ann's banns
And his, from Rev. Mr. Rice, twice, thrice:
White ribbons flourish, and a stout shout out,
That upward goes, shows Rose knows those bows' woes!

KATIE'S ANSWER

ANONYMOUS

Och, Katie's a rogue, it is thrue,
But her eyes, like the sky, are so blue,
   An' her dimples so swate,
   An' her ankles so nate,
She dazed, an' she bothered me, too—

Till one mornin' we wint for a ride;
Whin, demure as a bride, by my side,
   The darlint, she sat,
   With the wickedest hat,
'Neath a purty girl's chin iver tied.

An' my heart, arrah, thin how it bate
For my Kate looked so temptin' an' swate,
  Wid cheeks like the roses,
    An' all the red posies,
That grow in her garden so nate.

But I sat just as mute as the dead,
Till she said, wid a toss of the head,
  "If I'd known that to-day
    You'd have nothing to say,
I'd have gone wid my cousin instead."

Thin I felt myself grow very bowld,
For I knew she'd not scold if I towld
  Uv the love in my heart,
    That would never depart,
Tho I lived to be wrinkled an' owld.

An' I said, "If I dared to do so,
I'd lit go uv the baste, an' I'd throw
  Both arms 'round yer waist,
    An' be stalin' a taste
Uv them lips that are coaxin' me so."

Then she blushed a more illegent red,
As she said, widout raisin' her head,
  An' her eyes lookin' down
    'Neath her lashes so brown,
"Would ye like me to drive, Misther Ted?"

"'SPÄCIALLY JIM"

ANONYMOUS

I wus mighty good-lookin' when I was young,
  Peert an' black-eyed an' slim,
With fellers a-courtin' me Sunday nights,
  'Späcially Jim!

The likeliest one of 'em all was he,
  Chipper an' han'som' an' trim,
But I tossed up my head an' made fun o' the crowd,
  'Späcially Jim!

I said I hadn't no 'pinion o' men,
  An' I wouldn't take stock in him!
But they kep' up a-comin' in spite o' my talk,
  'Späcially Jim!

I got so tired o' havin' 'em roun'
  'Späcially Jim!
I made up my mind I'd settle down
  An' take up with him.

So we was married one Sunday in church,
  'Twas crowded full to the brim;
'Twas the only way to get rid of 'em all,
  'Späcially Jim.

AGNES, I LOVE THEE!

ANONYMOUS

I stood upon the ocean's briny shore;
And, with a fragile reed, I wrote
Upon the sand—"Agnes, I love thee!"
The mad waves rolled by, and blotted out
The fair impression.
Frail reed! cruel wave! treacherous sand!
I'll trust ye no more;
But, with giant hand, I'll pluck
From Norway's frozen shore
Her tallest pine, and dip its top
Into the crater of Vesuvius,
And upon the high and burnished heavens
I'll write,—"Agnes, I love thee!"—
And I would like to see any
Dog-goned wave wash that out!

THE GORILLA

ANONYMOUS

"O mighty ape!
  Half beast, half man,
Thy uncouth shape
  Betrays a plan
The gulf of Being at a bound to span.
Thou art the link between ourselves and brutes,
  Lifting the lower to a higher plane;
Thy human face all cavilers refutes,
  Who sneer at Darwin as a dreamer vain.
How camest thou beneath this canvas tent?
  Within this cage? behind these iron bars?
Thou, whose young days in tropic lands were spent,
  With strange companions, under foreign stars?
Art thou not lonely? What is life to thee
  Thus mewed in prison, innocent of crime,
Become a spectacle for crowds to see,
  And reckless boys to jeer at all the time?
Hast thou no feelings such as we possess?
  Art thou devoid of any sense of shame?
Rise up, O brother, and thy wrongs redress;
  Rise in thy might, and be no longer tame!"

I paused in my apostrophe. The animal arose;
He seized the bars that penned him in: my blood in terror froze.
He shook the cage from side to side; the frightened people fled;
Then, in a tone of savage wrath, the horrid monster said:
"I'm hired by the wake to wear the dhirty craythur's shkin;
I came from Tipperary, and me name is Micky Flynn!"

BANGING A SENSATIONAL NOVELIST

ANONYMOUS

The other day a stout woman, armed with an umbrella, and leading a small urchin, called at the office of a New York boys' story paper.

"Is this the place where they fight Indians?" she inquired of the young man in charge. "Is this the locality where the brave boy charges up the canyon and speeds a bullet to the heart of the dusky redskin?" and she jerked the urchin around by the ear and brought her umbrella down on the desk.

"We publish stories for boys, and——"

"I want to know if these are the premises on which the daring lad springs upon his fiery mustang, and, darting through the circle of thunderstruck savages, cuts the captive's cords and bears him away before the wondering Indians have recovered from their astonishment? That's the information I'm after. I want to know if that sort of thing is perpetrated here!" and she swung the umbrella around her head.

"I don't remember those specific facts, but——"

"I want to know if this is the precinct where the adventurous boy jumps on the back of a buffalo and with unerring aim picks off one by one the bloodthirsty pursuers who bite the dust at every crack of the faithful rifle! I'm looking for the place where that sort of thing happens!" and this time she brought the unlucky man a tremendous whack across the back.

"I think——"

"I'm in search of the shop in which the boy road-agent holds the quivering stage-driver powerless with his glittering eye, while he robs the male passengers with an adroitness born of long and tried experience, and kisses the hands of the lady passengers with a gallantry of bearing that bespeaks noble birth and a chivalrous nature! I'm looking for the apartment in which that business is transacted!"

"Upon my word, madam, I——"

"I want to be introduced to the jars in which you keep the

boy scouts of the Sierras! Show me the bins full of the boy
detectives of the prairie! Point out to me the barrels full of
boy pirates of the Spanish main!" and with each demand she
brought her umbrella down on the young man's head until he
jumped over the desk and sought safety in a neighboring canyon.

"I'll teach 'em!" she panted, grasping the urchin by the ear
and leading him off. "I'll teach 'em to make it good or dance.
Want to go fight Indians any more (*twisting the boy's ear*)?
Want to stand proudly upon the pinnacle of the mountain and
scatter the plain beneath with the bleeding bodies of uncounted
slain? Propose to spring upon the taffrail and with a ringing
word of command send a broadside into the richly-laden galley,
and then mercifully spare the beautiful maiden in the cabin,
that she may become your bride? Eh? Going to do it any more?"

The boy exprest his permanent abandonment of all the glories
enumerated.

"Then come along," said she, taking him by the collar. "Let
me catch you around with any more ramrods and carving knives,
and you'll think the leaping, curling, resistless prairie fire has
swept with a ferocious roar of triumph across the trembling
plains and lodged under your jacket to stay!"

HOPKINS' LAST MOMENTS

ANONYMOUS

Nurses in hospitals are inclined to lay too much stress on the
advantages received by the patients and their duty of thankful-
ness, but it is the poor soldier who suffers most from always having his cause to be grateful flung in his teeth. The following
true story took place between the chaplain and the hospital orderly:

Chaplain—"So poor Hopkins is dead. I should like to have
spoken to him once more and soothed his last moments. Why
didn't you call me?"

Hospital Orderly—"I didn't think you ought to be disturbed
for 'Opkins, sir; so I just soothed him as best I could myself."

Chaplain—"Why, what did you say to him?"
Orderly—"I sez, ' 'Opkins, you're mortal bad.'
" 'I am,' sez 'e."
" ' 'Opkins,' sez I, 'I don't think you'll get better.' "
" 'No,' sez 'e."
" ' 'Opkins,' sez I, 'you're going fast.' "
" 'Yes,' sez 'e."
" ' 'Opkins,' sez I, 'I don't think you can 'ope to go to 'eaven.' "
" 'I don't think I can,' sez 'e."
" 'Well, then, 'Opkins,' sez I, 'you'll go to 'ell.' "
" 'I suppose so,' sez 'e."
" ' 'Opkins,' sez I, 'you ought to be wery grateful as there's a place perwided for you, and that you've got somewhere to go.' And I think 'e 'eard, sir, for 'e just gave a little groan, turned over, and then 'e died."

THE FAIRIES' TEA

ANONYMOUS

Five little fairies went out to take tea,
Under the shade of a juniper tree.
Each had a cup from an acorn cut,
And a plate from the rind of a hickory nut.

The table was spread with a cloth all of lace,
Woven by spiders the banquet to grace.
Oh, what good things they all had to eat!—
Slices of strawberry,—my what a treat!

Honey the sweetest the wild bee could hive,
And a humming-bird's egg for each of the five.
Then they drank their host's health in their favorite drink,
Which was,—now what was it? Can anyone think?

Why the dew-drop that comes from the heart of the rose
Is the drink of the fairies, as everyone knows.

COUNTING EGGS

ANONYMOUS

Old Moses, who sells eggs and chickens on the streets of Austin for a living, is as honest an old negro as ever lived; but he has the habit of chatting familiarly with his customers, hence he frequently makes mistakes in counting out the eggs they buy. He carries his wares around in a small cart drawn by a diminutive donkey. He stopt in front of the residence of Mrs. Samuel Burton. The old lady herself came out to the gate to make the purchase.

"Have you any eggs this morning, Uncle Moses?" she asked.

"Yes, indeed I has. Jess got in ten dozen from de kentry."

"Are they fresh?"

"Fresh? Yes, indeed! I guantees 'em, an'—an'—de hen guantees 'em."

"I'll take nine dozen. You can just count them into this basket."

"All right, mum; (*he counts*) one, two, free, foah, five, six, seben, eight, nine, ten. You can rely on dem bein' fresh. How's your son comin' on de school? He must be mos' grown."

"Yes, Uncle Moses; he is a clerk in a bank in Galveston."

"Why, how ole am de boy?"

"He is eighteen."

"You don't tole me so! Eighteen, and getting a salary already! Eighteen (*counting*), nineteen, twenty, twenty-one, twenty-two, twenty-free, twenty-foah, twenty-five. And how's your gal comin' on? She was most growed up de last time I seed her."

"She is married and living in Dallas."

"Wall, I declar'; how time scoots away! And you say she has childruns? Why, how ole am de gal? She must be just about —"

"Thirty-three."

"Am dat so? (*Counting.*) Firty-free, firty-foah, firty-five, firty-six, firty-seben, firty-eight, firty-nine, forty, forty-one, forty-two, forty-free. Hit am singular dat you has sich ole childruns. You don't look more den forty years old yerseff."

"Nonsense, old man; I see you want to flatter me. When a person gets to be fifty-three years old——"

"Fifty-free! I jess dun gwinter bleeve hit; fifty-free, fifty-foah, fifty-five, fifty-six—I want you to pay 'tenshun when I count de eggs, so dar'll be no mistake—fifty-nine, sixty, sixty-one, sixty-two, sixty-free, sixty-foah. Whew! Dis am a warm day. Dis am de time ob year when I feels I'se gettin' ole myself; I ain't long fur dis world. You comes from an ole family. When your fadder died he was sebenty years ole."

"Seventy-two."

"Dat's old, suah. Sebenty-two, sebenty-free, sebenty-foah, sebenty-five, sebenty-six, sebenty-seben, sebenty-eight, sebenty-nine. And your mudder? She was one ob de noblest-lookin' ladies I eber see. You remind me ob her so much! She libed to mos' a hundred. I bleeves she was done past a centurion when she died."

"No, Uncle Moses; she was only ninety-six when she died."

"Den she wan't no chicken when she died, I know dat. Ninety-six, ninety-seben, ninety-eight, ninety-nine, one hundred, one, two, free, foah, five, six, seben, eight—dar, one hundred and eight nice fresh eggs—jess nine dozen; and here am one moah egg in case I have discounted myself."

Old Mose went on his way rejoicing. A few days afterward Mrs. Burton said to her husband:

"I am afraid that we will have to discharge Matilda. I am satisfied that she steals the milk and eggs. I am positive about the eggs, for I bought them day before yesterday, and now about half of them are gone. I stood right there, and heard Moses count them myself, and there were nine dozen."

THE OATMOBILE

ANONYMOUS

Ay yust bane oop by Minnesote
To sa my Onkle Yohn.
Ay stop me by St. Paul awhile
Yust for a little fun;

An' dere Ay saw one oatmobile—
  Dat bane de name you call;
Und yo could tak a ride on heem
  Mit out some horse at all.

Dat bane a purty nice machine
  Wit rubber tires an tings;
Yust sit heem lik a vagon on
  An' he run yust lik mit vings.
Ay ask dot man vot make heem go?
  He say, "My hade got vheels."
He say, "He feed heem plenty oat
  An' call heem Oat-mo-bile."

Ay say, "Ay know Ay bane grane Sweede
  Yust come from Nord Dakote,
But Ay dou belave he make heem go
  By feedin' vagin oat."
Ay say to heem, "Look here! Ay bane
  Some time in Missoure,
Ay know Ay'm grane, but yust de same
  Youbet me life, 'show me!'"

Dat feller lafe an' shake his head
  An' say, "Ay bane good show myself,"
Ay say, "Ay tink Ay punch your head
  An' lay you on de shelf."
Ay pick me oop a little stick
  Bane layin' on de seat
An bet me life, dot Oat-mo-bile
  Yust started oop de street.

Ay holler, "Wo-o-o!" but he don' stop
  An' den you bet my life
Ay wish Ay bane by Nord Dakote,
  At home mit Ann, my vife.

Dat Oat-mo-bile yust boomped me
　　Oop de side valk on an' stopt;
An' bucked me thro' de window
　　Of one dem butcher-shop.

He split me nose bay my face oop
　　He smash me almost dead;
He punch de inside of me mouth
　　All outside of me hade.
He hurt me eye so bad in one
　　Ay'm blin' yust like a beetle.
In oder one, Ay can see some
　　But only just a little.

De las Ay see of dat machine
　　He bané a buckin' still.
Ay tink he feed too many oat
　　Tod at old Oat-mo-bile.
Ay tell my wife, if I get vell
　　You bet I vill not monkey
Some anoder time with
　　Any Oat-mo-bile.

ALMOST BEYOND ENDURANCE

BY JAMES WHITCOMB RILEY

I ain't a-goin' to cry no more, no more!
I'm got earache, an' ma can't make it quit a-tall;
An' Carlo bite my rubber-ball
An' puncture it; an' Sis she take
An' poke my knife down through the stable-floor
An' loozed it,—blame it all!
But I ain't a-goin' to cry no more, no more!

An' Aunt Mame *wrote* she's comin' an' she *can't,*
Folks is come *there!*—An' I don't care if she *is* my aunt!
An' my eyes stings; an' I'm
Ist coughin' all the time,
An' hurts me so, an' where my side's so sore,
Grampa felt where, an' he
Says, "Maybe it's *pleurasy!*"
But I ain't a-goin' to cry no more, no more!

An' I clumbed up an' felled off the fence,
An' Herbert he ist laugh at me!
An' my fi' cents,
It sticked in my tin bank, an' I ist tore
Purt night my fum-nail off a-tryin' to git
It out—nen *smash* it! An' it's in there yet!
But I ain't a-goin' to cry no more, no more!

Oo! I'm so wicked! an' my breath's so *hot,*
Ist like I run an' don't rest none
But ist run on when I ought to not;
Yes, an' my chin
An' lips all warpy, an' teeth's so fast,
An's a place in my throat I can't swaller past,—
An' they all hurt so!
An' oh, my oh!
I'm a-startin' ag'in,—
I'm a-startin' ag'in, but I *won't* fer shore!
I ist ain't a-goin to cry no more, no more!

PROOF POSITIVE

ANONYMOUS

I stept into my room one day
And saw some children there at play.
I sought my little girl and found her
With half a dozen youngsters round her;
And from the way she slapped her rule,

I knew that they were "playing school."
I gave my little girl a kiss—
A pleasure that I never miss.
A murmur through the schoolroom ran,
A smile pervaded every feature,
"He must be a committeeman!"
They loud exclaimed. "He kissed the teacher!"

THE IRISH PHILOSOPHER

ANONYMOUS

LADIES AND GINTLEMEN:—I see so many foine-lookin' people sittin' before me, that if you'll excuse me I'll be after takin' a seat myself.

You don't know me, I'm thinkin,' or some of yees 'ud be noddin' to me afore this.

I'm a walkin' pedestrian, a traveling philosopher; Terry O'Mulligan's me name. I'm from Dublin, where many philosophers before me was raised and bred. Oh, philosophy is a foine study. I don't know anything about it, but it's a foine study. Before I kim over I attinded an important meetin' of philosophers in Dublin, and the discussin' and talkin' you'd hear there about the world 'ud warm the very heart of Socrates or Aristotle himself. Well, there was a great many *imminent* and learned min there at the meetin,' and I was there, too; and while we was in the very thickest of a heated argument a man comes up to me, and says he, "Do you know what we're talkin' about?" "I do," says I, "but I don't understand yees." "Could you explain the sun's motion round the earth?" says he. "I could," says I; "but I'd not know could you understand me or not." "Well," says he, "we'll see," says he.

Sure'n I didn't know anything how to get out of it then; so I piled in, for, says I to meself, never let on to anyone that you don't know anything, but make them believe that you do know all about it. So, says I to him, takin' up me shillalah this way (*holding up a very crooked stick horizontally*): "We will take that for

the straight line of the earth's equator." How's that for gehogg-
raphy? (*To the audience.*) Oh, that was straight till the other day
I bent it in an argument.

"Very good" says he. "Well," says I, "now the sun rises in the
east." (*Placing the disengaged hand at the eastern end of the
stick.*) Well, he couldn't deny that; "and," says I, "he-he-he-rises
in the mornin'." No more could he deny that. "Very early," says
I; "and when he gets up he

> " 'Darts his rosy beams
> Through the mornin' gleams.' "

Do you moine the poetry there? (*To the audience, with a
smile.*) "And he keeps on risin' an' risin' till he reaches his me-
ridan." "What's that?" says he. "His dinner-toime," says I.
"Sure'n that's my Latin for dinner-time. And when he gets his
dinner

> " 'He sinks to rest
> Behind the glorious hills of the west.' "

Oh, begorra, there's more poetry. I feel it croppin' out all
over me.

"There," says I, well satisfied with mesilf, "will that do for ye?"
"You haven't got done with him," says he.
"Done with him?" says I, kinder mad-like. "What more do you
want me to do with him? Didn't I bring him from the east to the
west? What more do you want?" "Oh," says he, "you have to
have him back agin in the east the next mornin'!"

By Saint Patrick, and wasn't I near betrayin' me ignorance.
Sure'n I thought there was a large family of suns, and they riz
one after the other; but I gathered meself quick, and says I to
him, "Well," says I, "I'm surprized you ax me that simple question. I thought any man 'ud know" says I, "when the sun sinks
to rest in the west that er—when the sun——" says I. "You
said that before" says he. "Well," I want to impress it strongly
upon you," says I. "When the sun sinks to rest behind the glorious hills of the east—no, west—why, he—why, he waits till it
grows very dark and then he *goes back in the noight-toime!*"

BELAGCHOLLY DAYS

ANONYMOUS

Chilly Dovebber with his boadigg blast
  Dow cubs add strips the beddow add the lawd
Eved October's suddy days are past—
    Add Subber's gawd!

I kdow dot what it is to which I cligg
  That stirs to sogg add sorrow, yet I trust
That still I sigg, but as the liddets sigg—
    Because I bust.

Add dow, farewell to roses add to birds,
  To larded fields and tigkligg streablets eke;
Farewell to all articulated words
    I faid would speak.

Farewell, by cherished strolliggs od the sward,
  Greed glades add forest shades, farewell to you;
With sorrowing heart I, wretched add forlord,
    Bid you—achew! ! !

A PANTOMIME SPEECH

ANONYMOUS

Have you ever realized what a funny thing it is to see a lot of people talking and gesticulating and not hear a single sound from them? The next time you are in a crowded dining-room, close your ears with your hands, and you will be quickly converted to the Darwinian theory.

This was forcibly imprest upon my mind at a political gathering. The hall was very large, but was crowded to the doors, so that when I reached there I was obliged to stand outside and on my toes to see the speakers. Please remember that altho I could in this way distinctly see the speakers, I was too far away to hear the slightest sound. It was simply a pantomime performance to me, and I shall try to give you a faithful representation of just what I saw.

Simply say: "The Chairman." The rest is pantomime. Seat yourself as an old man, put your right hand behind your ear as if listening to a side remark. Repeat to the left. Evidently some-one has told you it is time to begin. Take out your watch and compare it with the clock on the wall behind you. Bring out an imaginary pair of spectacles, clean them with your handkerchief, and as you put them on your nose draw down your face as old men do. Get up with seeming difficulty. The business here is *ad lib*. Point to the speaker of the evening, who is supposed to be sitting at your right. By silent movements of the lips seem to introduce him to the audience. Then suddenly remember that you have something else to say just as you are about to sit down. Repeat this two or three times. Then sit down at last with much difficuty.

Then say aloud: "The Speaker." Impersonate him as assuming a grandiloquent air. While he speaks in pantomime he rises on his toes and makes numerous gestures. He pounds fist on table. Someone evidently interrupts him from the audience. He looks in that direction and then replies. He seems to say to the man to come up on the platform or else get out of the hall. He talks for some time as if in argument, then dodges as if something has been thrown at him. Two or three times he has to dodge in this way and then something seems to have struck him in the face. He takes out his handkerchief and wipes off face and coat. Then things are thrown at him from right and left, while he continues to dodge. At last they come so thick that he rushes off the plat-form in great alarm.

THE ORIGINAL LAMB

ANONYMOUS

Oh, Mary had a little lamb, regarding whose cuticular
The fluff exterior was white and kinked in each particular.
On each occasion when the lass was seen perambulating,
The little quadruped likewise was there a gallivating.

One day it did accompany her to the knowledge dispensary,
Which to every rule and precedent was recklessly contrary.
Immediately whereupon the pedagog superior,
Exasperated, did eject the lamb from the interior.

Then Mary, on beholding such performance arbitrary,
Suffused her eyes with saline drops from glands called lachrymary,
And all the pupils grew thereat tumultuously hilarious,
And speculated on the case with wild conjectures various.

"What makes the lamb love Mary so?" the scholars asked the
     teacher.
He paused a moment, then he tried to diagnose the creature.
"Oh, *pecus amorem Mary habit omnia temporum.*"
"Thanks, teacher dear," the scholars cried, and awe crept darkly
     o'er 'em.

WHEN PA WAS A BOY

BY S. E. KISER

I wish 'at I'd of been here when
     My paw he was a boy;
They must of been excitement then—
     When my paw was a boy.
In school he always took the prize,
He used to lick boys twice his size—
I bet folks all had bulgin' eyes
     When my paw was a boy!

There was a lot of wonders done
  When my paw was a boy;
How grandpa must have loved his son,
  When my paw was a boy!
He'd git the coal and chop the wood,
And think up every way he could
To always just be sweet and good—
  When my paw was a boy!

Then everything was in its place,
  When my paw was a boy;
How he could rassle, jump and race,
  When my paw was a boy!
He never, never disobeyed;
He beat in every game he played—
Gee! What a record there was made!
  When my paw was a boy!

I wish 'at of been here when
  My paw was a boy;
They'll never be his like agen—
  Paw was the moddle boy.
But still last night I heard my maw
Raise up her voice and call my paw
The biggest goose she ever saw—
  He ought have stayed a boy.

By permission of Messrs. Forbes & Company, Chicago.

THE FRECKLED-FACED GIRL

(She entertains a visitor while her mother is dressing)

ANONYMOUS

"Ma's up-stairs changing her dress," said the freckled-faced little girl, tying her doll's bonnet-strings and casting her eye about for a tidy large enough to serve as a shawl for that double-jointed young person.

"Oh! your mother meedn't dress up for me," replied the female agent of the missionary society, taking a self-satisfied view of herself in the mirror. "Run up and tell her to come down just as she is in her every-day clothes, and not stand on ceremony."

"Oh! but she hasn't got on her every-day clothes. Ma was all drest up in her new brown silk, 'cause she expected Miss Diamond to-day. Miss Diamond always comes over here to show off her nice things, and ma don't mean to get left. When ma saw you coming, she said, 'The dickens!' and I guess she was mad about something. Ma said if you saw her new dress she'd have to hear all about the poor heathen, who don't have silk, and you'd ask her for more money to buy hymn-books to send to 'em. Say, do the nigger ladies use hymn-book leaves to do their hair up and make it frizzy? Ma says she guesses that's all the good the books do 'em, if they ever get any books. I wish my doll was a heathen!"

"Why, you wicked little girl, why do you want a heathen doll?" inquired the missionary lady, taking a mental inventory of the new things in the parlor to get material for a homily on worldly extravagance.

"So folks would send her lots of nice things to wear, and feel sorry to have her going about naked. I ain't a wicked girl, either, 'cause Uncle Dick—you know Uncle Dick, he's been out West, and he says I'm a holy terror, and he hopes I'll be an angel pretty soon. Ma'll be down in a minute, so you needn't take your cloak off. She said she'd box my ears if I asked you to. Ma's putting on that old dress she had last year, 'cause she said she didn't want you to think she was able to give much this time, and she needed a new muff worse than the queen of the cannon-ball islands needed religion. Uncle Dick says you ought to go to the islands, 'cause you'd be safe there, and the natifs'd be sorry they was such sinners if anybody would send you to 'em. He says he never seen a heathen hungry enough to eat you 'less 'twas a blind one, and you'd set a blind pagan's teeth on edge so he'd never hanker after any more missionary. Uncle Dick's awful funny, and makes pa and ma die laughing sometimes."

"Your Uncle Richard is a bad, depraved man, and ought to have remained out West, where his style is appreciated. He sets a bad example for little girls like you."

"Oh! I think he's nice. He showed me how to slide down the

banisters, and he's teaching me to whistle when ma ain't 'round. That's a pretty cloak you've got, ain't it? Do you buy all your good clothes with missionary money? Ma says you do."

Just then the freckled-faced little girl's ma came into the parlor and kissed the missionary lady on the cheek, and said she was delighted to see her, and they proceeded to have a real sociable chat. The little girl's ma can't understand why a person who professes to be so charitable as the missionary agent does should go right over to Miss Diamond's and say such ill-natured things as she did, and she thinks the missionary is a double-faced gossip.

WILLIE

BY MAX EHRMANN

A little boy went forth to school
  One day without his chum.
The teacher said, "Why, you're alone!
  Why doesn't Willie come?"
"O Willie!" sobbed the little boy,--
  There ain't no Willie now."
"What do you mean?" the teacher asked,
  With puzzled, knitted brow.
"Please, sir," the little boy replied,
  "We made a bet fur fun,--
Which one could lean the farthest out
  Our attic,--Willie won."

AMATEUR NIGHT

ANONYMOUS

It was one of those little evening entertainments where everyone talks at once, where everyone asks questions and does not wait for an answer. Mrs. Fitzgibbon, the hostess, finally broke into the babble:

"Sh! I want you all to be very quiet. Mr. Chooker—Mr. Chooker,—please don't talk,—don't talk, please,—Mr. Chooker is very excitable. Chooker,—yes, he is one of the Chookers. Young people come off the stairs. Sh! I have very great pleasure in introducing to you Mr. Chooker."

Mr. Chooker came forward with a malicious look, which seemed to say, "You all seem to be very happy,—very jolly,—and enjoying yourselves. Just wait a bit. I am about to recite a little poem of my own entitled, 'The Triple Suicide!'"

Then came the boy of the family, a kind of child prodigy, who, after giving a low and jerky bow, recited as follows: (*Here impersonate a boy in awkward style.*)

"A soldier of the Legion lay dying in Algiers,
There was lack of woman's nursing, there was dearth of woman's
    tears;—there was dearth of woman's tears." (*Stops.*)

"The women were crying, you know. Some were crying and others were weeping. Those that weren't weeping were crying!" (*Pauses, then bows low, and begins again.*)

"A soldier of the Legion lay dying in Algiers,
There was lack of woman's nursing, there was dearth of woman's
    tears;
But a comrade stood beside him, while his life-blood ebbed away—
while his life-blood ebbed away,—while his life-blood ebbed away
——"

"His blood was flowing along, you know. There was blood here and there. There was blood spattered over everything, and——" (*Pauses long, bows low, and begins again with great determination and in loud voice.*)

"A soldier of the Legion lay dying in Algiers,
There was lack of woman's nursing, there was dearth of woman's
    tears;
But a comrade stood beside him, while his life-blood ebbed away,—
ebbed away,—ebbed away (*gradually begins to cry*),—ebbed away (*as
if speaking to someone at the side*)—eh?" (*Exits slowly with hands
at eyes silently weeping.*)

The young miss of the family, recently graduated, next **gave** an original poem entitled "The Hen," as follows:

> "Tell me not in mournful numbers,
>   Life is but an empty dream!—
> For the hen is dead that slumbers,
>   And things are not what they seem.

> "Life is real, life is earnest,
>   And the shell is not its pen,
> Egg thou wert and egg remainest,
>   Was not spoken of the hen.

> "In the world's broad field of battle,
>   In the great barnyard of life,
> Be not like those lazy cattle,
>   Be a rooster in the strife.

> "Lives of roosters all remind us
>   We can make our lives sublime,
> And when roasted leave behind us
>   Hen-tracks on the sands of time.

> "Hen-tracks that perhaps another chicken
>   Drooping idly in the rain,
> Some forlorn and henpecked brother,
>   When he sees shall crow again."

The gem of the evening, however, was a recitation given in fine style by Mr. Chillingworth Chubb. He had rather a husky voice and a wooden arm. His memory, moreover, was defective. The effect of his wooden arm, which was made to perform the various actions of a real one, was highly amusing. (*Here the reciter may use "Excelsior," "The Speech of Mark Antony," or some similar selection. The left arm represents the wooden one. The hand should wear a right-hand, white kid glove, put on wrong way round with the finger-tips screwed into points. The arm should be assisted in all its movements by the right one. It should be made to move in a jerky and unnatural manner at all its joints. A violent push at the elbow raises it suddenly aloft, and it is brought again to the side by a tremendous slap from the right hand. Finally, the arm appears to get out of order, and moves violently in all directions, until at last the right hand, after vainly trying to reach it, pins it down to a table or to some other object. This imitation requires considerable practise, but when properly done never fails to send an audience into fits of laughter.)*

BOUNDING THE UNITED STATES

BY JOHN FISKE

Among the legends of our late Civil War there is a story of a dinner-party, given by the Americans residing in Paris, at which were propounded sundry toasts concerning not so much the past and present as the expected glories of the American nation. In the general character of these toasts, geographical considerations were very prominent, and the principal fact which seemed to occupy the minds of the speakers was the unprecedented bigness of our country.

"Here's to the United States!" said the first speaker,—"bounded on the north by British America, on the south by the Gulf of Mexico, on the east by the Atlantic Ocean, and on the west by the Pacific Ocean!" "But," said the second speaker, "this is far too limited a view of the subject, and, in assigning our boundaries, we must look to the great and glorious future, which is prescribed for us by the manifest destiny of the Anglo-Saxon race. Here's to the United States!—bounded on the north by the North Pole, on the east by the rising, and on the west by the setting, sun!"

Emphatic applause greeted the aspiring prophecy. But here arose the third speaker, a very serious gentleman, from the far West. "If we are going," said this truly patriotic gentleman, "to lessen the historic past and present, and take our manifest destiny into account, why restrict ourselves within the narrow limits assigned by our fellow countryman who has just sat down? I give you the United States!—bounded on the north by the Aurora Borealis, on the south by the precession of the equinoxes, on the east by the primeval chaos, and on the west by the Day of Judgment!"

DER DOG UND DER LOBSTER

ANONYMOUS

Dot dog, he vas dot kind of dog
    Vot ketch dot ret so sly,
Und squeeze him mit his leedle teeth,
    Und den dot ret vas die.

Dot dog, he vas onquisitive
    Vereffer he vas go,
Und like dot voman, all der time,
    Someding he vants to know.

Von day, all by dot market stand,
    Vere fish und clams dey sell,
Dot dog vas poke his nose aboud
    Und find out vot he smell.

Dot lobster, he vas dook to snooze
    Mit vone eye open vide,
Und ven dot dog vas come along,
    Dot lobster he vas spied.

Dot dog, he smell him mit his noze
    Und scratch him mit his paws,
Und push dot lobster all aboud,
    Und vonder vat he vas.

Und den dot lobster, he voke up,
    Und crawl yoost like dot snail,
Und make vide open ov his claws,
    Und grab dot doggie's tail.

Und den so quick as neffer vas,
    Dot cry vent to der sky,
Und like dot swallows vot dey sing,
    Dot dog vas homevard fly.

Yoost like dot thunderbolt he vent—
   Der sight vas awful grand,
Und every street dot dog vas turn,
   Down vent dot apple-stand.

Der children cry, der vimmin scream,
   Der mens fell on der ground,
Und dot boliceman mit his club
   Vas novare to pe found.

I make dot run, und call dot dog,
   Und vistle awful kind;
Dot makes no different vot I say,
   Dot dog don't look pehind.

Und pooty soon dot race vas end,
   Dot dog vas lost his tail—
Dot lobster, I vas took him home,
   Und cook him in dot pail.

Dot moral vas, I tole you 'boud,
   Pefore vas neffer known—
Don't vant to find out too much tings
   Dot vasn't ov your own.

HE LAUGHED LAST

ANONYMOUS

A young man was sitting in the Grand Central Depot the other day, holding a baby in his arms, when the child began to cry so lustily as to attract the attention of everyone around him. By and by a waiting passenger walked over to him with a smile of pity on his face and said:

"A woman gave you that baby to hold while she went to see about her baggage, didn't she?"

"Yes."

"Ha! ha! ha! I tumbled to the fact as soon as I saw you. You expect her back, I suppose?"

"Of course."

"Ha! ha! ha! This is rich! Looking for her every minute, aren't you?"

"Yes, and I think she'll come back."

"Well this makes me laugh,—ha! ha! ha! I had a woman play that same trick on me in a Chicago depot once, but no one ever will again. Young man, you've been played on for a hayseed. I would advise you to turn that baby over to a policeman and get out of here before some newspaper reporter gets hold of you."

"Oh, she'll come back, she'll come back."

"She will, eh? Ha! ha! ha! The joke grows richer and richer. Now what makes you think she'll come back?"

"Because she's my wife and this is our baby."

"Oh—um—I see," muttered the fat man, who got over feeling tickled all at once, and seeing a dog that a farmer had tied to one of the seats with a piece of clothes-line, he went over and gave it three swift kicks.

NORAH MURPHY AND THE SPIRITS

BY HENRY HATTON

Miss Honora Murphy, a young female engaged in the honorable and praiseworthy occupation of general housework, merely to dispel *ennui,* not hearing in some time from the "boy at home," to whom she was engaged to be married, was advised by the girl next door to consult the spirits. The result I shall give as detailed by her to her friend:

"How kem I by the black eye? Well, dear, I'll tell ye. Afther what yer wur tellin' me, I niver closed me eyes. The nixt marnin' I ast Maggie, the up-stairs gerrl, where was herself. 'In her boodoore,' sez Maggie, an' up I goes to her.

" 'What's wantin', Nora?' sez she.

" 'I've heerd as how me cousin's very sick,' sez I, 'an' I'm that frettin'. I must go an' see her.'

" 'Fitter fur ye to go ter yer worruk,' sez she, lookin' mighty cross, an' she the lazy hulks as niver does a turn from mornin' till night.

"Well, dear, I niver takes sass from anny av 'em; so I ups an' tould her, 'Sorra taste av worruk I'll do the day, an' av yer don't like it, yer can find some one else,' an' I flounced mesel' out av the boodoore.

"Well, I wint to me room ter dress mesel', an' whin I got on me sale-shkin sack, I thought av me poor ould mother—may the hivins be her bed!—could only see me, how kilt she'd be intoirely. Whin I was drest I wint down-stairs an' out the front-doore, an' I tell yer *I slammed it well after me.*

"Well, me dear, whin I got ter the majum's, a big chap wid long hair and a baird like a billy-goat kem inter the room. Sez he:

" 'Do yer want ter see the majum?'

" 'I do,' sez I.

" 'Two dollars,' sez he.

" 'For what?' sez I.

" 'For the sayants,' sez he.

" 'Faix, it's no aunts I want ter see,' sez I, 'but Luke Corrigan's own self.' Well, me dear, wid that he giv a laugh ye'd think would riz the roof.

" 'Is he yer husband?' sez he.

" 'It's mighty 'quisitive ye are,' sez I, 'but he's not me husband, av yer want ter know, but I want ter larn av it's alive or dead he is, which the Lord forbid!'

" 'Yer jist in the nick o' time,' sez he.

" 'Faix, Ould Nick's here all the time, I'm thinkin', from what I hear,' sez I.

"Well, ter make a long story short, I paid me two dollars, an' wint into another room, an' if ye'd guess from now till Aisther, ye'd never think what the majum was. As I'm standin' here, 'twas *nothin' but a woman!* I was that bet, I was almost spacheless.

" 'Be sated, madam,' sez she, p'intin' to a chair, 'yer must jine the circle.'

" 'Faix, I'll ate a triangle, av yer wish,' sez I.

" 'Yer must be very quiet,' sez she. An' so I set down along a lot av other folks at a table.

" 'First I'll sing a hymn,' sez the majum, 'an' thin do all yees jine in the chorus.'

" 'Yer must excuse me, mum,' sez I. 'I niver could sing, but rather than spile the divarshun of the company, av any wan'll whistle, I'll dance as purty a jig as ye'll see from here to Bal'na-sloe, tho it's meself as sez it.'

"Two young whipper-snappers begun ter laugh, but the look I gev them shut them up.

"Jist then, the big chap as had me two dollars kem into the room an' turned down the lights. In a minit the majum, shtickin' her face close to me own, whispers:

" 'The sperrits is about—I kin feel them!'

" 'Thrue for you, mum,' sez I, 'fur I kin shmell them!'

" 'Hush, the influence is an me,' sez the majum. 'I kin see the lion an' the lamb lying down together.'

" 'Bedad! it's like a wild beastess show,' sez I.

" 'Will yer be quiet?' sez an ould chap next ter me. 'I hev a question to ax.'

" 'Ax yer question,' sez I, 'an' I'll ax mine. I paid me two dollars, an' I'll not be put down.'

" 'Plaze be quiet,' sez the majum, 'or the sperrits 'll lave.'

"Jist then came a rap on the table.

" 'Is that the sperrit of Luke Corrigan?' sez the majum.

" 'It is not,' sez I, 'for he could bate any boy in Killballyowen, an' if his fisht hit that table 'twould knock it to smithereens.'

" 'Whist!' sez the majum, 'it's John Bunion.'

" 'Ax him 'bout his progress,' sez a woman wid a face like a bowl of stirabout.

" 'Ah, batherashin!' sez I. 'Let John's bunion alone, an' bring Luke Corrigan to the fore.'

" 'Hish!' whispers the majum, 'I feel a sperrit near me.'

" 'Feel av it has a lump on his nose,' sez I, 'for be that token ye'll know it's Luke.'

" 'The moment is suspicious,' sez the majum.

" 'I hope yer dont want to asperge me character,' sez I.

" 'Whist!' sez she, 'the sperrits is droopin'.'

" 'It's droppin' yer mane,' sez I, pickin' up a shmall bottle she let fall from her pocket.

" 'Put that woman out,' sez an ould chap.

" 'Who do you call a woman?' sez I. 'Lay a fing-er on me, an' I'll scratch a map of the County Clare on yer ugly phiz.'

" 'Put her out!' 'Put her out!' sez two or three others, an' they made a lep for me. But, holy rocket! I was up in a minute.

" 'Bring on yer fightin' sperrits,' I cried, 'from Julis Sazar to Tim Macould, an' I'll bate them all, for the glory of Ireland!'

"The big chap as had me money kem behind me, and put his elbow in me eye; but, me jewel, I tossed him over as ef he'd bin a feather, an' the money rolled out his pocket. Wid a cry of 'Faugh-a-ballah!' I grabbed six dollars, runned out av the doore, an' I'll niver put fut in the house again. An' that's how I kem be the black eye."

OPIE READ

BY WALLACE BRUCE AMSBARY

Dis language Anglaise dat dey spe'k,
    On State of Illinois,
Is hard for Frenchmen heem to learn,
    It give me moch annoy.
Las' w'ek ma frien', McGover*ane*
    He com' to me an' say:
"You mak' a toas' on Opie Read
    W'en dey geeve gran' banqay."

"I mak' a toas'? Not on your life!
    Dat man's wan frien' of me.
W'at for I warm heem op lak' toas'?
    De reason I can't see."
An' den John laugh out on hees eye
    W'en he is to me say:
"To mak' a toas' is not a roas',
    It's jus' de odder way."

Dat's how I learn dat toas' an' roas'
    Is call by different name,
Dough bot' are warm in dere own way,
    Dere far from mean de same.
An' so, ma frien', in lof' I clasp
    Your gr'ad, beeg, brawny han',
An' share vit you in fellowship,
    An' pay you on deman'.

You're built upon a ver' large plan,
    Overe seex feet you rise:
You need it all to shelter in
    Your heart dat's double size.
You are too broad for narrow t'ings,
    You gr'ad for any creed;
I'll eat de roas', but drink de toas',
    To ma frien', Opie Read.

THE VILLAGE CHOIR

After the Charge of the Light Brigade

ANONYMOUS

Half a bar, half a bar,
    Half a bar onward!
    Into an awful ditch
Choir and precentor hitch,
Into a mess of pitch,
    They led the Old Hundred.
Trebles to right of them,
Tenors to left of them,
Basses in front of them,
    Bellowed and thundered.
Oh, that precentor's look,
When the sopranos took
Their own time and hook
    From the Old Hundred!

Screeched all the trebles here,
Boggled the tenors there,
Raising the parson's hair,
    While his mind wandered;
Theirs not to reason why
This psalm was pitched too high:
Theirs but to gasp and cry
    Out the Old Hundred.
Trebles to right of them,
Tenors to left of them,
Basses in front of them,
    Bellowed and thundered.
Stormed they with shout and yell,
Not wise they sang nor well,
Drowning the sexton's bell,
While all the church wondered.

Dire the precentor's glare,
Flashed his pitchfork in air,
Sounding fresh keys to bear
    Out the Old Hundred.
Swiftly he turned his back,
Reached he his hat from rack,
Then from the screaming pack,
    Himself he sundered.
Tenors to right of him,
Tenors to left of him,
Discords behind him,
    Bellowed and thundered.
Oh, the wild howls they wrought:
Right to the end they fought!
Some tune they sang, but not,
    Not the Old Hundred.

BILLY OF NEBRASKA

BY J. W. BENGOUGH

'Twas out in Nebraska—a town they call Lincoln,
(I but mention the place, and everyone's thinkin'
Of W. J. B., the favorite son,
Who twice for the Washington sweepstakes has run),

But this is not a political story,
    And has nothing to do with the Silver question,
Or Rate-bills, or Trusts, or even Old Glory,—
    Tho Bryan's name may start the suggestion;
And he, as a matter of fact, is the source
Of the tale, which makes it much better, of course;
    For it goes to show
    What some may be slow
To believe,—that this Democrat, earnest and stern,
On whose lips the eloquent sentences burn,
And who never is known to drink or to smoke,
Has a fondness for fun and enjoys a good joke.

It appears that Billy—if I may make free,
    (Like the G. O. P. press) with the Commoner's name—
    Kept a goat, with a cognomen just the same,
(At least I suppose such was likely to be,
For Billy's the name of each goat that is *he*);
    And I likewise suppose,
    (Tho nobody knows)
That William's idea in keeping a goat
Was to make himself sound with the shantytown vote;
    But be that as it may,
    It happened one day
That he went to the court-house, did W. J.,—

To lodge in due form a complaint—to protest
'Gainst the manner in which his estate was assessed;
    And especially to kick
(For even a peace-arbitrationist hollers
    When you cut to the quick)—
To kick 'gainst the taxing at twenty-five dollars
Of Billy the goat. "I say it's too much,"
Cries Bryan, "and savors of kingcraft and such!
Tax-dodging's a thing I abhor, but I swear
This tax is unrighteous, unjust, and unfair;
'Tis a tax more odious than taxes on tea,
And illegal, moreover, for I fail to see
Where the law gives you power to impose such a rate,
For the statutes don't say that a goat's *real estate.*
I stand on my rights!"—Here he threw back his coat,
    And like Hampton of old
    Stood up brave and bold,
"I refuse," he declared, "to be taxed for my goat!"

The assessor, a gentle and mild-faced old chap,
    Most anxious to do only that which was right,
    Grew pale with affright
When he saw the great orators angry eyes snap;
    But he ventured to speak
    In a mild little squeak,
"If you will excuse me, I think you're astray;
The rules 'nd riglations is printed that way;
And I haint did nothin' but what I am bid;
I done it this year as I always have did;
    Here's the book;
    Take a look,
And read for yerself how the law sets it out,
And I guess you will see I know what I'm about.

"Your goat he runs on the highway, I guess?"
    "Well, yes, I suppose,"
    Says Bryan, "he does."
"And he butts, I presume, don't he, now, more or less?"

"Yes," says Bryan, "no doubt
     He butts when he's out,
But what has that got to do with ——"
     "See here!"
Says the old man, as one who had made his point clear:
"I calk'late, mister, you hain't read the laws,
If you'll just take a look at this here little clause;
Where the duties of 'sessors it specially notes;
     It says, as you see,
     Tax all property
Runnin' and a-buttin' on the highway!
And that has jest exactly bin *my* way;
     And the 'pinion's sound as oats
     That it taxes on billy-goats
So you can't git out o' payin' in such a sly way!"

DOT LAMBS VOT MARY HAF GOT

ANONYMOUS

Mary haf got a leetle lambs already;
Dose vool vas vite like shnow;
Und efery times dot Mary dit vent oued,
Dot lambs vent also oued mit Mary.

Dot lambs did follow Mary von day of der schoolhouse,
Vich vas obbosition to der rules of der schoolmaster,
Also, vich it dit caused dose schillen to schmile out loud,
Ven dey dit saw dose lambs on der inside of der schoolhouse.

Und zo dot schoolmaster dit kick dot lambs quick oued,
Likevize, dot lambs dit loaf around on der outsides,
Und did shoo der flies mit his tail off patiently bound,
Until Mary dit come also from dot schoolhouse oued.

Und den dot lambs dit run right away quick to Mary,
Und dit make his bet on Mary's arms,
Like he would say, "I doand vas schkared,
Mary would keep from drouble ena how."

"Vot vas der reason aboud it, of dot lambs und Mary?"
Dose schillen dit ask it dot schoolmaster;
Vell, doand you know it, dot Mary lov dose lambs already,
Dot schoolmaster dit zaid.

Moral

Und zo, alzo, dot moral vaz,
Boued Mary's lamb's relations;
Of you lofe dese like she lofe dose,
Dot lambs vas obligations.

GEORGA WASHINGDONE

ANONYMOUS

Georga Washingdone vos a vera gooda man. Hees fadda he keepa bigga place in Washingdone Street. He hada a greata bigga lot planta wees cherra, peacha, pluma, chesnutta, peanutta, an' banan trees. He sella to mena keepa de standa. Gooda mana to Italia mana was Georga Washingdone. He hata de Irish. Kicka dem vay lika dees.

One tay wen litta Georga, hees son, vos dessa high, like de hoppagrass, he take hees litta hatchet an' he beginna to fool round de place. He vos vera fresh, vos litta Georga. Poota soon he cutta downa de cherra tree lika dees. Dat spoila de cherra cropa for de season. Den he goa round trea killa de banan an' de peanutta.

Poota soon Georga's fadda coma rounda quicka lika dees. Den he lifta uppa hees fista looka lika big bunch a banan, an' he vos just goin' to giva litta Georga de smaka de snoota if he tola lie. Hees eyes blaze lika dees.

Litta Georga he say in hees minda, "I gitta puncha anyhow,

so I tella de square ting." So he holda up hees litta hands like
dees, an' he calla "Tima!"

Den he says, "Fadda, I cutta de cherra tree weesa mia own
litta hatchet!"

Hees fadda he say, "Coma to de barn weesa me! Litta Georga,
I wanta speeka weesa you!"

Den hees fadda cutta big club, an' he spitta hees handa, lika
dees!

Litta Georga say, "Fadda, I could notta tella de lie, because I
knowa you caughta me deada to rights!"

Den de olda man he smila lika dees, an' he tooka litta Georga
righta down to Wall Street, an' made him a present of de United
States!

DA 'MERICANA GIRL

BY T. A. DALY

I gatta mash weeth Mag McCue,
An' she ees 'Mericana, too!
Ha! w'at you theenk? Now mebbe so,
You weell no calla me so slow
Eef som' time you can looka see
How she ees com' an' flirt weeth me.
Most evra two, t'ree day, my frand,
She stop by dees peanutta-stand
An' smile an' mak' do googla-eye
An' justa look at me an' sigh.
An' alla time she so excite'
She peeck som' fruit an' taka bite.
O! my, she eesa look so sweet
I no care how much fruit she eat.
Me? I am cool an' mak' pretand
I want no more dan be her frand;
But een my heart, you bat my life,
I theenk of her for be my wife.
To-day I theenk: "Now I weell see
How moocha she ees mash weeth me,"

An' so I speak of dees an' dat,
How moocha playnta mon' I gat,
How mooch I makin' evra day
An' w'at I spend an' put away.
An' den I ask, so queeck, so sly:
"You theenk som' pretta girl weell try
For lovin' me a leetla beet?"—
O! my! she eesa blush so sweet!—
"An' eef I ask her lika dees
For geevin' me a leetla keess,
You s'pose she geeve me wan or two?"
She tal me: "Twanty-t'ree for you!"
An' den she laugh so sweet, an' say:
"Skeeddoo! Skeeddoo!" an' run away.

She like so mooch for keessa me
She gona geev me twanty-t'ree!
I s'pose dat w'at she say—"skeeddoo"—
Ees alla same "I lova you."
Ha! w'at you theenk! Now, mebbe so
You weell no calla me so slow!

BECKY MILLER

ANONYMOUS

I don'd lofe you now von schmall little bit,
My dream vas blayed oudt, so blease git up and git,
Your false-heardted vays I can't got along mit—
    Go vay, Becky Miller, go vay!

Vas all der young vomans so false-heardted like you,
Mit a face so bright, but a heart black and plue,
Und all der vhile schworing you lofed me so drue—
    Go vay, Becky Miller, go vay!

Vy, vonce I t'ought you vas a shtar vay up high;
I like you so better as gogonut bie;
But oh, Becky Miller, you hafe profed von big lie—
　　　Go vay, Becky Miller, go vay!

You dook all de bresents vat I did bresent,
Yes, gobbled up efery virst thing vot I sent;
All der vhile mit anoder rooster you vent—
　　　Go vay, Becky Miller, go vay!

Vhen first I found oudt you vas such a big lie,
I didn't know vedder to schmudder or die;
Bud now, by der chingo, I don't efen cry—
　　　Go vay, Becky Miller, go vay!

Don'd dry make belief you vas sorry aboudt,
I don'd belief a dings vot comes oudt by your moudt;
Und besides I don'd care, for you vas blayed oudt—
　　　Go vay, Becky Miller, go vay!

P. S. (pooty short)—Vell, he dold Becky to go avay enough dimes, enner how. I dinks he vas an uckly vellow. Vell, berhaps dot serfs Becky choost right for daking bresents from von vellow, vhile she vas vinking her nose by anoder vellow.

PAT AND THE MAYOR

ANONYMOUS

An Irishman named Patrick Maloney, recently landed, called upon the mayor to see if he could give him a position on the police force. The mayor, thinking he would have some fun with him, said:

"Before I can do anything for you, you will have to pass a Civil Service examination."

"Ah, dthin," said Pat, "and pfhat is the Civil Sarvice?"

"It means that you must answer three questions I put to you, and if you answer them correctly I may be able to place you."

"Well," said Pat, "I think I can answer dthim if they're not too hard."

"The first question is, 'What is the weight of the moon?'"

"Ah, now, how can I tell you that? Shure and I don't know."

"Well, try the second one, 'How many stars are in the sky?'"

"Now you're pokin' fun at me. How do I know how many stars there are in the shky?"

"Then try the third question, and if you answer it correctly I'll forgive you the others, 'What am I thinking of?'"

"Pfhat are you thinkin' of? Shure, how can any man tell what you politicians are thinkin' about. Bedad I don't belave you know pfhat you're thinkin' about yourself. I guess I'll be lookin' for work ilsewhere, so good-day to you!"

The mayor called Pat back and told him not to be discouraged, but to go home and think about it, and if on the morrow he thought he could answer the questions to come down again and he would give him another chance.

So Pat went home and told his brother Mike about it, whereupon Mike said:

"Now you give me dthim clothes of yours and I'll go down and answer his questions for him."

So next morning Mike went down bright and early, and the mayor recognizing Patrick as he thought, said:

"Ah, good morning, Patrick. Have you really come back to answer those three questions I put to you yesterday?"

"Yis, I have."

"Well the first question is, 'What is the weight of the moon?'"

"The weight of the moon is one hundred pounds, twenty-five pounds to each quarther, four quarthers make one hundred."

"Capital, Patrick, capital! Now the second question is, 'How many stars are in the sky?'"

"How many shtars are in the shky? There are four billion, sivin million, noine hundred and thirty-two tousand and one."

"Splendid, Patrick, splendid. Now look out for the last question which is, 'What am I thinking of?'"

"Pfhat are you thinkin' of? Well I know pfhat you're thinkin' of. You're thinkin' I'm Pat, but you're tirribly mistakin'; *I'm his brother Mike!*"

THE LIVERWING TESTIMONIAL

BY M. B. SPURR

Lord Liverwing, the eldest son of the Duke of Goosefield, had represented that borough for fifteen years in Parliament, and had faithfully carried out its traditions in the House by sleeping for it through the changing sessions. He once woke up, however, in time to introduce a bill for the better protection and preservation of crabs. He was now about to retire into private life, the strain upon his mental faculties, in the matter of those crabs, having proved too much for his intellect.

A public meeting was held to consider how most fittingly to commemorate the propitious event of his lordship's retirement, and it was resolved thereat that a testimonial should be presented to his lordship for his efforts on their behalf in the past, and also for the inestimable boon he was about to confer upon them by retiring. A committee was appointed to decide what form this testimonial should take, and a subscription list was opened, which was immediately filled in, everybody being anxious that his lordship should have no opportunity of drawing back. The committee, which consisted of the leading tradespeople of the town, met in a room at the "Golden Eggs," the chief hotel in Goosefield. The question was what particular form the presentation was to take. Peggs, the tailor, was the first to make a suggestion. He thought that a series of seven suits of clothes would be a very *suitable* present, and he would suggest that they would consist of a hunting, a riding, a bicycling, a lawn-tennis, a shooting and a morning and evening dress. Also, *he* would be glad to make the suits himself! Upon this, up rose Sands, the grocer, who observed that he had once a suit of clothes made for him by Peggs, and if the suits to be made for his lordship didn't fit him any better than *his* did, the only fit his lordship would be likely to have was an apoplectic one. Now, *he* could impartially recommend as a neat little present a stone—or more, if required— of his own unapproachable Gorgonzola cheese. This drew out Mr. Squills, the chemist, who stated that anyone who had ever got

within range of the aforesaid cheese would be quite ready to
grant its unapproachableness at any rate, from *one* point of view.
He thought that a more appreciable present would be a complete medicine chest—he would be glad to supply one of his own,
on the usual terms—to protect his lordship from and against
all forms of disease whatever. Mr. Forceps, the dentist, was re-
marking that he was not aware that his lordship was suffering
from any form or kind of disease whatever, unless he had been
rashly sampling one of Mr. Squill's medicine chests, and was
proceeding to propose that he should extract all his lordship's
remaining teeth, and should afterward supply him with a fresh
set, gold-mounted, patent swivel-pattern, and jeweled in seven
holes—when everyone seemed to have lost his temper. The heated
discussion was eventually calmed by the chairman—the only
person *not* in trade on the committee!—who informed his brother
members that he had observed in a certain jeweler's window a
silver toothpick, chastely and elaborately mounted, and a cheese-
toaster of remarkable elegance and beauty of design. He further
informed them that these articles could be had *cheap*, which would,
of course, allow of greater latitude when considering the expenses
of the committee. This shot went home, and so did the committee.
The chairman, who was accustomed to act as foreman of the jury
on the town inquests, proposed that they should now adjourn
and view the body—he meant the articles in question—so they
left for the purpose of doing so, and subsequently made arrange-
ments for the purchase of the toothpick and toaster, in due
course.

At last the memorable day arrived. In the evening the town-
hall was filled to overflowing with a motley crowd, while on the
platform sat a brilliant gathering of the lions of the borough,
among them being Sir Blinkaby Owlbush, the Honorable Augustus
Fitz-Gizzard, Mr. Jorkins, Mr. Cagmag, Mr. Wattles, Mr. Pottles,
Lady Liverwing, Lady Owlbush, Mrs. Tubbs and her six daughters
(all in lavender), Mrs. Fubbs, Miss Fubbs, Mrs. Wattles, Mrs.
Pottles, and Miss Gosling.

Amid loud and prolonged cheering, Sir Blinkaby Owlbush rose
to make the presentation. He said:

"It gives me great pleasure to assist in the retirement—I mean,

the—the proceedings connected with the retirement—of my
friend, Lord Liverwing. We are all here—I say, we are all here—
to express our heartfelt thanks to his lordship for his retiring.
I—I—I should say, for his untiring efforts on our behalf and on
behalf of humanity and on behalf of civilization and on behalf—
of the whole world in general! As instances of the good work
accomplished by his lordship I may mention such praiseworthy
acts as—as—such praiseworthy acts as—well, as he has done.
The whole of the civilized world, including Goosefield, knows
of Lord Liverwing's noble and unshellfish—I should say *unselfish*,
and successful efforts on behalf of the common crab of commerce.
More especially should we be grateful to his lordship for his
masterly handling of the clause of crabs—I mean the crab-
claws, which he has inserted, or claused—er, *caused*—to be
inserted in the statues of the realm. It is, at all times,
a most delicate matter to take up the clause of the cause
—er—the cause of the claws—er—to take up the cause of
crabs—er—the clause of crabs—the—er—clause in the laws of
the crab-clause—er, laws—and to insert those claws—er, laws,
—into the clause—er—the laws—rather, I should say, of the crab
claws laws. I have great pleasure in making this presentation."

Then Lord Liverwing, who was received with rapturous
applause, arose and spoke as follows:

"I am completely, and I might say, *quite* overwhelmed by the—
er—overwhelming and the highly complimentary—compliments—
I mean remarks—which have just fallen from the lips of my
learned friend and to which I have listened with a decided feeling
of—of—gratification and of—er—gratified—er—gratitude—er—
of the present day. The—er—elegant and pleasing *teeze-choaster*
—I mean to say *toes-cheester,* will always dwell in my—I mean to
say, will be perpetually associated with my mind—er—in my mind.
I accept it as a very handsome and appropriate *toast*imonial—er
—*test*imonial of your good wishes. I beg also to thank you—er
—most thankfully—-I mean cordially—er—for the accompanying
tooth-poster—or rather, *pooth-chick,* which I shall never use! I
mean, never use, without—er—without being reminded of this
eventful—er event—and er—occasion. Whether I look at the
chose-teester or at the *pease-chick,* I shall always say to myself

that the proudest day of my life—er proudest *existence* of my life—er—no, *day* of my life—I mean existence—er—was the day on which this *pose-ticker* and this *chooth-toast* were presented to me, on this day—er—in this room—er—in this place—er—in this way! The *peeth-toaster* and the *tick-cheese* will be handed down to my grandparents—I mean my grandchildren—and er—to their grandparents from time immemorial. They will be taught to contemplate with reverential reverence—er—this very elegant *choose-picker* and this beautiful and very handsome *teeth-poose!*"

UPS AND DOWNS OF MARRIED LIFE

ANONYMOUS

A well-drest woman walked into a prominent New York office building the other day and took one of the elevators. Her husband saw her from across the street, and hurrying over took the next elevator. He went to the office where he knew she had business, and found she had stept in only for a moment and had gone down again.

The elevator despatcher said to her: "Your husband just went up, and I think he's looking for you."

She took the next elevator up. Just then her husband came down. He looked all around and then inquired:

"Have you seen my wife here?"

"Yes, she went up this minute."

He took the next elevator and was just out of sight when she came down.

"Your husband has just gone up."

"Then I'll go right up, as he'll wait for me this time."

Down came her husband a second afterward.

"Did my wife come down again?"

"Yes, and just went up. She thought you'd wait for her."

After waiting a few moments he became impatient and went up again. She had been waiting for him, and came down.

"Husband just gone up."

"Then I'll wait here, as he will surely come down."

She waited a few moments and then hurried up again just as he came down.

"Wife here?"

"Just gone up!"

"Well I'm going home and you tell her ——" He paused, turned around and went up again. Down she came.

"Did he come down?"

"Yes, and he's gone up again as mad as a hornet."

"Then I had better go right up."

Up she went and down he came.

"Just gone up."

"Well, I'll be hanged if I'm going up again. No, sir! I've seen many ups and downs in my time, but this is the limit. I'm going to sit right here and wait if she never comes down!"

When they closed the building for the night, he was still sitting down-stairs, and she, equally determined, was waiting up-stairs, while the elevator man remarked:

"Well, I hope dey'll meet in heav'n!"

THE CROOKED MOUTH FAMILY

ANONYMOUS

In a locality not far removed from the city's busy hum, there lived a family noted for certain remarkable peculiarities of facial distortion. In the father the lower jaw protruded; in the mother it receded so that the upper jaw overhung it like a canopy; the daughter had her face drawn to the left side, while the son had his drawn to the right, and in addition to this deformity stammered most dreadfully. While he attempted to talk his face assumed an expression equally grotesque as the caricatures in a yellow journal.

The father kept a store and one day a man entered whose face, strangely enough, was drawn strongly to the right side. Addressing the daughter, who was standing back of the counter, he said,

"I want a pound of tea," his words coming from the corner of his mouth.

"What are you making fun of me for?" replied the girl, her face drawn in the opposite direction.

"I ain't making fun of you. Can't help it. I was born this way."

The young lady, however, was not satisfied that the stranger was telling the truth, so, stepping to the door she called to her father, "Pa, there's a man down here making fun of me."

The father put in an appearance and demanded of the customer why he had made fun of his daughter.

"I didn't make fun of her."

"Yes you did," said the girl.

"I s-s-saw y-y-you," stammered the brother, from out the corner of his twisted face.

"I tell you I didn't. I was born this way. Can't talk any other."

"Well," said the old man, "you would make a good match and you ought to marry each other."

This proposition meeting with a favorable consideration, the two were made one.

The entire family went on the wedding tour, and one night they spent at a country inn where candles were used for purposes of illumination. Picking up a candle the groom attempted to blow it out, but he nearly exhausted himself in the effort without accomplishing his purpose. The bride came to his rescue and blew, and blew, and blew, but with no better result. Papa appearing upon the scene, said, "Let me have it. I'll show you how to do it," and he went to work with a noise that sounded like the exhaust of a high-pressure engine, but the candle stubbornly refused to go out. The mother, hearing the racket, then came upon the scene, and learning of their quandary, put the candle on her head and blew upward but the flame merely flickered as tho fanned by a gentle zephyr. Just then they saw the watchman passing by, so, in their extremity, they called him to their aid and he promptly blew out the candle because he had a straight mouth.

"IMPH-M"

ANONYMOUS

When I was a laddie lang syne at the schule,
The maister aye ca'd me a dunce an' a fule;
For somehoo his words I could ne'er un'erstan',
Unless when he bawled, "Jamie, haud oot yer han'!"
　　　Then I gloom'd, and said, "Imph-m,"
　　　I glunch'd, and said, "Imph-m"—
I wasna owre proud, but owre dour to say—a-y-e!

Ae day a queer word, as lang-nebbits' himsel',
He vow'd he would thrash me if I wadna spell,
Quo I, "Maister Quill," wi' a kin' o' a swither,
"I'll spell ye the word if ye'll spell me anither:
　　　Let's hear ye spell 'Imph-m,'
　　　That common word 'Imph-m,'
That auld Scotch word 'Imph-m,' ye ken it means a-y-e!"

Had ye seen hoo he glour'd, hoo he scratched his big pate,
An' shouted, "Ye villain, get oot o' my gate!
Get aff to your seat! yer the plague o' the schule!
The de'il, o' me kens if yer maist rogue or fule!"
　　　But I only said, "Imph-m,"
　　　That pawkie word "Imph-m,"
He couldna spell "Imph-m," that stands for an a-y-e!

An' when a brisk wooer, I courted my Jean—
O' Avon's braw lasses the pride an' the queen—
When 'neath my gray pladie, wi' heart beatin' fain,
I speired in a whisper if she'd be my ain,
　　　She blushed, an' said, "Imph-m,"
　　　That charming word "Imph-m,"
A thousan' times better an' sweeter than a-y-e!

Just ae thing I wanted my bliss to complete—
Ae kiss frae her rosy mou', couthie an' sweet—
But a shake o' her head was her only reply—
Of course, that said no, but I kent she meant a-y-e,
  For her twa een said "Imph-m,"
  Her red lips said, "Imph-m,"
Her hale face said "Imph-m," an' "Imph-m" means a-y-e!

THE USUAL WAY

ANONYMOUS

There was once a little man, and his rod and line he took,
For he said, "I'll go a-fishing in the neighboring brook."
And it chanced a little maiden was walking out that day,
  And they met—in the usual way.

Then he sat down beside her, and an hour or two went by,
But still upon the grassy brink his rod and line did lie;
"I thought," she shyly whispered, "you'd be fishing all the day."
  And he was—in the usual way.

So he gravely took his rod in hand and threw the line about,
But the fish perceived distinctly, he was not looking out;
And he said, "Sweetheart, I love you," but she said she could not
 stay,
  But she did—in the usual way.

Then the stars came out above them, and she gave a little sigh,
As they watched the silver ripples, like the moments, running by;
"We must say good-by," she whispered, by the alders old and gray,
  And they did—in the usual way.

And day by day beside the stream, they wandered to and fro,
And day by day the fishes swam securely down below,
Till this little story ended, as such little stories may
  Very much—in the usual way.

And now that they are married, do they always bill and coo?
Do they never fret or quarrel, like other couples do?
Does he cherish her and love her? Does she honor and obey?
  Well, they do—in the usual way.

NOTHING SUITED HIM

ANONYMOUS

He sat at the dinner-table there,
  With discontented frown.
The potatoes and steak were underdone
  And the bread was baked too brown.
The pie too sour, the pudding too sweet,
  And the mince-meat much too fat,
The soup was greasy, too, and salt—
  'Twas hardly fit for a cat.

"I wish you could taste the bread and pies
  I have seen my mother make;
They were something like, and 'twould do you good
  Just to look at a slice of her cake."
Said the smiling wife: "I'll improve with age.
  Just now, I'm a beginner.
But your mother called to see me to-day
  And I got *her* to cook the dinner."

A LITTLE FELLER

ANONYMOUS

Say, Sunday's lonesome fur a little feller,
  With pop and mom a-readin' all the while,
An' never sayin' anything to cheer ye,
  An' lookin' 's if they didn't know how to smile;
With hook an' line a-hangin' in the wood-shed,
  An' lots o' 'orms down by the outside cellar,
An' Brown's creek just over by the mill-dam—
  Say, Sunday's lonesome fur a little feller.

Why, Sunday's lonesome fur a little feller
   Right on from sun-up when the day commences
Fur little fellers don't have much to think of,
   'Cept chasin' gophers 'long the corn-field fences,
Or diggin' after moles down in the wood-lot,
   Or climbin' after apples what's got meller,
Or fishin' down in Brown's creek an' mill-pond—
   Say, Sunday's lonesome fur a little feller.

But Sunday's never lonesome fur a little feller
   When he's a-stayin down to Uncle Ora's;
He took his book onct right out in the orchard,
   An' told us little chaps just lots of stories,
All truly true, that happened onct fur honest,
   An' one 'bout lions in a sort o' cellar,
An' how some angels came an' shut their mouths up,
   An' how they never teched that Dan'l feller.

An' Sunday's pleasant down to Aunt Marilda's;
   She lets us take some books that some one gin her,
An' takes us down to Sunday-school 't the schoolhouse;
   An' sometimes she has a nice shortcake fur dinner.
An' onct she had a puddin' full o' raisins,
   An' onct a frosted cake all white an' yeller.
I think, when I stay down to Aunt Marilda's,
   That Sunday's pleasant fur a little feller.

ROBIN TAMSON'S SMIDDY

BY ALEXANDER RODGER

My mither men't my auld breeks,
   An' wow! but they were duddy,
And sent me to get Mally shod
   At Robin Tamson's smiddy.
The smiddy stands beside the burn
   That wimples through the clachan,
I never yet gae by the door,
   But aye I fa' a-laughin'.

For Robin was a walthy carle,
  An' had ae bonnie dochter,
Yet ne'er wad let her tak' a man,
  Tho mony lads had sought her.
And what think ye o' my exploit?—
  The time our mare was shoeing,
I slippit up beside the lass,
  An' briskly fell a-wooing.

An' aye she e'ed my auld breeks,
  The time that we sat crackin',
Quo' I, "My lass, ne'er mind the *clouts,*
  I've new anes for the makin';
But gin ye'll just come hame wi' me,
  An' lea' the carle, your father,
Ye'se get my breeks to keep in trim,
  Mysel', an' a' thegither."

" 'Deed, lad," quo' she, "your offer's fair,
  I really think I'll tak' it,
Sae, gang awa', get out the mare,
  We'll baith slip on the back o't;
For gin I wait my father's time,
  I'll wait till I be fifty;
But na;—I'll marry in my prime,
  An' mak' a wife most thrifty."

Wow! Robin was an angry man,
  At tyning o' his dochter;
Through a' the kintra-side he ran,
  An' far an' near he sought her;
But when he cam' to our fire-end,
  An' fand us baith thegither,
Quo' I, "Gudeman, I've ta'en your bairn,
  An' ye may tak' my mither."

Auld Robin girn'd an' sheuk his pow,
  "Guid sooth!" quo' he, "you're merry,
But I'll just tak' ye at your word,
  An' end this hurry-burry."
So Robin an' our auld wife
  Agreed to creep thegither;
Now, I ha'e Robin Tamson's pet,
  An' Robin has my mither.

A BIG MISTAKE

ANONYMOUS

Recently our church has had a new minister. He is a nice, good, sociable man; but having come from a distant State, of course he was totally unacquainted with our people.

Therefore, it happened that during his pastoral calls he made several ludicrous blunders.

The other evening he called upon Mrs. Hadden. She had just lost her husband, and naturally supposed that his visit was relative to the sad occurrence. So, after a few commonplaces had been exchanged, she was not at all surprised to hear him remark:

"It was a sad bereavement, was it not?"

"Yes," faltered the widow.

"Totally unexpected?"

"Oh, yes; I never dreamed of it."

"He died in the barn, I suppose?"

"Oh, no; in the house."

"Ah—well, I suppose you must have thought a great deal of him."

"Of course, sir,"—this with a vim.

The minister looked rather surprized, but continued:

"Blind staggers was the disease, I believe?"

"No, sir," snapped the widow, "apoplexy."

"Indeed; you must have fed him too much."

"He was always capable of feeding himself, sir."

"Very intelligent he must have been. Died hard, didn't he?"

"He did."

"You had to hit him on the head with an ax to put him out of misery, I was told."

"Whoever told you so did not speak the truth. James died naturally."

"Yes," repeated the minister, in a slightly perplexed tone, "he kicked the side of the barn down in his last agonies, did he not?"

"No, sir, he didn't."

"Well, I have been misinformed, I suppose. How old was he?"

"Thirty-five."

"Then he did not do much active work. Perhaps you are better without him, for you can easily supply his place with another."

"Never, sir—never will I see one as good as he."

"Oh, yes, you will. He had the heaves bad, you know."

"Nothing of the kind!"

"Why, I recollect I saw him, one day, passing along the road, and I distinctly recollect that he had the heaves, and walked as if he had the string-halt."

"He could never have had the string-halt, for he had a cork leg!"

"A cork leg!—remarkable. But really, now, didn't he have a dangerous trick of suddenly stopping and kicking a wagon all to pieces?"

"Never; he was not a madman, sir!"

"Probably not. But there were some good points about him."

"I should think so!"

"The way in which he carried his ears, for example."

"Nobody else ever noticed that particular merit; he was warm-hearted, generous and frank!"

"Good qualities. How long did it take him to go a mile?"

"About fifteen minutes."

"Not much of a goer. Wasn't his hair apt to fly?"

"He didn't have any hair. He was bald-headed."

"Quite a curiosity?"

"No, sir; no more of a curiosity than you are."

"Did you use the whip much on him?"

"Never, sir."

"Went right along without it, eh?"

"Yes!"

"He must have been a very good sort of a brute!"

"The idea of you coming here and insulting me!" she sobbed. "If my husband had lived you wouldn't have done it. Your remarks in reference to that poor, dead man have been a series of insults. I won't stand it."

He colored and looked dumbfounded.

"Are you not Mrs. Blinkers, and has not your old gray horse died?"

"I never owned a h-horse, but my husband died a week ago!"

Ten minutes later the minister came out of that house with the reddest face ever seen on mortal man.

"And to think," he groaned, as he strode home, "that I was talking horse to that woman all the time, and she was talking husband."

LORD DUNDREARY'S LETTER

ANONYMOUS

(*He enters holding a letter in his hand and a monocle in his eye.*) I wonder who w-w-wote me this letter? I thuppose the b-b-best way to f-f-find out ith to open it and thee. (*Opens letter.*) Thome lun-lunatic hath w-w-witten me this letter. He hath w-w-witten it upthide down. I w-w-wonder if he th-thought I wath going to w-w-wead it thanding on my head. Oh, yeth, I thee; I had it t-t-turned upthide down.

"Amewica." Who do I know in Amewica? I am glad he hath g-g-given me hith addwess anyhow. Oh, yeth, I thee, it ith from Tham. I alwaths know Tham's handwiting when I thee hith name at the b-b-bottom of it.

"My dear bwother." Tham alwaths called me bwother, becauthe we never had any thisters. When we were boyths, we were ladths together—both of us. They used to g-g-get off a pwoverb when they thaw uth com-com-coming down the stweet. It ith awfully good, if I could only think of it. Iths—it iths the early bir-bir-bird—iths the early bir-bir-bird that knowths iths own f-f-father. What nonthense that iths! How co-co-could a b-b-bird know iths own father? Iths a withe child—iths a withe child—iths a wise child that geths the worm. T-t-that's not wite.

Wat nonthense that iths! No pa-pa-pawent would allow hiths child to ga-ga-gather worms. Iths a wyme. Fish of-of-of a feather,—fish of a f-f-feather,—now what nonthense that iths! Fish don't have feathers. Iths a b-b-bird—iths b-b-birds of a feather,—b-b-birds of a feather—flock together. B-b-birds of a f-f-feather! Just as if a who-who-whole flock of b-b-birds had only one f-f-feather. They'd all catch cold. Only one b-b-bird could have that f-f-feather, and he'd fly sidewithse. What con-confounded nonthense that iths! Flock to-to-together! Of courthse th-th-they'd flock together. Who ever heard of a b-b-bird being such a f-f-fool as to g-g-go into a corner and flock by himself? That's one of those things no fellow can find out.

"I wote you a letter thome time ago——" Thath's a lie; he d-d-didn't w-w-wite me a letter. If he had witten me a letter he would have posted it, and I would have g-g-got it; so, of courthse, he didn't post it, and then he didn't wite it. Thath's easy. Oh, yeths, I thee: "but I dwopped it into the poth-potht-office without putting any name on it." I wonder who the d-d-dickens got that letter. I w-w-wonder if the poth-pothman iths gwoin' awound asking for a fellow without any name. I wonder if there iths such a fellow, a fellow without any name? If there iths any fellow without any name, how doeths he know who he iths himself? I-I-I wonder if thuch a fellow could get mawaid. How could he ask a girl to take hiths name if he h-h-had no name? That's one of those things no fellow can find out.

"I have just made a startling dithcovery." Tham's alwaths d-d-doing thomthing. "I have dithcovered that my mother iths —that m-m-my mother iths not my m-m-mother; that a—the old nurthe iths my m-m-mother, and that you are not my b-b-bwother, and a—that-that-that I was changthed at my birth." How ca-ca-can a fellow be changthed at hith b-b-birth? If he hiths not him-thelf, who iths he? If Tham's m-m-mother iths not hiths m-m-mother, and the old nurthe iths hith m-m-mother, and Tham iths not my b-b-bwother, then who the dickens am I? Stope a minute. (*Points to forefinger of left hand.*) That's Tham's m-m-mother, and that's Tham's nurthe (*pointing to thumb of left hand*). Tham's nurthe ith only half the size of hith m-m-mother. Well, that's my m-m-mother (*pointing to second finger of left hand*).

I can't get my m-m-mother to stand up! (*All the fingers spring up.*) Hello, there's a lot of other fellows' m-m-mothers. Well, as far as I can make out, Tham hath left me no m-m-mother at all! That's one of those things no fellow can find out.

"I have just purchathed an ethstate som-som-somewhere——" Dothn't the idiot know wh-wh-where he hath bought it? Oh, yeth: "on the banks of the M-M-M-Mith-ith-ippi." Who iths Mit-this Thippi? I g-g-gueth iths Tham's m-m-mother-in-law. Tham's got mawaid. He thayths he felt awfully ner-ner-nervouths. S-s-speaking of m-m-mother-in-lawths, I had a fwiend who had a m-m-mother-in-law, and he didn't like her very well; and she felt the thame way toward him; and they went away on a steamer acwoths the ocean, and they got shipwecked, catht away on a waft, and they floated awound in the water, living on thuch things ath they could pick up—such ath thardines, ice-cweam, owanges, and other canned goods that were floating awound. When that was all gone, everybody ate everybody else. F-f-finally only himthelf and hiths m-m-mother-in-law waths left, and they played a game of c-c-checkers to thee who thould be eaten up—himthelf or hith m-m-mother-in-law. He w-w-won! He thays that wath the only time that he weally cared for his mother-in-law!

Oh, herthe a pothscript. "By the way, what do you think of the f-f-following widdle?" One of Tham's widdles. "If fourteen dogs with three legs each catch forty-eight rabbits with seventy-six legs in twenty-five minutes, how many legs must twenty-four rabbits have to get away from ninety-three dogs with two legs each in half an hour?" That's one of those things no fellow can find out.

SLANG PHRASES

ANONYMOUS

It is not strange that children misunderstand our slang phrases. Not long ago a gentleman about to go abroad, made the round of the steamship. When he came back he walked up to the captain and said: "Captain, what has become of the old steward? I do not see anything of him this trip."

"The old steward,—hm,—the old steward, well, he got too big for his breeches, and we fired him."

Now it happened that a little girl stood by and overheard the conversation, and not long after a second gentleman made the round of the ship, and coming up to a fellow traveler said:

"John, we do not see anything of the old steward this trip; what do you suppose has become of him?"

"I do not know, I am sure."

"I do," said a small voice.

They looked around and saw a little girl peeping out from a cabin door.

"Well, well, my little friend, could you tell us what has become of the old steward?"

"I don't like to say."

"Oh, that's a nice little girl, I am sure; was he discharged?"

"Yes, sir."

"What was the matter? What was the matter?"

"His pants were too short."

THE MERCHANT AND THE BOOK AGENT

ANONYMOUS

A book agent importuned James Watson, a rich merchant, living a few miles out of the city, until he bought a book entitled "The Early Christian Martyrs." Mr. Watson didn't want the book, but he bought it to get rid of the agent; then taking it under his arm he started for the train which takes him to his office in the city.

Mr. Watson had not been gone long before Mrs. Watson came home from a neighbor's. The book agent saw her, and went in and persuaded the wife to buy a copy of the book. She was ignorant of the fact that her husband had bought the same book in the morning.

When Mr. Watson came back in the evening, he met his wife with a cheery smile as he said: "Well, my dear, how have you enjoyed yourself to-day? Well, I hope."

"Oh, yes! had an early caller this morning."

"Ah, and who was she?"

"It wasn't a 'she' at all; it was a gentleman—a book agent."

"A what?"

"A book agent, and, to get rid of his importuning, I bought his book, the 'Early Christian Martyrs.' See, here it is."

"I don't want to see it."

"Why, husband?"

"Because that rascally book agent sold me the same book this morning. Now we've got two copies of the same book—two copies of the 'Early Christian Martyrs,' and——"

"But, husband, we can——"

"No, we can't, either! The man is off on the train before this. Confound it! I could kill the fellow——"

"Why, there he goes to the depot now!" said Mrs. Watson, pointing out of the window at the retreating form of the book agent making for the train.

"But it's too late to catch him, and I'm not drest. I've taken off my boots, and——"

Just then Mr. Stevens, a neighbor of Mr. Watson, drove by, when Mr. Watson pounded on the window-pane in a frantic manner, almost frightening the horse.

"Here, Stevens! You're hitched up! Won't you run your horse down to the train and hold that book agent till I come? Run! Catch 'im now!"

"All right," said Mr. Stevens, whipping up his horse and tearing down the road.

Mr. Stevens reached the train as the conductor shouted "All aboard!"

"Book agent!" he yelled, as the book agent stept on the train. "Book agent! hold on! Mr. Watson wants to see you."

"Watson? Watson wants to see me?" repeated the seemingly puzzled book agent. "Oh, I know what he wants; he wants to buy one of my books; but I can't miss the train to sell it to him."

"If that is all he wants, I can pay for it and take it to him. How much is it?"

"Two dollars for the 'Early Christian Martyrs,'" said the book agent as he reached for the money and passed the book out the car-window.

Just then, Mr. Watson arrived, puffing and blowing, in his shirt sleeves. As he saw the train pull out he was too full for utterance.

"Well, I got it for you," said Stevens; "just got it and that's all."

"Got what?"

"Got the book—'Early Christian Martyrs,' and paid——"

"By—the—great—guns!" moaned Watson, as he placed his hand to his brow and swooned right in the middle of the street.

THE COON'S LULLABY

ANONYMOUS

Heah, yo' Rastus, shet yo' sleepy head,
  Mammy's gwine tuh rock huh lamb tuh res'—
Ebry little possom coon am sleepin' in its bed,
  Yo's my precious honey—yes yo' am.
Swing oh; swing oh;—Lucy whar yo' bin so late?
  Lemme catch a niggah courtin' you, yes you!
Hurry up yo' rascals fo' dah's corn bread on de plate,
  Fo' mammy loves huh honey, yes she do!

(*Sings*)
Swing oh; swing oh; fo' mammy loves huh honey, yes she do.
Swing oh; swing oh; fo' mammy loves huh honey, yes she do.

Laws now, Rastus, I done gwine to swat yo' one ha'd,
  Slap yo' tuh a peak an' break it off—
Monst'us drefful Bogie man am waitin' in de ya'd—
  Mammy's only jokin', yes she am.
Swing oh; swing oh;—Petah, yes I see yo' git!
  Washin'ton, I'll cu'l yo' wool fo' you,
Neber in dis whole, roun' wo'ld I seen sich chilluns yit,
  But mammy loves huh honey, yes she do!

(*Sings*)

Swing oh; swing oh; fo' mammy loves huh honey, yes she do.
Swing oh; swing oh; fo' mammy loves huh honey, yes she do.

(After the last chorus the speaker should softly hum the tune
again, with an occasional "Sh!" to the audience, and with pantomime of putting the baby in the cradle, putting it to sleep, and
softly tiptoeing out.)

PARODY ON BARBARA FRIETCHIE

ANONYMOUS

Drough der streeds of Friedrichtown,
Mit der red-hot sun a-shinin' down,
Past dose saloons all filled mit beer,
Dose repel fellers valked on der ear.

All day drough Friedrichtown so fasd,
Hosses foot und sojers past,
Und der repel flag skimmerin' oud so pright,
You vould dink, py jiminy, id had a ridght.

Off all der flags dot flopped in der morning vind,
Nary a vone could enypody find.
Ub shumbed old Miss Frietchie den,
Who vas pent down py nine score years und den.

She took der flag the men hauled down,
Und stuck it fasd on her nighd-gown.
Und pud id in der vinder vere all could see
Dot dear old flag so free.

Yust den ub came Stonewall Jack,
Ridin' on his hosses' pack,
Under his prows he squinted his eyes,
By gracious, dot old flag make him much surprize.

"Halt!" Vell, efery man stood sdill,
"Fire!" vas echoed from hill to hill;
Id broke der strings of dot nighd-gown,
Put olt Miss Frietchie, she vas round.

She freezed on dot olt flag right quick,
Und oud of der vindow her head did stick:
"Scoot, if you must, dis olt cray head,
Put spare dot country's flag!" she said.

A look of shameness soon came o'er
Der face of Jack, und der tears did pour;
"Who pulls oud a hair of dot pauld head
Dies like a donkey!—skip along," he said.

All dot day and all dot night,
Undil der repels vas knocked oud of sight,
Und vay pehind from Friedrichtown,
Dot flag stuck fasd to dot olt nighd-gown.

Barbara Frietchie's vork vas done,
She don'd eny more kin hafe some fun;
Pully for her! und drop a tear
For dot olt gal midoud some fear.

BEFORE AND AFTER

BY CHARLES T. GRILLEY

Before

We had been engaged for just a week
　And now that we must part
The thought of it was maddening,
　And it nearly broke my heart.
As I waved her adieux from the steamer
　She answered back from the pier,
And I murmured softly to myself,
　"My, but isn't she dear!"

After

A year has passed of married life,
　I received a note to-day
Written in wifey's well-known hand:
　"Send me fifty right away!"
I thought of all she had cost me
　During that one brief year,
And then I murmured softly,
　"My, but isn't she dear!"

WHEN GREEK MEETS GREEK

ANONYMOUS

Stranger here? Yes, come from Varmount
   Rutland county. You've hern tell
Mebbe of the town of Granville?
   You born there? No! sho! Well, well!
You was born at Granville was you?
   Then you know Elisha Brown,
Him as runs the old meat market
   At the lower end of town!
Well! well! well! Born down in Granville!
   And out here, so far away!
Stranger, I'm homesick already,
   Tho it's but a week to-day
Since I left my good wife standin'
   Out there at the kitchen door,
Sayin' she'd ask God to keep me;
   And her eyes were runnin' o'er!
You must know ole Albert Withers,
   Henry Bell and Ambrose Cole?
Know them all? And born in Granville!
   Well! well! well! Why, bless my soul!
Sho! You're not old Isaac's nephew!
   Isaac Green, down on the flat!
Isaac's eldest nephew,—Henry?
   Well, I'd never thought of that!
Have I got a hundred dollars
   I could loan you for a minute,
Till you buy a horse at Marcy's?
   There's my wallet! Just that in it!
Hold on tho! You have ten, mebbe,
   You could let me keep; you see
I might chance to need a little
   Betwixt now and half past three!
Ten. That's it; you'll owe me ninety;
   Bring it round to the hotel.
So you're old friend Isaac's nephew?
   Born in Granville! Sho! Well, well!

What! policeman, did you call me?
That a rascal going there?
Well, sir, do you know I thought so,
    And I played him pretty fair;
Hundred-dollar bill I gave him—
    Counterfeit—and got this ten!
Ten ahead. No! you don't tell me!
    This bad, too? Sho! Sold again!

MR. POTTS' STORY

BY MAX ADELER

While I was over at Jersey City, the other day, I called on the Potts. Mr. Potts is liable to indulge in extravagance in his conversation, and as Mrs. Potts is an extremely conscientious woman where matters of fact are concerned, she's obliged to keep her eye on him. Potts was telling me about an incident that occurred in the town a few days before, and this is the way he related it:

Potts.—"You see old Bradley over here is perfectly crazy on the subject of gases, and the atmosphere, and such things—absolutely wild; and one day he was disputing with Green about how high up in the air life could be sustained, and Bradley said an animal could live about forty million miles above the earth, if——"

Mrs. Potts.—"Not forty millions, my dear; only forty miles, he said."

P.—"Forty, was it? Thank you. Well sir, old Green, you know, said that was ridiculous; and he said he'd bet Bradley a couple of hundred thousand dollars that life couldn't be sustained half that way up, and so——"

Mrs. P.—"William, you are wrong; he offered to bet only fifty dollars."

P.—"Well, anyhow, Bradley took him up quicker'n a wink, and they agreed to send up a cat in a balloon to decide the bet. So what does Bradley do but buy a balloon about twice as big as our barn, and begin to——"

Mrs P.—"It was only about ten feet in diameter, Mr. Adeler; William forgets."

P.—"Begin to inflate her. When she was filled, it took eighty men to hold her, and——"

Mrs. P.—"Eighty men, Mr. Potts? Why, you know Mr. Bradley held the balloon himself."

P.—"He did, did he? Oh, very well; what's the odds? And when everything was ready, they brought out Bradley's tom-cat, and put it in the basket, and tied it in so that it couldn't jump, you know. There were about one hundred thousand people looking on, and, when they let go, you never heard such a——"

Mrs. P.—"There were not more than two hundred people there. I counted them myself."

P.—"Oh, don't bother me! I say you never heard such a yell, as the balloon went scooting up into the sky, pretty near out of sight. Bradley said she went up about one thousand miles, and —now don't interrupt me, Henrietta; I know what the man said— and that cat, mind you, a-howling like a hundred fog-horns, so's you could a' heard her from here to Peru. Well, sir, when she was up so's she looked as small as a pin-head, something or other burst. I dunno how it was, but pretty soon down came that balloon a-flickering toward the earth at the rate of fifty miles a minute, and old——"

Mrs. P.—"Mr. Potts, you know that the balloon came down as gently as——"

P.—"Oh, do hush up! Women don't know anything about such things. And old Bradley, he had a kind of a registering thermometer fixt in the balloon along with that cat. Some sort of a patent machine; cost thousands of dollars, and he was expecting to examine it; and Green had an idea he'd lift out a dead cat and scoop in the stakes. When all of a sudden, as she came pelting down, a tornado struck her—now, Henrietta, what in the thunder are you staring at me in that way for? It was a tornado—a regular cyclone—and it struck her and jammed her against the lightning-rod on the Baptist Church steeple, and there she stuck —stuck on that spire, about eight hundred feet up in the air."

Mrs. P.—"You may get just as mad as you like, but I am positively certain that steeple's not an inch over ninety-five feet."

P.—"Henrietta, I wish to gracious you'd go up-stairs and look after the children. Well, about half a minute after she struck out stept that tom-cat on to the weathercock. It made Green sick. And just then the hurricane reached the weathercock, and it began to revolve six hundred or seven hundred times a minute, the cat howling until you couldn't hear yourself speak—now, Henrietta, you've had your put; you keep quiet. That cat stood on that weathercock about two months——"

Mrs. P.—"Mr. Pott., that's an awful story; it only happened last Tuesday."

P. (confidentially)—"Never mind her. And on Sunday the way that cat carried on and yowled, with its tail pointing due east, was so awful that they couldn't have church. And Sunday afternoon the preacher told Bradley if he didn't get that cat down he'd sue him for a million dollars damages. So Bradley got a gun, and shot at the cat fourteen hundred times—now, you didn't count 'em, Henrietta, and I did—and he banged the top of the steeple all to splinters, and at last fetched down the cat, shot to rags, and in her stomach he found the thermometer. She'd ate it on her way up, and it stood at eleven hundred degrees, so old——"

Mrs. P.—"No thermometer ever·stood at such a figure as that."

P. (indignantly)—"Oh, well, if you think you can tell the story better than I can, why don't you tell it? You're enough to worry the life out of a man."

Then Potts slammed the door and went out, and I left. I don't know whether Bradley got the stakes or not.

AT FIVE O'CLOCK TEA

BY MORRIS WADE

"So good of you to come!"

"Ah, thanks."

"So good of you to come!"

"As if I could get along without you! The obligation is all on my side."

"How sweet of you to say so!"

"Now I want you to meet Mrs. Slambang. Mrs. Slambang, let me present to you my deah friend, Mrs. Twiddle-twaddle."

"So glad to know you, Mrs. Slambang! I have so often heard

deah Mrs. Sweet speak of you that I feel quite as if I knew you. Beautiful day, isn't it?"

"Chawming!"

"What a lovely wintah we are having."

"Chawming! So very, very gay, isn't it?"

"Oh, very, very gay! Haven't I met you at Mrs. Titters' teas?"

"I daresay you have. Isn't she a deah?"

"Oh, I am extravagantly fond of her!"

"I am, too. So clevah!"

"Of course you go to the opera?"

"Oh, I couldn't exist without it. Oh, Melba! Melba!"

"And Nordica! I rave over them all!"

"I fairly CRY over them. And, do you know, I have a friend who does not care in the least for them. She isn't a bit musical."

"Oh, how sad! I would die if I did not——Who is the tall lady in black over by the piano?"

"I'm sure I do not know. What exquisite lace on her gown! Do you know that I just simply rave over beautiful lace!"

"Really?"

"Yes, indeed! I care more for it than for jewels, because it—— Do you know the tall, fine-looking man who has just come in?"

"I'm sure I have seen him somewhere, and yet I can not ——Yes, thank you, I think I *will* have a cup of tea. How lovely the dining-room looks!"

"Lovely!"

"Mrs. Sweet has such exquisite taste!"

"EXQUISITE! I often say——How *do* you do, my deah? So glad to see you!"

"Thanks! So glad to meet YOU!"

"So good of you to say so! Quite well, deah?"

"Oh, vulgarly so. I really must say good-by to dear Mrs. Sweet and go. I must look in at Mrs. Shoddy's for a few minutes."

"So must I. We'll go together."

"HOW LOVELY! Good-by, deah Mrs. Sweet. Have had *such* a chawming time!"

"Must you go so soon?"

"Yes, really! Such a lovely time!"

"So glad! But it is quite naughty of you to go so soon. So glad you came!"

"By-by, deah."

"By-by. You will come to see me soon?"

"Yes, indeed."

"You MUST. By-by!"

"By-by!"

And as she gathers up her trailing skirts to walk down the steps she says: "Thank goodness, that's over!"

Reprinted from *Lippincott's Magazine*.

KEEP A-GOIN'!

BY FRANK L. STANTON

If you strike a thorn or rose,
    Keep a-goin'!
If it hails or if it snows,
    Keep a-goin'!
'Taint no use to sit an' whine
When the fish ain't on your line;
Bait your hook an' keep on tryin'—
    Keep a-goin'!

When the weather kills your crop,
    Keep a-goin'!
When you tumble from the top,
    Keep a-goin'!
S'pose you're out of every dime?
Gittin' broke ain't any crime;
Tell the world you're feelin' prime,—
    Keep a-goin'!

When it looks like all is up,
    Keep a-goin'!
Drain the sweetness from the cup,
    Keep a-goin'!
See the wild birds on the wing!
Hear the bells that sweetly ring—
When you feel like sighin'—sing!
    Keep a-goin'!

A LOVER'S QUARREL

BY CYNTHIA COLES

"O Kitty, you *are* so sweet, and I *do* love you so. Tell me you love me, dearie."

"I do love you, Dick; why, I never supposed I *could* love anybody so much."

"O little girl, I only wished you loved me half as much as I love you."

"Half as much! Why, dear, I love you more than you love me—a great deal more——"

"Now. don't be silly, pet. It would be impossible for you to love me as much as I love you. Of course, I love you best."

"Of course you don't! You love me, I know, but not as much as I love you."

"Now, Kitty, be reasonable."

"I will if you'll admit that I do love you best."

"How can I admit what isn't true?"

"Well, you might say it was so just to please me."

"Oh, no, dear, I can't do that."

"Because you don't love me enough!"

"Oh, the idea!"

"If you *did* love me the best, you'd say anything I asked you to, whether it was true or not."

"Would *you* do that?"

"Of course I would."

"All right, then you admit that I love you best, because I ask you to do so!"

"O Dick, how horrid you are! How can you be so cruel to me?"

"There, there, don't cry. I'll admit that you love me best, but I only admit it *because* you ask me to."

"Then that's all right."

"But, don't you see, Kitty, when I say that because you ask me to, and you *won't* say it when I ask you to, that *proves* I love you best after all."

"There you go on again! I do think you're too mean for anything!"

"Well, never mind, sweetheart, let's kiss and be friends. You *do* love me best I'm sure."

"Oh, no, I don't, Dick. Oh, you are so sweet. You love me best, darling."

"Oh, no, I don't, love. You love me best!"

"No, my Dick, *you* love *me* best——"

CASEY AT THE BAT

BY PHINEAS THAYER

It looked extremely rocky for the Mudville nine that day;
The score stood two to four, with but an inning left to play.
So, when Cooney died at second, and Burrows did the same,
A pallor wreathed the features of the patrons of the game.

A straggling few got up to go, leaving there the rest,
With that hope which springs eternal within the human breast,
For they thought: "If only Casey could get a whack at that,"
They'd put up even money now, with Casey at the bat.

But Flynn preceded Casey, and likewise so did Blake,
And the former was a puddin', and the latter was a fake,
So on that stricken multitude a deathlike silence sat,
For there seemed but little chance of Casey's getting to the bat.

But Flynn let drive a "single," to the wonderment of all,
And the much-despised Blakey "tore the cover off the ball."
And when the dust had lifted, and they saw what had occurred,
There was Blakey safe at second, and Flynn a-huggin' third.

Then, from the gladdened multitude went up a joyous yell,
It rumbled in the mountain-tops, it rattled in the dell;
It struck upon the hillside and rebounded on the flat;
For Casey, mighty Casey, was advancing to the bat.

There was ease in Casey's manner as he stept into his place;
There was pride in Casey's bearing, and a smile on Casey's face.
And when, responding to the cheers, he lightly doffed his hat,
No stranger in the crowd could doubt 'twas Casey at the bat.

Ten thousand eyes were on him as he rubbed his hands with dirt,
Five thousand tongues applauded when he wiped them on his
        shirt;
Then while the New York pitcher ground the ball into his hip,
Defiance gleamed in Casey's eye, a sneer curled Casey's lip.

And now the leather-covered sphere came hurling through the air,
And Casey stood a-watching it in haughty grandeur there.
Close by the sturdy batsman the ball unheeded sped—
"That ain't my style," said Casey. "Strike one," the umpire said.

From the benches, black with people, there went up a muffled
        roar,
Like the beating of storm waves on a stern and distant shore.
"Kill him! Kill the umpire!" shouted some one on the stand.
And it's likely they'd have killed him had not Casey raised a
        hand.

With a smile of Christian charity great Casey's visage shone;
He stilled the rising tumult; he bade the game go on:
He signaled to Sir Timothy, once more the spheroid flew;
But Casey still ignored it, and the umpire said, "Strike two."

"Fraud!" cried the maddened thousands, and echo answered
        "Fraud!"
But one scornful look from Casey and the audience was awed.
They saw his face grow stern and cold, they saw his muscles
        strain,
And they knew that Casey wouldn't let that ball go by again.

The sneer is gone from Casey's lip, his teeth are clenched in hate;
He pounds with cruel violence his bat upon the plate.
And now the pitcher holds the ball, and now he lets it go,
And now the air is shattered by the force of Casey's blow.

Ah, somewhere in this favored land the sun is shining bright;
The band is playing somewhere, and somewhere hearts are light.
And somewhere men are laughing, and somewhere children shout:
But there is no joy in Mudville—mighty Casey has struck out.

FAMILIAR LINES

ANONYMOUS

(Arranged so that the little ones can always remember them)

The boy stood on the burning deck,
    His fleece was white as snow;
He stuck a feather in his hat,
    John Anderson, my Jo!

"Come back, come back!" he cried in grief,
    From India's coral strands,
The frost is on the pumpkin and
    The village smithy stands.

Am I a soldier of the cross
    From many a boundless plain?
Should auld acquaintance be forgot
    Where saints immortal reign?

Ye banks and braes o' bonny Doon
    Across the sands o' Dee,
Can you forget that night in June—
    My country, 'tis of thee!

Of all sad words of tongue or pen,
  We're saddest when we sing,
To beard the lion in his den—
  To set before the king.

Hark! from the tombs a doleful sound,
  And Phœbus gins arise;
All mimsy were the borogroves
  To mansions in the skies.

A FRIENDLY GAME OF CHECKERS

ANONYMOUS

"Now, my dear," said Mr. Italics, as he drew on his slippers and settled himself for the evening, "if you will get the checker-board, I'll play you a game—you're learning so rapidly that it's really a pleasure to try quits with you."

Mrs. Italics giggled with delight, kissed her husband on the top of the head and fluttered away to find the board and checkers. After she had found them, she plumped herself down in a rocking-chair about a foot and a half lower than his easy-chair and arranged the apparatus at an angle of fifty degrees, whereupon Mr. Italics said:

"I think you misapprehend my suggestion. I didn't propose to go sliding down hill at this season of the year, neither do I intend to shoot the chutes. My idea was a game of checkers and if you think those men are going to stand around on a board tipped up on one end and wait to be moved, you are not familiar with their habits."

"Perhaps I had better put a book under it; or if you could lower your knees a little it would come even."

"Oh, that's your idea, is it? My knees weren't constructed with special regard to playing checkers. They were put where they are and fastened and they won't run up and down like a flag. Do you think I'm the india-rubber man from the circus, or the cork-legged man from Oskoloosa? If you can't hold up your side of the board, we won't play."

"Now, dear, it's all right. Let me see, is it your move, or mine?"

"What are you trying to play? Do you think this is a game of baseball? Don't you know you've got to move cattecornered? 'Taint your move anyway. Put that back. There. Now I'll move there."

"Oh, I know you're going to jump me and take my man," said Mrs. Italics, picking up the checker she had moved before and putting it in her mouth. "If I put it here, you'll——"

"SWALLOW IT, why don't you? If you don't want it taken, why don't you masticate it? Can't you leave the thing alone until you get ready to move? Put it down before it chokes you."

"There, dear (*swallowing it*), I've put it down, but it hurt my throat."

"What in thunder do you mean by eating up my set of checkers. When I said 'put it down' I meant put it back on the board. Will you please play this game instead of masticating it."

"If I put this man there, you'll jump it."

"Just watch and see."

"Now, I'll put this man there,—no,—perhaps I had better move here,—or I think I'll——"

"Going to move in six places at once? Think this is the first of May and that you're looking for a new flat? 'Taint your move anyway. Now will you please hold the board straight? D'ye think this is a washboard? Well it isn't and it isn't a teeter-board either. Now, I'll move into your king row. Ha! ha!"

"Then do I jump these two men and get a king? Of course, I do. Crown me! I've got the first king!"

"No, you haven't. I didn't mean that move. If you can't play checkers without cackling like a hen you'd better stop. I'll take back that move. Now, so. Now you can move."

"Over here."

"Certainly. That's splendid. Now I'll take these two men."

"I didn't see that, I'd rather put it here."

"Too late now. You can't take back a move in this game. You should study your moves first."

"Well, if I jump here I get another king."

"What do you want to tumble them all over for? Haven't

you got any sense scarcely? You make more fuss over a measly king than most women over a mouse. Don't you know it's my move? Give me back those men. Can't you hold the board straight? What's that? Oh, of course, you know. You know it all. All you want is a pair of hinges and painted sides to be a checker-box. If ever I want to play with some good player I'll put the coal-scuttle on your head and move you around for a king. There goes the whole business! Now, are you satisfied? Do you wonder a man won't play checkers with a woman? I'll throw the measly things out of the window so that I won't waste any time playing with you again." And Mr. Italics suited the action to the word. But then Mr. Italics was such an *odd type*.

MODERN ROMANCE

BY HENRY M. BLOSSOM, JR.

Information, speculation; fluctuation; ruination.
Dissipation, degradation; reformation or starvation.
Application, situation; occupation, restoration.
Concentration, enervation, nerve prostration. A vacation.
Destination, country station. Nice location, recreation.
Exploration, observation; fascination—a flirtation.
Trepidation, hesitation, conversation, simulation;
Invitation, acclamation, sequestration, cold libation.
Stimulation, animation; inspiration, new potation.
Demonstration, agitation, circulation, exclamation!
Declaration, acceptation, osculation, sweet sensation.
Exultation, preparation, combination, new relation.

From *The Smart Set*, New York.

LULLABY

BY PAUL LAURENCE DUNBAR

Kiver up yo' haid, my little lady,
  Hyeah de win' a-blowin' out o' do's.
Don' you kick, ner projick wid de comfo't,
  Less'n fros'll bite yo' little toes.
Shut yo' eyes an' snuggle up to mammy,
  Gi' me bofe yo' han's, I hol' 'em tight;
Don' you be afeard an' 'mence to trimble
  Des ez soon ez I blows out de light.

Angels is a-mindin' you, my baby,
  Keepin' off de Bad Man in de night.
What de use o' bein skeered o' nuffin'?
  You don' fink de dakness gwine to bite?
What de crackin' soun' you heah erroun' you?
  Lawsey, chile, you tickles me to def:—
Dats de man what brings de fros', a paintin'
  Picters on de winder wid his bref.

Mammy ain' afeard, you hyeah huh laffin'?
  Go' away, Mistah Fros', you can't come in;
Baby ain' receivin' folks this evenin',
  Reckon dat you'll have to call agin.
Curl yo' little toes up so, my possum—
  Umph, but you's a cunnin' one fu' true!
Go to sleep, de angels is a-watchin',
  An' yo' mammy's mindin' of you, too.

THE REASON WHY

BY MARY E. BRADLEY

"When I was at the party," said Betty (aged just four),
"A little girl fell off her chair, right down upon the floor;
And all the other little girls began to laugh but me—
I didn't laugh a single bit," said Betty, seriously.
"Why not?" her mother asked her, full of delight to find
That Betty—bless her little heart—had been so sweetly kind.
"Why didn't you laugh, darling, or don't you like to tell?"
"I didn't laugh," said Betty, " 'cause it was me that fell!"

HOW A BACHELOR SEWS ON A BUTTON

ANONYMOUS

This is a very laughable piece of pantomime. It is well to have
a small table and a chair, but everything else is left to the
imagination of the audience. The success of the selection depends
upon the varied facial expression and other business. It is ad-
visable to first practise with a needle and thread so as to get a
correct imitation.

First say to the audience: "Ladies and gentlemen, I shall endeavor to give you an imitation of how a bachelor sews on a
button." Then seat yourself and take from the table an imaginary
spool of thread. Hold it in your left hand and pull out several
lengths with your right hand. Then bite the thread off and put
the spool back on the table. Hold the end of the thread in your
left hand, then wet the first finger and thumb of your right
hand and make the thread into a point. Now start to thread
your needle. The thread refuses to find the eye of the needle
and there is a lot of laughable business here. Change your
position frequently, and at every turn vary the facial expression.
Then blow through the eye of the needle. Just as you think you
have at last put the thread through, the needle is lost and you

look all over for it. After some difficulty you find it on the floor. Then as you seat yourself again you find the thread in a snarl, so you take the spool again and pull off several fresh lengths. Try again to thread the needle and as you get it through the needle's eye, turn it very carefully around and take hold of the thread with your teeth, drawing it through slowly with appropriate facial expression. Now tie a knot in your thread and to make it secure bite it with your teeth. Reach to the table for your imaginary button and place it on the *inside* of your coat. Begin to sew, with difficulty at first, pulling the thread through at arm's length. At the third stitch prick your finger and jump as if in great pain. The thread gradually gets shorter. As you seem to gain facility you begin to smile. Then wind the thread around the button, make several short stitches, and bite it off with your teeth. Now stand and try to button your coat. You first feel for the button but can not find it. Then you look down at your coat, but there is no button there. You turn the coat over and discover that you have sewed the button on the inside. With a look of anger you pull the button off the coat, throw it violently on the floor, and exit hastily.

CHRISTOPHER COLUMBUS

ANONYMOUS

Deesa man liva in Italia a gooda longa time ago. He hada a greata heada ever since he was a kidda. Not a bigga heada likea de politicians nowaday—not a swella heada. His fadda keepa de standa in Italia. Sella de peanutta and de banan. Maka plente de mon. Christopher Colum he say, "Fadda, gimma de stamp, I go finda de new world." His fadda he laugh, "Ha! ha!" just so. Den Christopher he say, "Whata you maka fun? I betta you I finda new world." After a long time his fadda say, "You go finda new world, and bringa it over here." Den de olda man he buy him a grip-sack, an' giva him boodle, an' maka him a present of three ships to come over to deesa contra. Well, Christopher Colum he saila an' saila for gooda many day. He don't see any landa. An' he say, "I giva fiva-dollar-bill if I was back in Italia!" Well, he saila, an' he saila, an' vera soon he strika Coney Island. Den dat maka him glad! Very soon he coma to Castle Garden, an' den he walka up Broadway an' he feel very bada. He finda outa dat de Irish gang has gotta possession of New Yorka! He don't lika de Irish, an' de Shamrocka donta lika him. He donta go vera far before a pleasanter mana speaks to him. He say, "How-a-you do, Mista Jones? How a-de folks in Pittaburg?" Christopher Colum he say, "I notta Mista Jones; I reada the papers; I tinka you sella de green goods, ha? You go away, or I broka your jaw!" Den he shaka hees fista deesa way, an' de man he skedaddle. Den he tries to crossa de Broad-a-way, but it fulla de mud an' he canta swim. Very soon he sees a policeman cluba de mana, one, two, three times, an' he feel secka de stom'! Next he meeta de politicians uppa Tammany Hall an' dees wanta him to runna for Alderman. He getta plenty friend. He learna to "settom up" at de bar many times. Next day he hava heada lika deesa!

His fadda writa: "Why you notta bringa back de new world? I like to hava de earth!" Christopher Colum he writa back dat New Yorka is already in de hands of de Shamrocka. Den he goes to Ohio and buys a place an' calla it after himself—Colum. Soon he goa broka an' taka de nexta train home in disgusta, because he reada in de paper dat de Fair in '93 will be holda in Chicago!

THE FLY

ANONYMOUS

The following is told in child dialect. She finds a fly and speaks to it affectionately:

"Poor little fly! Ain't you got anyone to love you? Ain't you got any brothers or any sisters, little fly? Ain't you got any aunts, little fly? Ain't you got anyone to love you? Your mother loves you, little fly. (*She slaps her hand and kills the fly.*) Go home to your mother!"

THE YARN OF THE "NANCY BELL"

BY W. S. GILBERT

'Twas on the shores that round our coast
  From Deal to Ramsgate span,
That I found alone on a piece of stone
  An elderly naval man.

His hair was weedy, his beard was long,
  And weedy and long was he,
And I heard this wight on the shore recite
  In a singular minor key:

"Oh, I am a cook, and a captain bold,
  And the mate of the *Nancy* brig,
And a bo'sun tight, and a midshipmite,
  And the crew of the captain's gig!"

And he shook his fists, and he tore his hair,
  Till I really felt afraid,
For I couldn't help thinking the man had been drinking,
  And so I simply said:

"O elderly man, it's little I know
  Of the duties of men of the sea,
And I'll eat my hand if I understand
  How you can possibly be

"At once a cook and a captain bold,
  And the mate of the *Nancy* brig,
And a bo'sun tight, and a midshipmite,
  And the crew of the captain's gig."

Then he gave a hitch to his trousers, which
  Is a trick all seamen larn,
And having got rid of a thumpin' quid,
  He spun this painful yarn:

" 'Twas in the good ship *Nancy Bell*
　　That we sailed to the Indian sea,
And there on a reef we come to grief,
　　Which has often occurred to me.

"And pretty nigh all o' the crew was drowned,
　　(There was seventy-seven o' soul),
And only ten of the *Nancy's* men
　　Said 'Here!' to the muster roll.

"There was me, and the cook, and the captain bold,
　　And the mate of the *Nancy* brig,
And the bo'sun tight, and a midshipmite,
　　And the crew of the captain's gig.

"For a month we'd neither wittles nor drink,
　　Till a-hungry we did feel,
So we drawed a lot, and accordin' shot
　　The captain for our meal.

"The next lot fell to the *Nancy's* mate,
　　And a delicate dish he made;
Then our appetite with the midshipmite
　　We seven survivors stayed.

"And then we murdered the bo'sun tight,
　　And he much resembled pig;
Then we wittled free, did the cook and me,
　　On the crew of the captain's gig.

"Then only the cook and me was left,
　　And the delicate question, 'Which
Of us two goes to the kettle?' arose,
　　And we argued it out as sich.

"For I loved that cook as a brother, I did,
　　And the cook he worshiped me;
But we'd both be blowed if we'd either be stowed
　　In the other chap's hold, you see.

" 'I'll be eat if you dines of me,' says Tom
  'Yes, that,' says I, 'you'll be.'
'I'm boiled if I die, my friend,' quoth I;
  And 'Exactly so,' quoth he.

"Says he, 'Dear James, to murder me
  Were a foolish thing to do,
For don't you see that you can't cook *me*,
  While I can—and will—cook *you?*'

"So he boils the water, and takes the salt,
  And the pepper in portions true
(Which he never forgot), and some chopped shalot
  And some sage and parsley, too.

" 'Come here,' says he, with a proper pride,
  Which his smiling features tell,
' 'Twill soothing be if I let you see
  How extremely nice you'll smell.'

"And he stirred it round and round and round,
  And he sniffed at the foaming froth—
When I ups with his heels, and smothers his squeals
  In the scum of the boiling broth.

"And I eat that cook in a week or less,
  And—as I eating be
The last of his chops, why, I almost drops,
  For a wessel in sight I see.

.   .   .   .   .

"And I never grieve, and I never smile,
  And I never larf nor play,
But I sit and croak, and a single joke
  I have—which is to say:

"Oh, I am a cook, and a captain bold,
  And the mate of the *Nancy* brig,
And a bo'sun tight, and a midshipmite,
  And the crew of the captain's gig!"

I TOL' YER SO

BY JOHN L. HEATON

John Jones he was the beatenus cuss,
Allus a-pickin' 'n' sayin' to us:
  "I tol' yer so, I tol' yer so!"
No matter what happened, he'd up an' say:
"Yer sorry ye done it, haint ye, hey?
  Well, well, I tol' yer so!"

When Kerin-Happuck wuz tuk down sick
From the pizen ivy she'd gin a lick,
  He'd tol' us so, he'd tol' us so.
'N' Shadrack's fuss with his mother-in-law,
Before the weddin' John Jones foresaw;
  Well, well, he tol' us so.

If a fellow wuz hit by a fallin' tree,
Or kicked by a horse, says Jones, says he:
  "I tol' yer so, I tol' yer so!"
If a barn tuck fire, or a well-sweep broke,
We might a-knowed it before Jones spoke,
  The time he tol' us so.

It got so tejus, says Bill one day:
"Ye're a dern ol' idjit, 'ith nothin' ter say
  But 'tol' yer so,' 'n 'tol' yer so,'—
A mean, contemptible, sneakin' cuss!"
'N' jes from habit, Jones sez to us:
  "Well, well, I tol' yer so!"

"YOU GIT UP!"

BY JOE KERR

There's lots of folks that has good times,
  There's lots that never does;
But the ones that don't like morning naps
  Is the meanest ever wuz.
It's very nice to eat a meal
  With pie for its wind-up;
'Taint half so sweet's th' nap pa spoils
  When he yells, "You git up!"

I'd rather lay in bed and snooze,
  Jest one small minit more
In the morning, when the sunshine
  Comes a-creeping o'er the floor,
Then to go to Barnum's circus or
  To own a bulldog pup.
The meanest thing pa ever said
  Wuz, "Come now—you git up!"

I like to go in swimming,
  And I like to play baseball;
I like to fight and fly a kite,
  'N' I sometimes like to bawl;
But them thare forty winks of sleep
  Pa tries to interrup',
Is better 'n' all. It breaks my heart
  When pa yells, "You git up!"

I'd stand the hurt and ache and pain
  And all the smart and itch
Of having him turn the bedclothes down
  To wake me with a switch,
Ef he 'ud on'y jest go 'way
  And let me finish up
The nap I started jest before
  He yelled out, "You git up!"

You bet, when I git growed up big,
    Es rich 'n' old as pa,
'N' never haf to go to school,
    Nor work nor stand no jaw—
I'll sleep all day and all night, too,
    And only jest git up
When I git 'nough sleep to suit me
    Ef all the world yells, "You git up!"

By permission of G.W. Dillingham Company.

PRESENTATION OF THE TRUMPET

ANONYMOUS

In the days of the old volunteer fire department there existed in this city a certain hose company noted for the bravery of its foreman, whose reckless daring in time of danger, coupled with his pugilistic attainments, had made him a local celebrity.

The members of his company decided to present him with a handsome silver trumpet, as an expression of their regard and appreciation of his pluck, courage and fighting qualities. One of the members was chosen to prepare a fitting speech for the occasion, and after some weeks of labor announced himself as being thoroughly prepared for the task.

In the meantime, the foreman, who was supposed to be in blissful ignorance of all the preparations being made to surprize him, was let into the "secret" through the kindness of one of the boys. He recognized this as his supreme opportunity to display his literary qualifications in the shape of a speech of acceptance. He secured the services of a literary friend to write a glowing oration, replete with metaphors, similes, and sweet-sounding poetry, expressing his "unworthiness of the honor," the "deep gratitude which words failed him to adequately express," etc.

The night in question at last arrived. The building was filled to overflowing. The band played "See the Conquering Hero Comes," and the boys gave three hearty cheers and a "tiger" for the proud foreman.

The chairman advanced to the front, holding the massive trumpet in one hand, while his other hand grasped convulsively at the collar of his shirt.

After staring around the room and giving a few preparatory coughs, he said:

"Mr. Foreman, and Members of Hose Company Number 10: I—a—a—I—a—I——(*Looks hard at the floor. Begins again with great determination.*) Mr. Foreman, and Members of Hose Company Number 10: I—a—a—I—a—feel—I feel a——(*Puts one hand in his pocket and looks very foolish. Begins again, shouting, and looking very angry.*) Mr. Foreman, and Members of Hose Company Number 10: I—I—I—I feel a—much a pleas—— (*Word sticks in his throat. Very angrily, and striding toward the foreman.*) Ah! take your trumpet!"

A look of consternation spread over the faces of the boys at the failure of their spokesman, and there were many whisperings of "I told you so!"

It was now the foreman's turn. He drew his hand across his mouth and began as follows:

"Mr. Chairman, and Members of Hose Company Number 10: It is—it is—it is—it is with a—with a——(*Looks at ceiling, and shifts his position uneasily. Begins over again, with a very confident air.*) Mr. Chairman, and Members of Hose Company Number 10: It is with—with a—with a—with a—a—a—a heart ——(*Stops, stares wildly at the ceiling, floor and company. Begins over again, very angrily, and with his body in fighting attitude.*) Mr. Chairman, and Members of Hose Company Number 10: I—I—I—it is—it is with a heart—with a heart full— full——(*Stops. Very loud and violently.*) Ah! give us yer trumpet!"

DON'T USE BIG WORDS

ANONYMOUS

In promulgating your esoteric cogitations, or articulating your superficial sentimentalities and amicable, philosophical or psychological observations, beware of platitudinous ponderosity. Let your conversational communications possess a clarified conciseness, a compact comprehensibleness, coalescent consistency, and a concatenated cogency. Eschew all conglomerations of flatulent garrulity, jejune babblement and asinine affectations. Let your extemporaneous descantings and unpremeditated expatiations have intelligibility and veracious vivacity, without rhodomontade or thrasonical bombast. Sedulously avoid all polysyllabic profundity, pompous prolixity, psittaceous vacuity, ventriloquial verbosity, and vaniloquent vapidity. Shun double-entendres, prurient jocosity, and pestiferous profanity, obscurant or apparent.

In other words, talk plainly, briefly, naturally, sensibly, truthfully, purely. Keep from "slang"; don't put on airs; say what you mean; mean what you say. And don't use big words!

DER MULE SHTOOD ON DER STEAMBOAD DECK

ANONYMOUS

Der mule shtood on der steamboad deck,
    For der land he wouldn't dread,
Dhey tied a halder rount his neck,
    Und vacked him over der headt.

But obstinate und braced he shtood,
    As born der scene to rule,
A creature of der holt-back brood—
    A shtubborn, shtedfast mule.

Dhey curst und shwore, but he vould not go
    Undill he felt inclined,
Und dhough dhey dundered blow on blow,
    He aldered nod his mind.

Der boats-boy to der shore complained,
    "Der varmint's bound do shtay,"
Shtill ubon dot olt mule's hide
    Der sounding lash made blay.

His masder from der shore reblied,
  "Der boats aboud do sail;
As oder means in vain you've dried,
  Subbose you dwist his dail.

"I dhink dot dat will magke him land,"
  Der boats-boy brave, dhough bale,
Den near drew mit oudstretched hand,
  Do magke der dwist avail.

Dhen game a kick of thunder sound!
  Dot boy—oh, vhere vas he?
Ask of der vaves dot far around
  Beheld him in der sea.

For a moment nod a voice vas heard,
  Bud dot mule he vinked his eye,
As dhough to ask, to him occurred,
  "How vas dot for high?"

THE NEW SCHOOL READER

ANONYMOUS

I will now give you a selection from my New School Reader. It is built upon the lines of the school-books in use in the years preceding our early childhood. It is one of the selections that unfortunate boys would render in an heroic attitude, and in stilted, unnatural tones:

"The October sun was shining down upon an avenue of trees, and gilding with its golden splendor the chromatic nose of a solitary horseman, who reigned up his steed at the sight of a small boy with a school-book on his shoulder. 'Where do you live, my fine fellow?' said the stranger, in low, pleasing tones. 'In yonder cottage, near the glen; my widowed mother and her thirteen chil-

dren dwell with me,' replied the boy, in a rich, mellow voice.
'And is your father dead?' asked the stranger with a rising
inflection. 'Extremely so,' murmured the lad, 'and that is why
my mother is a widow.' 'And how does your mother gain a live-
lihood?' asked the horseman, his voice dropping to a gentle whisper. 'I support the family,' proudly replied George. 'You support the family? Why, what can such a little fellow as you do?'
'I dig wells during the day, and help my mother at night. I have
a good education and am able to dig wells almost as well as a
man.' 'But you must have to work very hard,' said the stranger,
wiping a tear from his eyebrow. 'Indeed I do, sir, and since my
little sister Ann got married, and brought her husband home to
live with us, I have to work with more assiduity than ever. I am
enabled to barely maintain our family in a precarious manner;
but, oh, sir, should my other sisters marry, I fear that some of
my brothers-in-law would have to suffer.' 'My boy,' asked the
solitary horseman, looking at the youth proudly, 'what would you
say if I told you your father was not dead?' 'Sir,' replied the boy
respectfully, 'I am too polite to tell you what I would say,—
besides you are much larger than I am.' 'But, my brave lad,'
said the man in low, musical tones, 'do you not recognize your
parent on your father's side?—do you not know me, Georgie? O
George!' 'I must say,' replied George, 'that you have the advan-
tage of me. While I may have met you before, I can not at this
moment place you, sir!' At this the stranger opened his valise
and took therefrom a large-sized strawberry mark, which he placed
on his right arm. Immediately the boy recognized him as his
long-lost parent, and he, drawing the lad to his bosom, ejaculated,
'O my son, my son!' 'But how did you escape, father?' said the
boy through his tears, in a voice broken by emotion. 'We were
far away at sea,' said the heartbroken man. 'The winds howled
and the waves threatened to engulf our frail bark. When everybody was lost, the rest of the crew turned and sprang into the
foaming billows and swam several miles. At last I felt my feet
touch something *hard,*—it was Jersey City!' "

THE POOR WAS MAD

A FAIRY SHTORY FOR LITTLE CHILDHER

BY CHARLES BATTELL LOOMIS

Wance upon a toime the poor was virry poor indade, an' so they wint to a rich leddy that was that rich she had goold finger-nails, an' was that beautiful that it'u'd mek you dopey to luke at her. An' the poor asht her would she give thim the parin's of her goold finger-nails fer to sell. An' she said she would that, an' that ivery Chuesdeh she did be afther a-parin' her nails. So of a Chuesdeh the poor kem an' they tuke the gold parin's to a jewel-ery man, an' he gev thim good money fer thim. Wasn't she the koind leddy, childher? Well, wan day she forgot to pare her nails, an' so they had nothin' to sell. An' the poor was mad, an' they wint an' kilt the leddy intoirely. An' when she was kilt, sorra bit would the nails grow upon her, an' they saw they was silly to kill her. So they wint out to sairch fer a leddy wid silver finger-nails. An' they found her, an' she was that beautiful that her face was all the colors of the rainbow an' two more besides. An' the poor asht her would she give thim the parin's of her finger-nails fer to sell. An' she said that she would that, an' that every Chuesdeh she did be afther a-parin' her nails. So of a Chuesdeh the poor kem an' they tuk the silver parin's to the jewel-ery man, an' he giv thim pretty good money fer thim, but not nair as good as fer the goold. But he was the cute jewel-ery man, wasn't he, childher? Well, wan day she forgot to pare her nails an' so they had nothin' to sell. An' the poor was mad, an' they wint an' kilt the leddy intoirely. An' when she was kilt, sorra bit would the nails grow upon her, an' they saw they was silly to kill her. So they wint out to sairch for a leddy with tin finger-nails. An' they found her, and she was that beautiful that she would mek you ristless. An' the poor asht her would she give thim the parin's of her tin finger-nails fer to sell. An' she said she would that, an' that ivery Chuesdeh she did be afther a-parin' her nails. So of a Chuesdeh the poor kem. An' did they get the tin nails, childher? Sure, that's where y are out. They did not, fer the leddy had lost a finger in a mowin'-machine, an' she didn't have tin finger-nails at arl, at arl—only noine.

LIDES TO BARY JADE

ANONYMOUS

The bood is beabig brighdly love,
   The sdars are shidig, too;
While I ab gazing dreabily
   Add thigkig, love, of you;
You caddot, oh, you caddot kdow,
   By darlig, how I biss you,—
(Oh, whadt a fearful cold I've got—
   Ck-*tish*-u! Ck-ck-*tish*-u!)

I'b sittig id the arbor, love
   Where you sat by by side,
Whed od that calb, Autubdal dight
   You said you'd be by bride.
Oh, for wud bobedt to caress
   Add tederly to kiss you;
Budt do! we're beddy biles apart—
   (Ho-*rash*-o! Ck-ck-*tish*-u!)

This charbig evedig brigs to bide
   The tibe whed first we bet;
It seebs budt odly yesterday,
   I thigk I see you yet.
Oh, tell be, ab I sdill your owd?
   By hopes, oh, do dot dash theb!
(Codfoud by cold, 'tis gettig worse—
   Ck-*tish*-u! Ck-ck-*thrash*-eb!)

Good-by, by darlig Bary Jade
  The bid-dight hour is dear,
Add it is hardly wise by love
  For be to ligger here!
The heavy dews are fallig fast;
  A fod good-dight I wish you;
(Ho-*rash*-o!—there it is agaid—
  Ck-*tish*-u! Ck-ck-*thrash*-eb!`

"CHARLIE MUST NOT RING TO-NIGHT"

Parody on "Curfew Must not Ring To-night"

ANONYMOUS

Slowly England's sun was setting o'er a mansion old and grey;
Filling all the land with glory, in the usual kind of way.
And its bright rays tinged the foreheads of a man and maiden
  fair:
He with powdered head and whiskers, she with locks of—some-
  one's hair.
She was clutching at it wildly, as, with lips all cold and white,
She was saying, "Listen, Thomas,—Charlie must not ring to-
  night!"

"Thomas," Bessie's white lips murmur'd, as she feverishly laid
  hold
Of the buttons of his liv'ry—lobster-red with spots of gold—
"Freddie Smith will call this evening; he'll be ringing by and by;
Charlie does not know about him; if they met here I should die!
Tell him I am out, dear Thomas; gone to call on Mrs. Blight;
Tell him any lie you like but—Charlie must not ring to-night."

"Bessie," calmly said the flunkey—ev'ry word was like a dart
Barbed with poison, entering in that damsel's heart—
"For the last three weeks that pusson—w'ich 'is name are Charlie
  Power—
Hev'ry hevenink's called to see you, jest about the dinner-hour.
'E' as never failed to tip me—w'ich is only just and right—
So I still must do my duty, should that pusson ring to-night!"

She with quick steps bounded upward, till she reached the cham-
ber-door,
Seized her purse, and quick returning, threw it wildly on the
floor.
"Take it, Thomas," cried the maiden, with her eyes and cheeks
aglow,
"Take it all and welcome—what there is I do not know—
But 'tis yours, ay, ev'ry farthing; gold and precious silver bright,
Only, take good care, dear Thomas, Charlie must not ring to-
night!"

She had fled to dress for Freddie; Thomas seeks the front door-
bell.
He will muffle up the clapper, in a way he knows full well.
See! The bell is being shaken; 'tis the fateful moment now!
Thomas hastes to "do his dooty," with a firm, determined brow.
Shall he let it ring? No, never; he has touched the guerdon
bright,
So he grasps the clapper, whisp'ring, "Charlie *shall* not ring to-
night!"

It was o'er; the youth ceased pulling, and the maiden breathed
once more.
But, alas! that fickle maiden wept as maid ne'er wept before
When she learn'd that he who'd called there, promptly at the
dinner-hour,
Was the long-expected Freddie, *not* the hated Charlie Power.
While the tried and trusted Thomas, knowing not her evil plight,
Open'd wide the door for Charlie when that "pusson" called
that night!

A SHORT ENCORE

Man wants but little here below,
    He's not so hard to please;
But woman (bless her little heart)
    Wants everything she sees!

MY DOUBLE, AND HOW HE UNDID ME

BY EDWARD EVERETT HALE

I am, or rather, was a minister, and was settled in an active, wide-awake town with a bright parish and a charming young wife. At first it was all delightful, but as my duties increased I found myself leading a double life—one for my parish, whom I loved, and the other for a vague public, for whom I did not care two straws. It was then that on my wife's suggestion I looked for a double—some one who would pass for me and fill the many engagements I wanted to shirk. I found him. When he was discovered his name was Dennis Shea, and he was not shaved, had no spectacles, and his style of dress was not at all like mine; but these difficulties were soon surmounted, for, by application to the Judge of Probate, his name was soon changed to Frederick Ingham—my name. As for appearance, he was so much like me that by the united efforts of Polly and myself and a tailor he was made to look the exact image of me. Then in four successive afternoons I taught him four speeches, which were to be his stock in trade:

No. 1—"Very well, thank you; and you?" (This for an answer to casual salutations.)

No. 2—"I am very glad you liked it." (This in response to a compliment on a sermon.)

No. 3—"There has been so much said, and on the whole so well said, that I will not occupy the time." (This for public meetings when called to speak.)

No. 4—"I agree in general with my friend on the other side of the room." (This when asked for an opinion of his own.)

Thus equipped, my double attended a number of conventions and meetings which I was too busy to notice and was very success-ful. He gained a good reputation for me, and people began to say I was less exclusive than I used to be, and that I was more punctual, less talkative, etc. His success was so great that one evening I risked him at a reception. I could ill afford the time to go, and so I sent him with Polly, who kept her eye on him, and afterward told me about it. He had to take a very talkative

lady—Mrs. Jeffries—down to supper, and at sight of the eatables
he became a little excited, and attempted one of his speeches to
the lady. He tried the shortest one in his most gallant manner:
"Very well, thank you; and you?" Polly, who stood near his
chair, was much frightened, as this speech had no connection
with anything that had been said, but Mrs. Jeffries was so much
engrossed with her own talking that she noticed nothing. She
rattled on so busily that Dennis was not obliged to say anything
more until the eating was over, when he said, to fill up a pause:
"There has been so much said, and on the whole so well said,
that I will not occupy the time." This again frightened Polly,
but she managed to get him away before he had done anything
serious.

After this my double relieved me in so many ways that I grew
quite light-hearted. That happy year I began to know my wife
by sight. We saw each other sometimes, and how delightful it
was! But all this could not last; and at length poor Dennis,
my double, undid me!

There was some ridiculous new movement on foot to organize
some kind of a society, and there was to be a public meeting.
Of course I was asked to attend and to speak. After much urging
I consented to go and sit on the platform, upon condition that
I would not be called upon to make a speech. This was agreed
upon, and I went—that is, Dennis went, having been told to say
nothing on any subject. He sat resplendent on the platform,
and kept his peace during the preliminary exercises, which were
rather dry. Governor Blake called the meeting to order, but
as he really did not know what the object of the gathering was,
he said that there were other gentlemen present who could entertain them better than he. Then there followed an awkward
scene, for nobody wanted to speak, and every one that was
called upon was either absent or unprepared; and finally a
wretched boy in the gallery called out, "Ingham! Ingham!" The
governor thought I would respond, and as nothing had been said
so far, he ventured to ask me, saying: "Our friend, Mr. Ingham,
is always prepared, and tho we had not relied upon him, he
will say a word perhaps." Applause followed, which turned
Dennis' head. He rose and tried speech No. 3: "There has been

so much said, and on the whole so well said, that I will not longer
occupy the time!"

Then he sat down, looking for his hat—for things seemed
squally. But the people cried, "Go on! Go on!" and some applauded. Dennis still confused, but flattered by the applause,
rose again, and this time tried No. 2: "I am very glad you like
it." Which, alas! should only be said when complimented on a
sermon. My best friends stared, and people who didn't know me
yelled with delight. A boy in the gallery cried out: "It's all
a humbug!" just as Dennis, waving his hand, commanded silence,
and tried No. 4: "I agree in general with my friend on the other
side of the room." The poor governor, doubting his senses,
crossed to stop him, but too late. The same gallery boy shouted:
"How's your mother?" And Dennis, completely lost, tried as
his last shot No. 1: "Very well, thank you; and you?" The
audience rose in a whirl of excitement. Some other impertinence
from the gallery was aimed at Dennis; he broke all restraint and
to finish undoing me, he called out: "Any wan o' ye blatherin'
rascals that wants to fight, can come down an' I'll take any five
o' yez, single-handed; ye're all dogs and cowards! Sure an'
I've said all his riverance an' the mistress bade me say!"

That was all; my double had undone me.

Reprinted by permission of Little, Brown & Co., Boston, Mass.

ROMANCE OF A HAMMOCK

ANONYMOUS

Shady tree—babbling brook,
Girl in hammock—reading book.

Golden curls—tiny feet,
Girl in hammock—looks so sweet.

Man rides past—big mustache,
Girl in hammock—makes a "mash."

"Mash" is mutual—day is set,
Man and maiden—married get.

Married now a year and a day,
Keeping house in Avenue A.

Red-hot stove—beefsteak frying,
Girl got married—cooking trying.

Cheeks all burning—eyes look red,
Girl got married—almost dead.

Biscuit burnt up—beefsteak charry,
Girl got married—awful sorry.

Man comes home—tears mustache,
Mad as blazes—got no cash.

Thinks of hammock—in the lane;
Wishes maiden—back again.

Maiden also—thinks of swing,
And wants to go back, too, poor thing!

Hour of midnight—baby squawking;
Man in bare feet—bravely walking;

The baby yells—now the other
Twin, he strikes up—like his brother.

Paregoric—by the bottle
Poured into—the baby's throttle.

Naughty tack—points in air,
Waiting some one's—foot to tear.

Man in bare feet—see him there!
O my gracious!—hear him swear!

Raving crazy—gets his gun
Blows h.s head off—dead and gone.

Pretty widow—with a book
In the hammock—by the brook.

Man rides past—big mustache;
Keeps on riding—nary "mash."

FINNIGIN TO FLANNIGAN

BY S. W. GILLINAN

Superintindent wuz Flannigan;
Boss av the siction wuz Finnigin;
Whiniver the kyars got offen the thrack,
An' muddled up things t' th' divil an' back,
Finnigin writ it to Flannigan,
Afther the wrick wuz all on ag'in;
      That is, this Finnigin
      Repoorted to Flannigan.

Whin Finnigin furst writ to Flannigan,
He writed tin pages—did Finnigin,
An' he tould jist how the smash occurred;
Full minny a tajus, blunderin' wurrd
Did Finnigin write to Flannigan
Afther the cars had gone on ag'in.
      That wuz how Finnigin
      Repoorted to Flannigan.

Now Flannigan knowed more than Finnigin—
He'd more idjucation, had Flannigan;
An' it wore'm clane an' complately out
To tell what Finnigin writ about
In his writin' to Muster Flannigan.
So he writed back to Finnigin:
    "Don't do sich a sin ag'in;
    Make 'em brief, Finnigin!"

Whin Finnigin got this from Flannigan,
He blushed rosy rid, did Finnigin;
An' he said: "I'll gamble, a whole month's pa-ay
That it will be minny an' minny a da-ay
Befoore Sup'rintindint—that's Flannigan—
Gits a whack at this very same sin ag'in.
    From Finnigin to Flannigan
    Repoorts won't be long ag'in."

.   .   .   .   .   .

Wan da-ay, on the siction av Finnigin,
On the road sup'rintinded by Flannigan,
A rail gave way on a bit av a curve,
An' some kyars went off as they made the swerve.
"There's nobody hurted," sez Finnigin,
"But repoorts must be made to Flannigan."
    An' he winked at McCorrigan,
    As married a Finnigin.

He wuz shantyin' thin, wuz Finnigin,
As minny a railroader's been ag'in,
An' the shmoky ol' lamp wuz burnin' bright
In Finnigin's shanty all that night—
Bilin' down his repoort, was Finnigin!
An' he writed this here: "Muster Flannigan:
    Off ag'in, on ag'in,
    Gone ag'in—Finnigin."

From *Life*, by courtesy of the publishers.

AN INTRODUCTION

BY MARK TWAIN

"Ladies—and—gentlemen:—By—the request of the—Chairman of the—Com-mit-tee—I beg leave to—introduce—to you—the reader of the evening—a gentleman whose great learning—whose historical ac-curacy—whose devotion—to science—and—and—whose veneration for the truth—are only equaled by his high moral character—and—his—majestic presence. I allude—in these vague general terms—to my-self. I—am a little opposed to the custom of ceremoniously introducing a reader to the audience, because it seems—unnecessary—where the man has been properly advertised! But as—it is—the custom—I prefer to make it myself—in my own case—and then I can rely on getting in—all the facts! I never had but one introduction—that seemed to me just the thing—and the gentleman was not acquainted with me, and there was no nonsense. Ladies and gentlemen, I shall waste no time in this introduction. I know of only two facts about this man: first, he—has never been in the state prison; and second, I can't—imagine why."

THE HARP OF A THOUSAND STRINGS

A Hard-shell Baptist Sermon

BY JOSHUA S. MORRIS

(This characteristic effusion first appeared in a New Orleans paper. The sermon is supposed to have been preached at a village on the bank of the Mississippi River, whither the volunteer parson had brought his flatboat for the purpose of trade.)

I may say to you, my brethring, that I am not an edicated man, an' I am not one of them as beleeves that edication is necessary for a Gospel minister, for I beleeve the Lord edicates his preachers jest as He wants 'em to be edicated; an' altho I say it that oughtn't to say it, yet in the State of Indianny, whar I live, thar's no man as gits bigger congregations nor what I gits.

Thar may be some here to-day, my brethring, as don't know
what persuasion I am uv. Well, I must say to yu, my brethring,
that I'm a Hard-shell Baptist. Thar's some folks as don't like
the Hard-shell Baptists, but I'd rather have a hard shell as no
shell at all. You see me here to-day, my brethring, drest up in
fine clothes; you mout think I was proud, but I am not proud,
my brethring; and altho I've been a preacher of the Gospel for
twenty years, an' altho I'm capting of the flatboat that lies at
your landing, I'm not proud, my brethring.

I am not gwine to tell edzactly whar my tex may be found;
suffice to say, it's in the leds of the Bible, and you'll find it
somewhar between the fust chapter of the book of Generations
and the last chapter of the book of Revolutions; and ef you'll go
and sarch the Scriptures, you'll not only find my tex thar, but
a great many other texes as will do you good to read; and my
tex, when you shall find it, you shall find it to read thus: "And
he played on a harp uv a thousand strings, sperits uv jest men
made perfeck."

My tex, my brethring, leads me to speak of sperits. Now,
thar's a great many kinds of sperits in the world. In the fust
place, thar's the sperits as some folks call ghosts; and thar's
the sperits of turpentine; and thar's the sperits as some folks
call liquor, an' I've got as good an artikel of them kind of sperits
on my flatboat as ever was fotch down the Mississippi River.
But thar's a great many other kinds of sperits, for the tex says,
"He played on a harp uv a t-h-o-u-s-and strings, sperits uv jest
men made perfeck."

But I tell you the kind uv sperits as is meant in the tex is
FIRE. That's the kind uv sperits as is meant in the tex, my
brethring. Now, thar's a great many kinds uv fire in the world.
In the fust place, there's the common sort of fire you light your
cigars or pipe with; and then thar's foxfire and camphire, fire
before you're ready, and fire and fall back, and many other kinds
of fire—for the tex say, "He played on a harp uv a *thous*and
strings, sperits uv jest men made perfeck."

But I'll tell you the kind of fire as is meant in the tex, my
brethring: its HELL-FIRE! An' that's the kind uv fire as
a great many uv you'll come to, ef you don't do better nor what

you have been doin'—for "He played on a harp uv a *thous*and strings, sperits uv jest men made perfeck."

Now, the different sorts of fire in the world may be likened unto the different persuasions of Christians in the world. In the fust place, we have the Piscapalions, an' they are a high-sailin' and highfalutin' set; and they may be likened unto a turkey buzzard that flies up in the air, and he goes up, and up, and up, till he looks no bigger than your finger-nail, and the fust thing you know, he cums down, and down, and down, and is a-fillin' himself on the carkiss of a dead hoss by the side of the road—and "He played on a harp uv a *thous*and strings, sperits uv jest men made perfeck."

And then thar's the Methodis, and they may be likened unto the squirril runnin' up into a tree, for the Methodis beleeves in gwine on from one degree of grace to another, and finally on to perfection; and the squirril goes up and up, and up and up, and he jumps from limb to limb, and branch to branch, and the fust thing you know he falls, and down he cums kerflumix; and that's like the Methodis, for they is allers fallin' from grace, ah!— and "He played on a harp uv a *thous*and strings, sperits uv jest men made perfeck."

And then, my brethring, thar's the Baptists, ah! and they have been likened unto a 'possum on a 'simmon tree, and thunders may roll and the earth may quake, but that 'possum clings thar still, sh! and you may shake one foot loose, and the other's thar, and you make shake all feet loose, and he laps his tail around the limb, and clings, and he clings furever—for "He played on a harp uv a *thous*and strings, sperits uv jest men made perfeck."

THE DIFFICULTY OF RIMING

ANONYMOUS

We parted by the gate in June,
   That soft and balmy month,
Beneath the sweetly beaming moon,
   And (wonth-hunth-sunth-bunth—I can't
find a rime to month).

Years were to pass ere we should meet.
　　A wide and yawning gulf
　Divides me from my love so sweet,
　　　While (ulf-sulf-dulf-mulf—stuck again; I
can't get any rime to gulf.　I'm in a gulf myself).

　　Oh, how I dreaded in my soul
　　　To part from my sweet nymph,
　While years should their long seasons roll
　　　Before (hymph-dymph-symph—I guess I'll
have to let it go at that).

　Beneath my fortune's stern decree
　　　My lonely spirits sunk,
　For I a weary soul should be,
　　　And a (hunk-dunk-runk-sk—that will
never do in the world).

　She buried her dear lovely face
　　　Within her azure scarf,
　She knew I'd take the wretchedness,
　　　As well as (parf-darf-harf-and-harf—
that won't answer either).

　Oh, I had loved her many years.
　　　I loved her for herself;
　I loved her for her tender tears,
　　　And also for her (welf-nelf-self-pelf—no,
no; not for her pelf).

　I took between my hands her head,
　　　How sweet her lips did pouch!
　I kissed her lovingly and said—
　　　(Bouch-mouch-louch-ouch—not a bit of it
did I say ouch!).

I sorrowfully wrung her hand,
   My tears they did escape,
My sorrow I could not command,
   And I was but a (sape-dape-fape-ape;
well, perhaps I did feel like an ape).

I gave to her a fond adieu,
   Sweet pupil of love's school,
I told her I would e'er be true,
   And always be a (dool-sool-mool-fool; since
I come to think of it, I was a fool, for she fell in love
with another fellow before I was gone a month).

SO WAS I

BY JOSEPH BERT SMILEY

My name is Tommy an' I hates
That feller of my sister Kate's.
He's bigger'n I am an' you see
He's sorter lookin' down on me,
An' I resents it with a vim;
I think I'm just as good as him.
He's older, an' he's mighty fly
But he's a kid,—an' so am I.

One time he came,—down by the gate,
I guess it must been awful late,—
An' Katie, she was there, an' they
Was feelin' very nice and gay,
An' he was talkin' all the while,
About her sweet an' lovin' smile,
An' everythin' was nice as pie,
An' they was there,—an' so was I.

They didn't see me, 'cause I slid
Down underneath a bush, an' hid,
An' he was sayin' that his love
Was greater'n all the stars above
Up in the glorious heavens placed;
An' then his arm got round her waist,
An' clouds were floatin' in the sky,
An' they was there,—an' so was I.

I didn't hear just all they said,
But by an' by my sister's head
Was droopin' on his shoulder, an'
I seen him holdin' Katie's hand,
An' then he hugged her closer, some,
An' then I heered a kiss—*yum, yum!*
An' Katie blushed an' drew a sigh,
An' sorter coughed,—an' so did I.

An' then that feller looked around
An' seed me there, down on the ground,
An'—*was* he mad?—well, betcher boots
I gets right outer there an' *scoots*.
An' he just left my sister Kate
A-standin' right there by the gate;
An' I seen blood was in his eye,
An' he runned fast,—an' so did I.

I runned the very best I could
But he cotched up,—I's 'fraid he would,
An' then he said he'd teach me how
To know my manners, he'd allow;
An' then he shaked me *awful*. Gee!
He jest—he frashed the ground with me.
An' then he stopt it by and by,
'Cause he was tired,—an' so was I.

An' then he went back to the gate
An' couldn't find my sister Kate,
'Cause she went to bed, while he
Was runnin' round an' thumpin' me.
I got round in a shadder dim,
An' made a face, an' guffed at him;
An' then the moon larfed, in the sky,
'Cause he was there,—an' so was I.

THE ENCHANTED SHIRT

BY JOHN HAY

The king was sick. His cheek was red,
  And his eye was clear and bright;
He ate and drank with a kingly zest,
  And peacefully snored at night.

But he said he was sick—and a king should know;
  And doctors came by the score;
They did not cure him. He cut off their heads,
  And sent to the schools for more.

At last two famous doctors came,
  And one was as poor as a rat;
He had passed his life in studious toil
  And never found time to grow fat.

The other had never looked in a book;
  His patients gave him no trouble;
If they recovered, they paid him well,
  If they died, their heirs paid double.

Together they looked at the royal tongue,
  As the king on his couch reclined;
In succession they thumped his august chest,
  But no trace of disease could find.

The old sage said, "You're as sound as a nut."
"Hang him up!" roared the king, in a gale,—
In a ten-knot gale of royal rage;
    The other leach grew a shade pale;

But he pensively rubbed his sagacious nose,
    And thus his prescription ran:
"The king will be well if he sleeps one night
    In the shirt of a happy man."

Wide o'er the realm the couriers rode,
    And fast their horses ran,
And many they saw, and to many they spake,
    But they found no happy man.

They saw two men by the roadside sit,
    And both bemoaned their lot;
For one had buried his wife, he said.
    And the other one had not.

At last they came to a village gate;
    A beggar lay whistling there;
He whistled and sang and laughed, and rolled
    On the grass in the soft June air.

The weary couriers paused and looked
    At the scamp so blithe and gay,
And one of them said, "Heaven save you, friend,
    You seem to be happy to-day?"

"Oh, yes, fair sirs," the rascal laughed,
    And his voice rang free and glad;
"An idle man has so much to do
    That he never has time to be sad."

"This is our man." the courier said,
  "Our luck has led us aright.
I will give you a hundred ducats, friend,
  For the loan of your shirt to-night."

The merry rascal lay back on the grass
  And laughed till his face was black;
"I would do it," said he, and roared with the fun,
  "But I haven't a shirt to my back!"

Each day to the king the reports came in
  Of the unsuccessful spies;
And the sad panorama of human woes,
  Passed daily under his eyes.

And he grew ashamed of his useless life,
  And his maladies hatched in gloom;
He opened his windows and let the free air
  Of the heavens into his room.

And out he went into the world and toiled
  In his own appointed way,
And the people blest him, the land was glad,
  And the king was well and gay.

DER OAK UND DER VINE

BY CHARLES FOLLEN ADAMS

I don'd vas preaching voman's righdts,
  Or anyding like dot,
Und I likes to see all beoples
  Shust gontended mit dheir lot;
But I vants to gontradict dot shap
  Dot made dis leedle shoke:
"A voman vas der glinging vine,
  Und man, der shturdy oak."

Berhaps, somedimes, dot may be drue;
  Budt, den dimes oudt off nine,
I find me oudt dot man himself
  Vas peen der glinging vine;
Und ven hees friendts dhey all vas gone
  Und he vas shust "tead proke,"
Dot's vhen der voman shteps righdt in,
  Und peen der shturdy oak.

Shust go oup to der paseball groundts
  Und see dhose "shturdy oaks"
All planted roundt ubon der seats—
  Shust hear dheir laughs und shokes!
Dhen see dhose vomens at der tubs,
  Mit glothes oudt on der lines:
Vhich vas der shturdy oaks, mine frendts,
  Und vhich der glinging vines?

Ven sickness in der householdt comes,
  Und veeks und veeks he shtays,
Who vas id fighdts him mitout resdt,
  Dhose veary nighdts und days?
Who beace und gomfort alvays prings,
  Und cools dot fefered prow?
More like id vas der tender vine
  Dot oak he glings to, now.

"Man vants budt leedle here pelow,"
  Der boet von time said;
Dhere's leedle dot man he *don'd* vant,
  I dink id means, inshted;
Und vhen der years keep rolling on,
  Dheir cares und droubles pringing,
He vants to pe der shturdy oak,
  Und, also, do der glinging.

Maype, vhen oaks dhey gling some more,
  Und don'd so shturdy peen,
Der glinging vines dhey haf some shance
  To helb run life's masheen.
In helt und sickness, shoy und pain,
  In calm or shtormy veddher,
'Tvas beddher dot dhose oaks und vines
  Should alvays gling togedder.

THE SHIP OF FAITH

ANONYMOUS

A certain colored brother had been holding forth to his little flock upon the ever-fruitful topic of *Faith,* and he closed his exhortation about as follows:

"My bruddren, ef yous gwine to git saved, you got to git on board de Ship ob Faith. I tell you, my bruddren, dere ain't no odder way. Dere ain't no gitten up de back stairs, nor goin' 'cross lots; you can't do dat away, my bruddren, you got to git on board de Ship ob Faith. Once 'pon a time dere was a lot ob colored people, an' dey was all gwine to de promised land. Well, dey knowed dere w'an't no odder way for 'em to do but to git on board de Ship ob Faith. So dey all went down an' got on board, de ole granfaders, an' de ole granmudders, an' de pickaninnies, an' all de res' of 'em. Dey all got on board 'ceptin' one mons'us big feller, he said he's gwine to swim, he was. 'W'y!' dey said, 'you can't swim so fur like dat. It am a powerful long way to de promised land!' He said: 'I kin swim anywhur, I kin. I git board no boat, no, 'deed!' Well, my bruddren, all dey could say to dat poor disluded man dey couldn't git him on board de Ship of Faith, so dey started off. De day was fair, de win' right; de sun shinin' and ev'ryt'ing b'utiful, an' dis big feller he pull off his close and plunge in de water. Well, he war a powerful swimmer, dat man, 'deed he war; he war dat powerful he kep' right 'long side de boat all de time; he kep' a hollerin' out to de people on de boat, sayin': 'What you doin' dere, you folks, brilin' away in de sun; you better come down heah in de water, nice an'

cool down here.' But dey said: 'Man alive, you better come up
here in dis boat while you got a chance.' But he said: 'No, in-
deedy! I git aboard no boat; I'm havin' plenty fun in de water.'
Well, bimeby, my bruddren, what you tink dat pore man seen?
A horrible, awful shark, my bruddren; mouf wide opne, teef
more'n a foot long, ready to chaw dat pore man all up de minute
he catch him. Well, when he seen dat shark he begun to git
awful scared, an' he holler out to de folks on board de ship:
'Take me on board, take me on board, quick!' But dey said:
'No, indeed; you wouldn't come up here before, you swim now!'

"He look over his shoulder an' he seen dat shark a-comin' an'
he let hisself out. Fust it was de man an' den it was de shark,
an' den it was de man again, dat away, my bruddren, *plum to de
promised land.* Dat am de blessed troof I'm a-tellin' you dis
minute. But what do you t'ink was a-waitin' for him on de odder
shore when he got dere? *A horrible, awful lion,* my bruddren,
was a-stan'in' dere on de shore, a-lashin' his sides wid his tail,
an' a-roarin' away fit to devour dat poor nigger de minit he git
on de shore.

"Well, he *war* powerful scared den, he don't know what he
gwine to do. If he stay in de water de shark eat him up; if he
go on shore de lion eat him up; he dunno what to do. But he
put his trust in de Lord, an' went for de shore. Dat lion he give
a fearful roar an' bound for him; but, my bruddren, as sure as
you live an' breeve, dat horrible, awful lion he jump clean ober
dat pore feller's head into de water; an' *de shark eat de lion.*
But, my bruddren, don't you put your trust in no such circum-
stance; dat pore man he done git saved, but I tell you *de Lord
ain't a-gwine to furnish a lion fo' every nigger!*"

HE WANTED TO KNOW

ANONYMOUS

Early one moonlight morning, in the city of London, a man was
vainly trying to find his home, but being unable to locate it he
called upon the services of a passer-by.

"Hey! M-m-mister (hic), will you take me to twenty-two?"

"Number twenty—Why you are standing right in front of it!"

"Oh, no you d-d-don't,—that's two-two, two-two!"

"Why, no, it's twenty-two."

"Say, you can't fool me. 'Nuther fellow tried to d-d-do that. He-he-he told me the other side of the street was (hic) on this side,—an' 'tisn't,—s-sit's over there. Please t-t-take me (hic) to twenty-two, will you?"

The man walked him around the block and back again.

"Now, then, get out your key. I must be going."

"Say, it was m-m-mighty (hic) jolly of you to bring me all this l-l-long way ho-ho-home, old chap!"

"That's all right. Now get your key,—hurry up."

"I'm ever so much obliged to you for bringing me all this long way ho-ho-home."

"That's all right. I must go now. Good-night."

The man had walked but a little distance when he heard his friend trying to whistle to him.

"Hey! (*Tries to whistle*). C-co-come here, I want ter speak to you. Now d-d-don't get mad (hic), old chap, it's important."

"Well, what do you want?"

"I just want to (hic) tell you how much obliged I'm to you for bringing me all this long way home."

"You had better go to bed now, so good-night."

"'Hold up, old chap, you're a-a-a—would you mind telling me what your name is?"

Here the clock in St. Paul's struck two.

"My name—is St. Paul."

"Good enough, Miss Saint 'All. Much obliged to you for bring —me——"

"Never mind, good-night."

"Hey! Hi! (*Tries to whistle*). Mister Saint 'All—Miss Saint P-all, co-co-come here, I want to ask (hic) you something."

"What!"

"Old f-f-friend, I d-d-d-d-didn't mean that, Misser Saint Faull, —I just want to ask you a persh-pershonal question, Mis-Mis——"

"Well, what is it?"

"Misser Saint Paul, would you mind telling me whether you ever got answers to those letters you wrote to the Ephesians?"

AN OPPORTUNITY

ANONYMOUS

I dropt into the post-office this morning for my mail, and just inside the door I found a little boy crying very bitterly. Naturally I asked him the cause of his trouble, and lifting his tear-stained face to mine he said:

"I had two quarters, and a feller come along just now and took one away from me."

"What!" said I, "right here in the post-office?"

"Yes, sir."

"Well, why didn't you tell some one?"

"I did; I hollered, 'Help! help!'" (*Said very weakly.*)

"Well," I said, "is that as loud as you can holler?"

"Yes, sir."

So *I* took the other quarter.

GAPE-SEED

ANONYMOUS

A farmer, walking the streets of one of our big cities, looked through a window at a lot of men writing very rapidly on type-writers; and as he stood at the door with his mouth open, one of the men called out to him, "Do you wish to buy some gape-seed?" Passing on a short distance, he asked a man what the business was of the men he had just seen in the office he had passed. He was told that they wrote letters dictated by others, and transcribed all sorts of documents. The farmer returned to the office, and inquired if one of the men would write a letter for him, and was answered in the affirmative. He asked the price, and was told one dollar. After considerable talk, the bargain was made; one of the conditions being that the scribe should write just what the farmer told him to, or he should receive no pay. The man said he was ready, and the farmer dictated as follows:

"Dear wife," and then asked, "Have you got that down?"

"Yes; *go on.*"

"I went for a ride the other day—have you got that down?"

"Yes; *go on, go on.*"

"And I harnessed up the old mare into the wagon—have you got that down?"

"Yes, yes, long ago; *go on.*"

"Why, how fast you write!—And I got into the wagon, and sat down, and drew up the reins, and took the whip in my right hand—have you got that down?"

"Yes, long ago; *go on.*"

"Dear me, how fast you write! I never saw your equal.—And I said to the old mare, '*Go 'long,*' and I jerked the reins pretty hard—have you got that down?"

"Yes; and I am impatiently waiting for more. I wish you wouldn't bother me with so many foolish questions. Go on with your letter."

"Well, the old mare wouldn't stir out of her tracks, and I hollered, '*Go 'long, you old jade! go 'long*'—have you got that down?"

"Yes, indeed, *you pestiferous fellow; go on.*"

"And I licked her, and licked her, and licked her——" (*continuing to repeat these words as rapidly as possible*).

"Hold on there! I have written two pages of 'licked her,' and I want the rest of the letter."

"Well, and she kicked, and she kicked, and she kicked——"(*continuing to repeat these words with great rapidity*).

"Do go on with your letter; I have several pages of 'she kicked.'"

(*The farmer clucks as in urging horses to move, and continues the clucking noise with rapid repetition for some time.*)

The scribe jumps up from the typewriter.

"*Write it down! write it down!*"

"I can't!"

"Well, then, I won't pay you."

(*The scribe, gathering up his papers.*) "What shall I do with all these sheets upon which I have written your nonsense?"

"You might use them in doing up your *gape-seed!* Good-day!"

LARIAT BILL

ANONYMOUS

"Well, stranger, 'twas somewhere in 'sixty-nine
   I wore runnin' the 'Frisco fast express;
An' from Murder Creek to Blasted Pine,
   Were nigh onto eighteen mile, I guess.
The road were a down-grade all the way,
   An' we pulled out of Murder a little late,
So I opened the throttle wide that day,
   And a mile a minute was 'bout our gait.

"My fireman's name was Lariat Bill,
   A quiet man with an easy way,
Who could rope a steer with a cowboy's skill,
   Which he had learned in Texas, I've heard him say:
The coil were strong as tempered steel,
   An' it went like a bolt from a crossbow flung,
An' arter Bill changed from saddle to wheel,
   Just over his head in the cab it hung.

"Well, as I were saying, we fairly flew
   As we struck the curve at Buffalo Spring,
An' I give her full steam an' put her through,
   An' the engine rocked like a living thing;
When all of a sudden I got a scare—
   For thar on the track were a little child!
An' right in the path of the engine there
   She held out her little hands and smiled!

"I jerked the lever and whistled for brakes,
   The wheels threw sparks like a shower of gold;
But I knew the trouble a down-grade makes,
   An' I set my teeth an' my flesh grew cold.
Then Lariat Bill yanked his long lasso,
   An' out on the front of the engine crept—
He balanced a moment before he threw,
   Then out in the air his lariat swept!"

He paused. There were tears in his honest eyes;
  The stranger listened with bated breath.
"I know the rest of the tale," he cries;
  "He snatched the child from the jaws of death!
'Twas the deed of a hero, from heroes bred,
  Whose praises the very angels sing!"
The engineer shook his grizzled head,
  And growled: "He didn't do no sich thing.

"He aimed at the stump of a big pine tree,
  An' the lariat caught with a double hitch,
An' in less than a second the train an' we
  Were yanked off the track an' inter the ditch!
'Twere an awful smash, an' it laid me out,
  I ain't forgot it, and never shall;
Were the passengers hurt? Lemme see—about—
  Yes, it killed about forty—but saved the gal!"

THE CANDIDATE

BY BILL NYE

The heat and the venom of each political campaign bring back
to my mind with wonderful clearness the bitter and acrimonious
war, and the savage factional fight, which characterized my own
legislative candidacy in what was called the Prairie Dog District
of Wyoming, about ten years ago.

I hesitated about accepting the nomination because I knew that
vituperation would get up on its hind feet and annoy me greatly,
and, indeed, this turned out to be the case.

In due time I was nominated, and one evening my heart swelled
when I heard a campaign band coming up the street, trying to
see how little it could play and still draw its salary. The band
was followed by men with torches, and speakers in carriages.
A messenger was sent into the house to tell me that I was about
to be waited upon by my old friends and neighbors, who desired

to deliver to me their hearty endorsement, and a large willow-covered two-gallon Godspeed as a mark of esteem.

The spokesman, as soon as I had stept out on my veranda, mounted the improvised platform previously erected, and after a short and debilitated solo and chorus by the band, said as follows, as near as I can now recall his words:

" *Mr. Nye*—

"Sir:—We have read with pain the open and venomous attacks of the foul and putrid press of our town, and come here to-night to vindicate by our presence your utter innocence *as* a man, *as* a fellow citizen, *as* a neighbor, *as* a father, mother, brother or sister.

"No one could look down into your open face, and deep, earnest lungs, and then doubt you *as* a man, *as* a fellow citizen, *as* a neighbor, *as* a father, mother, brother, or sister. You came to us a poor man, and staked your all on the growth of this town. We like you because you are still poor. You can not be too poor to suit us. It shows that you are not corrupt.

"Mr. Nye, on behalf of this vast assemblage (*tremulo*), I am glad that you are POOR ! ! !"

Mr. Limberquid then said:

"Sir:—What do we care for the vilifications of the press—a press hired, venial, corrupt, reeking in filth and oozy with the slime of its own impaired circulation, snapping at the heels of its superiors, and steeped in the reeking poison and pollution of its own shop-worn and unmarketable opinions?

"What do we care that homely men grudge our candidate his symmetry of form and graceful, upholstered carriage? What do we care that calumny crawls out of its hole, calumniates him a couple of times and then goes back?

"We like him for the poverty he has made. Our idea in running him for the Legislature is to give him a chance to accumulate poverty, and have some saved up for a rainy day."

Several people wept here, and wiped their eyes on their alabaster hands. The band then played, "See the Conquering Hero Comes," and yielding to the pressing demands of the populi, I made a few irrelevant, but low, passionate remarks, as follows:

"Fellow Citizens and Members of the Band:—We are not here,

as I understand it, solely to tickle our palates with the twisted doughnuts of our pampered and sin-cuʒst civilization, but to unite and give our pledges once more to the support of the best men. In this teacup of foaming and impervious cider from the Valley of the Jordan I drink to the success of the best men. Fellow citizens and members of the band, we owe our fealty to the old party. Let us cling to the old party as long as there is any juice in it and vote for its candidates. Let us give our suffrages to men of advanced thought who are loyal to their party but poor. Gentlemen, I am what would be called a poor but brainy man. When I am not otherwise engaged you will always find me engaged in thought. I love the excitement of following an idea and chasing it up a tree. It is a great pleasure for me to pursue the red-hot trail of a thought or the intellectual spoor of an idea. But I do not allow this habit to interfere with politics. Politics and thought are radically different. Why should man think himself weak on these political matters when there are men who have made it their business and life study to do the thinking for the masses?

"This is my platform. I believe that a candidate should be poor; that he should be a thinker on other matters, but leave political matters and nominations to professional political ganglia and molders of primaries who have given their lives and the inner coating of their stomachs to the advancement of political methods by which the old, cumbersome and dangerous custom of defending our institutions with drawn swords may be superseded by the modern and more attractive method of doing so with overdrawn salaries.

"Fellow Citizens and Members of the Band:—In closing let me say that you have seen me placed in the trying position of postmaster for the past year. For that length of time I have stood between you and the government at Washington. I have assisted in upholding the strong arm of the government, and yet I have not allowed it to crush you. No man here to-night can say that I have ever, by word or deed, revealed outside the office the contents of a postal card addrest to a member of my own party or held back or obstructed the progress of new and startling seeds sent by our representative from the Agricultural Department.

I am in favor of a full and free interchange of interstate red-
eyed and pale beans, and I favor the early advancement and
earnest recognition of the merits of the highly offensive partizan.
I thank you, neighbors and band (*husky and pianissimo*), for
this gratifying little demonstration. Words seem empty and
unavailing at this time. Will you not accept the hospitality of
my home? Neighbors, you are welcome to these halls. Come in
and look at the family album."

ONE AFTERNOON

ANONYMOUS

The events narrated in the following story take place about the
middle of the twentieth century. At that date the institution
known as the department store had reached its full development.
There was not a single article of any kind that could not be
purchased at one of these mammoth emporiums. It is well to
bear this fact in mind, for the whole action of this story takes
place under the roof of Sniggle Scooper's Department Store.

Scene the First. When Charlie Hussel entered Sniggle
Scooper's refreshment department on that beautiful summer afternoon, he had no more idea of getting married than most millionaires have of paying full taxes on all their property. Charlie sat down at the counter and ordered a plain soda. He had
been at the club the night before and his nerves were somewhat
unstrung. While waiting for his soda he noticed a young lady
by his side toying with an ice cream soda marked down from
seven cents to four and a half. She was as fair as a poet's dream
and the young man's heart beat tumultuously within him as he
gazed at her. He longed for an opportunity of speaking to her
and at last it came. She dropt her purse,—whether by accident I leave you to conjecture. Picking up the pocketbook our
hero handed it to the young lady with a bow. She took the pocketbook, but returned the bow.

"Thank you," she murmured; "you are very kind."

"No," said he, "I am not kind. I'm a selfish brute!"

"Then why did you trouble yourself to pick up my purse?"

"Because, to tell the truth, I wanted to hear your voice."

"And now that you have heard it?"

"I wish I could hear it always. Consent to be my wife. You love me, do you not?"

"Yes! What is your name?"

"Charlie Hussel,—and yours, dear?"

"Mildred Uptodate. Now, Charlie, you must ask father's consent."

"All right, Mabel. There is a telephone on the next floor. Come along and I'll ask him."

They ascended by the escalator.

SCENE THE SECOND. Mr. Uptodate readily gave his consent, for he knew of Charlie Hussel in a business way.

"Now, Mildred, let us set the time for the wedding. It is now five minutes after one. Suppose we say four o'clock?"

"Oh, dear, no, I can't possibly get ready before to-morrow afternoon."

"Of course you can. Why, you can get everything you need right here in this store."

"Well, Charlie, if you insist, I suppose I must yield. But it seems a terribly short engagement."

"Yes, sweetheart, but then our married life will be so much longer. Run along, now, darling, and get your wedding-gown, while I get a suit of clothes and attend to the license. Meet me in the chapel on the top floor at half past four sharp."

At the appointed hour the happy couple were made one by the department store clergyman. A few minutes later they were seated in the café enjoying their wedding dinner. How happy they were as they planned for the future!

SCENE THE THIRD. Dinner was over and the happy pair went hand-in-hand toward the transportation department to arrange for their wedding tour. As they passed a bargain counter, the bride exclaimed rapturously:

"O Charlie, I see some lovely bargains over there. Do let me have two dollars."

A moment later the proud husband was watching his wife as with the ease born of long practise she fought her way through the crowd and reached the counter. After a little while she returned waving triumphantly a folded paper, exclaiming:

"Wasn't I lucky? I got the last one they had."

"What is it?"

"Why, don't you know? It's a divorce!"

The young man grew pale.

"I thought," he said, "you loved me."

"Why, of course I love you, but I simply couldn't resist such a bargain as that."

She pointed to a sign. Charlie looked at it and read:

THIS DAY ONLY!

OUR REGULAR DIVORCES MARKED DOWN

FROM $2.75 TO $1.69

NOT IN IT

ANONYMOUS

They built a church at his very door—
    "He wasn't in it."
They brought him a scheme for relieving the poor—
    "He wasn't in it."
Let them work for themselves, as he had done,
They wouldn't ask help from any one
If they hadn't wasted each golden minute—
    "He wasn't in it."
So he passed the poor with haughty tread—
    "He wasn't in it."

When men in the halls of virtue met
He saw their goodness without regret;
Too high the mark for him to win it—
    "He wasn't in it."
A carriage crept down the street one day—
    "He was in it."
The funeral trappings made a display—
    "He was in it."
St. Peter received him with book and bell;
"My friend, you have purchased a ticket to—well,
Your elevator goes down in a minute."
    "He was in it!"

A TWILIGHT IDYL

BY ROBERT J. BURDETTE

One summer evening, Mr. Ellis Henderson, a popular young man, went out walking with two of the sweetest girls in town. Mr. Henderson wore a little straw hat with a navy blue band, a cutaway coat, a pair of white trousers, a white vest, a button-hole bouquet, and fifteen cents. The evening was very hot, and as they walked, they talked about the baseball match, the weather, and sunstrokes. By and by one of the young ladies gave a delicate little shriek.

"OO-oo! What a funny sign!"

"Ha—yes," said Mr. Henderson, in troubled tones, looking gently but resolutely at the wrong side of the street.

"How funny it is spelled; see, Ethel."

"Why," said Ethel, "it is spelled correctly. Isn't it, Mr. Henderson?"

"Hy—why—aw—why, yes, to be sure," said Mr. Henderson, staring at a window full of house-plants.

"Why, Mr. Henderson," said Elfrida, "how can you say so? Just see, 'i—c—e, ice, c—r double e—m, cream'; that's not the way to spell cream."

And Mr. Henderson, who was praying harder than he ever prayed before that an earthquake might come along and swallow up either himself or all the ice-cream parlors in the United States, looked up at the chimney of the house and said:

"That? Oh, yes, yes; of course, why certainly. How very much cooler it has grown within the past few minutes. That cool wave from Manitoba is nearing us once more."

He took out his handkerchief and swabbed a face that would scorch an iceberg brown in ten minutes.

"Is it true, Mr. Henderson," asked Ethel, "that soda fountains sometimes explode?"

"Oh, frequently," said he, and they scatter death and destruction everywhere. In some of our Eastern cities they have been abolished by law,—and they ought to do the same thing here! Why, in New York, all the soda fountains have been removed far outside the city limits and are now located side by side with powder houses."

"I am not afraid of them," said Ethel, "and I don't believe they are a bit dangerous."

"Nor I," echoed Elfrida, "I would not be afraid to walk up to one and stand by it all day. Why are you so afraid of them, Mr. Henderson?"

"Because once I had a fair, sweet young sister blown to pieces by one of those terrible engines of destruction while she was drinking at it, and I can not look at one without growing faint."

"How do they make soda water, Mr. Henderson?"

He was about to reply that it was composed chiefly of dirt and poison, when Ethel read aloud four ice-cream signs, and said, "How comfortable and happy all those people look in there."

Then young Mr. Henderson, who had been clawing at his hair, and tearing off his necktie and collar, and pawing the air, shouted in tones of wild frenzy:

"Oh, yes, yes, yes! Come in; come in and gorge yourselves. Everybody come in and eat up a whole week's salary in fifteen minutes. Set 'em up! Strawberry, chocolate, vanilla, pineapple, raspberry, lemon, peach, apricot, tutti frutti, nesselrode pudding, water-ice, cake and sherbet. Set 'em up! The treat's on me. Oh, yes, I can stand it. Ha, ha! I'm Astorbilt in disguise. Oh, yes; it doesn't cost anything to take an evening walk! Put out your frozen pudding! Ha, ha, ha!"

They carried him home to his boarding house, and put him to bed, and sent for his physician. He is not yet out of danger, but will recover. The exact trouble is a mystery to the doctor, but he thinks it must be hydrosodia, as the sight of a piece of ice throws the patient into the wildest and most furious paroxysms.

LAVERY'S HENS

ANONYMOUS

Michael Lavery, a thrifty Irishman, lived in a small cottage, on Devarsey Street, South Side, Chicago. It had no yard in front, and the rear was ditto. It had a cellar, however, and it occurred to Lavery that he might make something out of it by using it as a hen-house; but one cold night, during the following winter, the water-pipes burst, flooded the cellar, and drowned the chickens. Friends of Lavery told him the city would make good his loss if he made proper application. So Mr. Lavery went down to the city hall, and entering the room of the clerk, said:

"Good marnin'. Me name is Michael Lavery, and I live in Devarsey Street, on the South Side, and I kape chickens in me cellar, and the water came in and drowned thim; what'll I do?"

"What's that?"

"Me name is Michael Lavery, and I live in Devarsey Street, on the South Side, and I kape chickens in me cellar, and the water came in and drowned thim; what'll I do?"

"What's that?"

"Me name is Michael Lavery, and I live in Devarsey Street, on the South Side, and I kape chickens in me cellar, and the water came in and drowned thim; what'll I do?"

"The water came in and drowned your chickens; what will you do?"

"Yis, sir."

"Well, you step into the next room and see the mayor. You will find him at his desk; tell him what you want."

"All right, sir, I will." (*Exit Lavery to next room.*)

"Good marnin'. Me name is Michael Lavery, and I live in Devarsey Street, on the South Side, and I kape chickens in me cellar, and the water came in and drowned thim; what'll I do?"

(*Gruffly.*) "What, sir?"

"Me name is Michael Lavery, and I live in Devarsey Street, on the South Side, and I kape chickens in me cellar, and the water came in and drowned thim; what'll I do?"

"What's that?"

(*Very loud.*) "Me name is Michael Lavery, and I live in Devarsey Street, on the South Side, and I kape chickens in me cellar, and the water came and drowned thim; what'll I do?"

"I don't understand one word you say, sir!"

(*Very softly and sarcastically, and working up into loud voice.*) "Me name is Michael Lavery, and I live in Devarsey Street, on the South Side, and I kape chickens in me cellar, and the water came in and drowned thim; what'll I do?"

"The water came in and drowned your chickens; what will you do?"

"Yis, sir."

"Well I can do nothing for you, so good-morning, sir!"

(*Clerk whispers to Lavery as he is passing out.*) "Well, Mr. Lavery, what did he say to you?"

"*Kape ducks!*"

LISP

ANONYMOUS

Thome folks thay I listhp,
But then I don't perthieve it.
Juth listhen while I call the cat:
"Here Pusthy! Pusthy! Pusthy!"
Now thee I don't listhp.

THEY MET BY CHANCE

ANONYMOUS

They met by chance,
  They had never met before.
They met by chance,
  And she was stricken sore.

They never met again,
  Don't want to, I'll allow!
They met but once:
  'Twas a freight-train and a cow!

THE BRIDEGROOM'S TOAST

ANONYMOUS

(*Speaks while seated.*) "I know a story,—what? (*Laughs.*) I know another story,—eh? Oh, don't ask me. I never made a speech in my life. I am willing to do anything to make you fully enjoy——(*This is broken by applause, which the reader may imitate by rapping on a chair, or on a table.*) I will only make a fool of myself——(*Attempting to get up. More applause. Sits down again.*) I would rather not. (*After much difficulty and persuasion he rises to his feet and begins.*) Ladies and gentlemen, I have been suddenly called upon to propose a toast, which I think you will admit,—I am suddenly called upon, —very suddenly,—to propose and——(*Sits down. More applause. Rises again.*) Ladies and gentlemen, you are very kind (*clears throat*) and I will do my best, and I only hope that unaccustomed as I am to public houses,—speaking,—I sometimes find I have some difficulty in the,—of course I don't mean to say,—I don't mean to say what I mean when I mean what I say! At all events, ladies and gentlemen, I am very, very much obliged for the kind remarks in which you have drunk my health. (*Sits down. Rises again.*) I am called upon to propose a toast *(makes a motion as if someone has thrown something at him from behind striking him on the head)* upon—to propose a toast, but have forgotten it. Considering it is the most important toast of the evening you will understand—(*Aside*: *'What is the toast?'*) —the toast of the ladies. Of course we all know (*runs his hand up and down the back of the chair*) whatever may be said against them,—whatever people may say about the ladies, there is no doubt the ladies are really a very excellent—institution! I don't agree with those people who—I think, I say, that far from being a uniform success they are the reverse. I am bold enough to say, I don't agree that they are very nearly as good as we are. I know (*again he is hit in the back*) there are few drink the health of the army and navy,—I mean ladies. Shakespeare says that 'when a woman' (*hit again*)—I had it just now. Shakespeare says, 'When a woman,'—oh, yes, the immortal bard says, 'We won't go home till morning!'" (*Sits down in great confusion.*)

REHEARSING FOR PRIVATE THEATRICALS

BY STANLEY HUNTLEY

"Now, my dear," said Mr. Spoopendyke, opening the book and assuming the correct dramatic scowl—"now my dear, we'll rehearse our parts for Specklewottle's theatricals. I'm to be Hamlet and you're to be the queen, and we want this thing to go off about right. The hardest part we have to play together is where I accuse you of poisoning my father, and we'd better try that until we get it perfect. I'll commence:

"Now, mother, what's the matter?"

"Well, I was thinking whether I had better wear my black silk or my maroon suit. Do queens wear——"

"Will you be kind enough to tell me what pack of cards you got that idea of a queen from? Do you suppose the queen sent for Hamlet to get his opinion about bargains in dry-goods? When I say that you must say, 'Hamlet, thou hast thy father much offended!'"

"Oh, I understand, I thought you asked me what I was thinking about. I didn't know you had commenced to play. Try it again."

"Well you be careful this time, this is a play, this is. Think you know the difference between a play and a bankrupt sale? Know the distinction between a play and a millinery-shop opening? Now, I'll begin again and you try to do it decently."

"Now, mother, what's the matter!"

"There's nothing the matter now; go on, dear. I understand it now."

"Say it, can't ye! Haven't ye studied this business? Don't ye know your part?"

"What shall I say, dear?"

"Say! Sing a hymn! If you don't know your part, get off a psalm! Didn't I tell you what to say? Look here. Have you ever read this play? Have you conceived any kind of a notion of what it's all about?"

"Why, yes, you come in and stab Mr. Specklewottle behind the ears and I scream. Isn't that right, dear?"

"Hear her! Stab Specklewottle behind the ears! That is all right; now you scream! Scream, why don't you? You know so much about your measly part, why don't you play it?"

"We-e-e-e-e! I knew I could do it right as soon as you showed me how. Will that do?"

"Oh, that was queenly! Just do that again! Four of those dramatic efforts will make this play the greatest of modern entertainments! Do it once more!"

"It hurts my throat. Can't we make it do with one scream, dear?"

"Mrs. Spoopendyke, there's been some mistake made in this thing. You should have been cast for Ophelia. That was the part intended for you."

"I would just as soon play it. What does he do?"

"He was an idiot from his birth and afterward went crazy. That was the part for you."

"Then I'd rather be queen. Now, dear, let's commence all over and I'll do it right this time."

"You can't do it worse. I'll try it once more, just to see what kind of foolishness you can work off."

"Now, mother, what's the matter?"

"We-e-e-e, Hamlet, oh, Hamlet! We-e-e-e-e!"

"Turn it off! Be quick and break off the end! What's the matter?"

"We-e-e-e-e!"

"What's the matter with you, anyway?"

"We-e-e-e-e! My dear, you are just splendid as Hamlet. You should have been an actor."

"Will ye ever shut up? Who ever told ye to yell like that? Don't ye know anything at all scarcely? Think Hamlet's a lunatic asylum? Got some kind of a notion that the queen's a fog-horn? Where'd ye get your idea of this thing, anyway?"

"I did just as you told me, dear. You said I was to scream when you asked me what the matter was. Didn't I do it right?"

"Oh, that was right! You struck the keynote of high art both times! With that yell and your knowledge of the text all you want now is a fire and a free list to be a theater with a restaurant attachment! Such talent as that can't be wasted on any cheap Shakespeare plays while I've got the money and influence to get you a job in the legitimate circus!" And Mr. Spoopendyke bolted from the house, thoroughly disgusted with private theatricals.

By permission of *The Brooklyn Eagle*.

.

THE V-A-S-E

BY JAMES JEFFREY ROCHE

Far from the crowd they stood apart,
The maidens four and the Work of Art;

And none might tell from sight alone
In which had culture ripest grown,—

The Gotham Millions fair to see,
The Philadelphia Pedigree,

The Boston Mind of azure hue,
Or the Soulful Soul from Kalamazoo,—

For all loved Art in a seemly way,
With an earnest soul and a capital A.

.   .   .   .

Long they worshiped, but no one broke
The sacred stillness, until up spoke

The Western one from the nameless place,
Who blushing said, "What a lovely vace!"

Over three faces a sad smile flew,
And they edged away from Kalamazoo.

But Gotham's haughty soul was stirred
To crush the stranger with one small word.

Deftly hiding reproof in praise,
She cries, " 'Tis, indeed, a lovely vaze!"

But brief her unworthy triumph when
The lofty one from the home of Penn,

With the consciousness of two grandpapas,
Exclaims, "It is quite a lovely vahs!"

And glances round with an anxious thrill,
Awaiting the word of Beacon Hill.

But the Boston maid smiles courteouslee,
And gently murmurs, "Oh, pardon me!

"I did not catch your remark, because
I was so entranced with that charming vaws!"

And then each nose was a sight to see
Turned up in contempt at the other three.

PAPA AND THE BOY

BY J. L. HARBOUR

Charming as is the merry prattle of innocent childhood, it is not particularly agreeable at about one o'clock in the morning. There are young and talkative children who have no more regard for your feelings or for the proprieties of life than to open their eyes with a snap at one or two in the morning, and to seek to engage you in enlivening dialog of this sort.

"Papa."

You think you will pay no heed to the imperative little voice, hoping that silence on your part will keep the youngster quiet; but again that boy of three pipes out sharply:

"Papa!"

"Well?" you say.

"You 'wake, papa?"

"Yes."

"So's me."

"Yes, I hear that you are," you say with cold sarcasm. "What do you want?"

"Oh! nuffin."

"Well, lie still and go to sleep then."

"I isn't s'eepy, papa."

"Well, I am, young man."

"Is you? I isn't—not a bit. Say, papa, papa! If you was wich what would you buy me?"

"I don't know—go to sleep."

"Wouldn't you buy me nuffin?"

"I guess so; now you——"

"What, papa?"

"Well, a steam engine, may be; now you go right to sleep."

"With a bell that would ring, papa?"

"Yes, yes; now you——"

"And would the wheels go wound, papa?"

"Oh! yes (*yawning*). Shut your eyes now, and——"

"And would it go choo, choo, choo, papa?"

"Yes, yes; now go to sleep."

"Say, papa."

No answer.

"Papa!"

"Well, what now?"

"Is you 'fraid of the dark?"

"No" (*drowsily*).

"I isn't either. Papa!"

"Well?"

"If I was wich I'd buy you somefin.'"

"Would you?"

"Yes; I'd buy you some ice-cweam and some chocolum drops and a toof brush and panties wiv bwaid on like mine, and a candy wooster, and——"

"That will do. You must go to sleep now."

Silence for half a second, then—

"Papa! papa!"

"Well, what now?"

"I want a jink."

"No, you don't."

"I do, papa."

Experience has taught you that there will be no peace until you have brought the "jink," and you scurry out to the bathroom in the dark for it, knocking your shins against everything in the room as you go.

"Now I don't want to hear another word from you to-night," you say, as he gulps down a mouthful of the water he didn't want. Two minutes later he says:

"Papa!"

"See here, laddie, papa will have to punish you if——"

"I can spell 'dog,' papa."

"Well, nobody wants to hear you spell at two o'clock in the morning."

"B-o-g—dog; is that right?"

"No, it isn't. But nobody cares if——"

"Then it's d-o-g, isn't it?"

"Yes, yes; now you lie right down and go to sleep instantly."

"Then I'll be a good boy, won't I, papa?"

"Yes; you'll be the best boy on earth. Good-night, dearie."

"Papa!"

"Well, well! What now?"

"Is I your little boy?"

"Yes, yes; of course."

"Some mans haven't got any little boys; but you have, haven't you?"

"Yes."

"Don't you wish you had two, free, nine, 'leben, twenty-six, ninety-ten, free hundred little boys?"

The mere possibility of such a remote and contingent calamity so paralyzes you that you lie speechless for ten minutes during which you hear a yawn or two in the little bed by your side, a little figure rolls over three or four times, a pair of heels fly into the air once or twice, a warm, moist little hand reaches out and touches your face to make sure that you are there, and the boy is asleep with his heels where his head ought to be.

THE OBSTRUCTIVE HAT IN THE PIT

BY F. ANSTEY

SCENE: *The Pit of a London theatre during Pantomime Time.*

An Overheated Matron (*to her husband*)—"Well, they don't give you much room in 'ere, I must say. Still, we done better than I expected, after all that crushing. I thought my ribs was gone once—but it was on'y the umbrella's. You pretty comfortable where you are, eh, father?"

Father—"Oh, I'm right enough, I am."

Jimmy (*their small boy with a piping voice*)—"If father is it's more nor what I am. I can't see, mother, I can't!"

Mother—"Lor' bles' the boy! there ain't nothen to see yet; you'll see well enough when the curting goes up. (*Curtain rises on opening scene.*) Look, Jimmy, ain't that nice, now? All them himps, dancin' round and real fire comin' out of the pot—which I 'ope it's quite safe—and there's a beautiful fairy just come on drest so grand, too!"

Jimmy (*whimpering*)—"I can't see no fairy—nor yet no himps —no nothen!"

Mother (*annoyed*)—"Was there ever such an aggravating boy? Set quiet, do, and don't fidget, and look at the hactin'!"

Jimmy—"I tell yer I can't see no hactin', mother. It ain't my fault—it's this lady in front of me, with the 'at."

Mother—"Father, the pore boy says he can't see where he is, 'cause of a lady's 'at in front."

Father—"Well, I can't 'elp the 'at, can I? He must put up with it, that's all!"

Mother—"No—but I thought, if you wouldn't mind changing places with him; you're taller than him."

Father—It's always the way with you—never satisfied, you ain't! Well, pass the boy across! I'm for a quiet life, I am (*changing seats*). Will this do for you?" (*He settles down immediately behind a very large, furry hat which he dodges for some time.*)

Father (*suddenly*)—"Blow the 'at."

Mother—"You can't wonder at the boy not seeing! P'r'aps the lady wouldn't mind taking it off, if you asked her?"

Father—"Ah! (*touching the owner of the hat on the shoulder*). Excuse me, mum, but might I take the liberty of asking you to kindly remove your 'at?" (*The owner of the hat deigns no reply.*)

Father (*more insistently*)—"Would you 'ave any objection to oblige me by taking off your 'at, mum? (*Same result.*) I don't know if you 'eard me, mum, but I've asked you twice, civil enough, to take that 'at of yours off. I'm playin' 'ide-and-seek be'ind it 'ere!" (*No answer.*)

Mother—"People didn't ought to be allowed in the Pit with sech 'ats! Callin' 'erself a lady, and settin' there in a great 'at and feathers like a 'ighlander's, and never answering no more nor a stuffed himage!"

Father (*to the husband of the owner of the hat*)—"Will you tell your good lady to take her 'at off, sir, please?"

The Owner of the Hat (*to her husband*)—"Don't you do nothing of the sort, Sam, or you'll 'ear of it!"

Mother—"Some people are perlite, I must say. Parties might be'ave as ladies when they come in the Pit! It's a pity her 'usband can't teach her better manners!"

Father—"'Im teach her! 'E knows better. 'E's got a Tartar there, 'e 'as!"

The Owner of the Hat—"Sam, are you going to set by and hear me insulted like this?"

Her Husband (*turning round tremulously*)—"I—I'll trouble you to drop making these personal allusions to my wife's 'at, sir. It's puffickly impossible to listen to what's going on on the stage, with all these remarks be'ind!"

Father—"Not more nor it is to see what's going on on the stage with that 'at in front! I paid 'arf-a-crown to see the Pantermime, I did; not to 'ave a view of your wife's 'at! . . . 'ere, Maria, blowed if I can stand this 'ere game any longer. Jimmy must change places again, and if he can't see, he must stand up on the seat, that's all!" (*Jimmy goes back and mounts upon the seat.*)

A Pit-ite Behind Jimmy (*touching Jimmy's father with an umbrella*)—"Will you tell your little boy to set down, please, and not to block the view like this?"

Father—"If you can indooce that lady to take off her 'at, I will, but not before. Stay where you are, Jimmy."

The Pit-ite Behind—"Well, I must stand myself then, that's all. I mean to see somehow!" (*He rises.*)

People Behind (*sternly*)—"Set down there, will yer?" (*He resumes his seat expostulating.*)

Jimmy—"Father, the man behind is a-pinching of my legs!"

Father—"Will you stop pinching my little boy's legs. He ain't doing you no 'arm, is he?"

The Pinching Pit-ite—"Let him sit down, then!"

Father—"Let the lady take her 'at off!"

Murmurs Behind—"Order there! Set down! Put that boy down! Take off that 'at! Silence in front there! Turn 'em out! Shame! . . ."

The Husband of the Owner of the Hat (*in a whisper to his wife*)—"Take off the blessed 'at, and 'ave done with it, do!"

The Owner of the Hat—"What, now? I'd sooner die in the 'at!" (*An attendant is called.*)

Attendant—"Order, there, gentlemen, please, unless you want to get turned out! No standing allowed on the seats; you're disturbing the performance 'ere, you know!" (*Jimmy is made to sit down, and weeps silently; the hubbub subsides, and the Owner of the Hat triumphs.*)

Mother—"Never mind, my boy, you shall have mother's seat in a minute. I dessay, if all was known, the lady 'as reasons for keeping her 'at on, pore thing!"

Father—"Ah, I never thought o' that. So she may. Very likely her 'at won't come off—not without her 'air!"

Mother—"Ah, well, then we mus'n't be 'ard on her."

The Owner of the Hat (*removing the obstruction*)—"I 'ope you're satisfied now, I'm sure?"

Father (*handsomely*)—"Better late nor never, mum, and we take it kind of you. Tho why you shouldn't ha' done it at fust, I dunno; for you look a deal 'ansomer without the 'at than what you did in it—don't she Maria?"

The Owner of the Hat (*mollified*)—"Sam, ask the gentleman behind if his boy would like a ginger-nut." (*This olive-branch is accepted; compliments pass; cordiality is restored, and the pantomime then proceeds without any further disturbance in the audience.*)

HULLO

BY S. W. FOSS

W'en you see a man in wo,
Walk right up an' say "Hullo!"
Say "Hullo" an' "How d'ye do?
How's the world a-usin' you?"
Slap the fellow on the back;
Bring your hand down with a whack;
Walk right up, an' don't go slow;
Grip an' shake, an' say "Hullo!"

Is he clothed in rags? Oh! sho;
Walk right up an' say "Hullo!"
Rags is but a cotton roll
Jest for wrappin' up a soul;
An' a soul is worth a true
Hale and hearty "How d'ye do?"
Don't wait for the crowd to go
Walk right up an' say "Hullo!"

When big vessels meet, they say
They saloot an' sail away.
Jest the same are you an' me
Lonesome ships upon a sea;
Each one sailin' his own log,
For a port behind the fog.
Let your speakin' trumpet blow;
Lift your horn an' cry "Hullo!"

Say "Hullo!" an' "How d'ye do?"
Other folks are good as you.
W'en you leave your house of clay
Wanderin' in the far away,
W'en you travel through the strange
Country t'other side the range,
Then the souls you've cheered will know
Who ye be, an' say "Hullo."

THE DUTCHMAN'S TELEPHONE

ANONYMOUS

"I guess I haf to gif up my delephone already," said an old
citizen, as he entered the office of the company with a very
long face.

"Why, what's the matter now?"

"Oh! eferytings. I got dot delephone in mine house so I
could shpeak mit der poys in der saloon down town, und mit

my relations in Springwells, but I haf to gif it up. I never
haf so much droubles."

"How?"

"Vhell, my poy Shon, in der saloon, he rings der pell and calls
me oop und says an old frent of mine vhants to see how she vorks.
Dot ish all right. I say, 'Hello!' und he says, 'Come closer.' I
goes closer und helloes again. Den he says, 'Shtand a little
off.' I shtands a little off und yells vunce more, und he says,
'Shpeak louder.' I yells louder. I goes dot vhay for ten minutes,
und den he says, 'Go to Texas, you old Dutchman!' You see?"

"Yes."

"Und den mein brudder in Springwells he rings der pell und
calls me oop und says, 'How you vhas dis eafnings?' I says I vhas
feeling like some colts, und he says, 'Who vhants to puy some
goats?' I says, 'Colts—colts—colts!' und he answers, 'Oh!
coats. I thought you said goats!' Vhen I goes to ask him ef he
feels petter I hear a voice crying out, 'Vhat Dutchman is dot on
dis line?' Den somepody answers, 'I doan' know, but I likes to
punch his headt!' You see?"

"Yes."

"Vhell, somedimes my vhife vhants to shpeak mit me vhen I
am down in der saloon. She rings mein pell und I says, 'Hello!'
Nopody shpeaks to me. She rings again, und I says, 'Hello,' like
dunder! Den der Central Office tells me to go aheadt, und den
tells me holdt on, und den tells mein vhife dot I am gone avhay.
I yells oudt, 'Dot ish not so,' und somepody says, 'How can I talk
if dot old Dutchmans doan' keep shtill?' You see?"

"Yes."

"Und vhen I gets in bedt at night, somepody rings der pell like
der house vas on fire, und vhen I shumps oud und says, 'Hello,' I
hear somepody saying, 'Kaiser, doan' you vhant to puy a dog?'
I vhants no dog, und vhen I tells 'em so, I hear some peoples
laughing, 'Haw! haw! haw!' You see?"

"Yes."

"Und so you dake it oudt, und vhen somepody likes to shpeak
mit me dey shall come right avay to mein saloon. Oof my brudder ish sick he shall get better, und if somepody vhants to puy
me a dog, he shall come vhere I can punch him mit a glub."

HOW BILL ADAMS WON THE BATTLE OF WATERLOO

BY G. H. SNAZELLE

LADIES AND GENTLEMEN:

Last summer I was touring in Kent, and came to a small village of probably about seven hundred inhabitants. Being a very hot day, I went into the village ale-house to get a glass of—ginger ale. There was no one in the bar, but I could hear a buzzing sound coming from an apartment marked "Tap-room." The door was slightly open, and I peeped in, and saw a crowd of yokels sitting motionless and open-mouthed listening with absorbing interest to a grizzly old man, who appeared to be relating some intensely exciting story. I went back to the bar, and knocked sharply on the counter. Presently the landlord sauntered out of the tap-room, and I mildly remarked that I had been waiting full five minutes.

"Very zorry, zur," said the landlord, "but you zee, zur, I couldn't get out of the tap-room just then. The fact is, zur, Bill Adams is in there."

"How do you mean you could not get out? Was he holding you?"

"Noa, zur," answered the landlord, and then in a tone of voice implying the most profound veneration for the person alluded to, he added, "It's Bill Adams, zur; 'ee's in the tap-room, zur!"

I naturally remarked, "Well, and who is Bill Adams?"

"Whoi, 'ee doan't mean to tell me that you've never 'eerd o' Bill Adams?"

I confess I never had. Mine host favored me with a stare of undisguised astonishment and incredulity at such lamentable ignorance, and burst out—"Whoi, wherever wos you brought up, zur,—in the back'oods of 'Meriky, or in the bush in Australy? Never 'eerd o' Bill Adams! Well, you do surprize me, sure-*ly*. Whoi, Bill Adams is the most celebratedest mon in these 'ere parts."

"Oh, **indeed**!" I said, "what is he celebrated for? What did he do?"

"Whoi, zur, it wos Bill Adams and the Duke of Wellington as won the Battle of Worterloo!"

Here was news, indeed, to hear for the first time in an obscure little village in Kent. And this is what I complain about, that all our history books at school, and historical literature in the broader arena of the world, place before us the—until now—undisputed fact that the Duke of Wellington won that battle, and had never given poor old Bill Adams a chance of a "show."

I very humbly apologized to the landlord for my ignorance, and said that I should be only too happy to gain any information about so important an historical event in the history of the country.

"Well, zur, you're in luck's way; th'old gentleman's in the tap-room, jest agoin' to tell the boys all about it. 'Ee's jest told 'em what 'ee did in the Peninsoolar; 'ee gave 'em snuff there; but that's nothing to what 'ee did at Worterloo. Please go in, zur, and 'ear it; it'll supprize yer."

Well, I went in, and heard the old gentleman's yarn, and it certainly did surprize me.

Mr. William Adams, after surveying me with a semi-military critical eye, cleared his throat with a loud "Ahem" or two, and began his tale.

"Well, yer see, boys, it wos like this 'ere at Worterloo: There wos me and the Dook and the rest on us a standin' there with our staff. The Dook ony got about a 'undered men awailable, and when 'ee puts up 'is hopera glass 'ee see Bonyparty a comin' over the 'ill with about four 'undered thousan' men—picked men they wos, most on 'em. Well, the Dook 'ee didn't like the looks on it at all; so 'ee turns round to Sir Garnet Wolseley and 'ee sez, 'Garnet,' sez 'ee, ''ere's a tough job as we got cut out. Who's a-goin' to take this 'eer job on?'

" 'Not me,' sez Sir Garnet, 'but it's all right, guv'nor,' 'ee sez, '' 'ere's Nelson a-comin' up.'

"Well, just then Nelson comes a-gallopin' up on 'is white 'orse. He git off, a-salutin' me and the Dook and the rest on us, and a-stickin' 'is wooden leg in the sand—yer know, boys, Nelson had a wooden leg, wot 'ee lost at—at—let's see—ah! Sringapatam. The Dook 'ee turn to 'im and 'ee sez, '' 'Oratio, I'm in a fix, I've ony

got about a 'undered and fifty men awailable, and 'ere's Bonyparty a-comin' over the 'ill with seven 'undered and twenty-eight
thousan' men—picked men, most on 'em. Can you take the job
on ?'

" 'No,' sez Nelson, ' 'tain't fair to arst me. Tain't in my line,'
sez 'ee. 'Ain't Garnet a-goin' to do it?'

" 'No,' sez the Dook, 'Garnet won't touch it.'

" 'Wot about yerself, guv'nor?' Nelson sez.

" 'No,' sez the Dook, 'it's amost too much for me.'

" 'Well, then,' sez Nelson, 'there's only one man as I knows on
wot can take this 'ere job on.'

" 'Who's that?' sez the Dook.

" 'Why, Bill Adams,' sez Nelson.

" 'Well, o' course,' sez the Dook, 'why, wot a hold juggins I
must a-bin not to a-thought o' Bill! Course, Bill's the werry man
for the job!' and the Dook 'ee whistles me up.

"I was jest down in the canteen a-havin' a—half a cup o' tea,
and I goes up and I sez, 'Well, Nosey, wot's up; wot is it?' I
mostly called 'im Nosey; we wos werry familiar, we wos, them
times.

" 'Well,' 'ee sez, 'Bill, I won't deceive yer; I'm in a bit of an
'ole. I've only got about a 'undered and fifty men awailable, and
'ere's Bonyparty a-comin' over the 'ill with a million o' men—
picked men, most on 'em. Can you take the job on?'

" 'Well, Harthur,' I sez, 'I think I can pull yer through. How
mony men wos yer thinkin' o' givin' me?'

" 'Well,' he sez, 'take wot yer want, William.' Well, I takes
about a 'undered on 'em. I knowed jest wot they could do; and
we goes a-marchin' up the 'ill.

"Jest as we gets to the top, and we wos a-gettin' ready to wipe
'em out, I looks round the corner, and I see Bonyparty and Napoleon and Blucher a-hidin' behind a tree.

"Napoleon and Bonyparty wos a larfin' at our little lot; but
hold Blucher 'ee looks round the other side the tree, and when 'ee
see me, 'ee turns white as a sheet. Then 'ee sez to Bonyparty and
Napoleon, 'You're a-larfin' at 'em, gentlemen, ain't yer, but,' sez
'ee, 'do yer see who's a-leadin' these 'ere men?'

" 'No,' sez Bonyparty, 'can't say as I knows 'im. Who is it?'

" 'Well,' sez Blucher, 'doan't yer go and do nothin' rash. That's Bill Adams! !'

" '*What! !* ' sez Bonyparty, 'is that Bill a-leadin' on 'em?'

" 'It is,' sez Blucher.

" 'Why, good grashus,' sez Bony, 'so it is. It's old Bill Adams, wot gave me such pepper at Balaclava.'

"Then 'ee turns round to 'is army, and 'ee shouts out:

" 'Right about turn; there won't be no fight. Get off the grass, if yer doan't all want to be eat up. 'Ere's Bill Adams a-comin'!'

"Well, that's the way me and the Dook of Wellington won the Battle of Worterloo, boys."

THE RULING PASSION

BY WILLIAM H. SIVITER

She had never mailed a letter before, and so she approached the stamp clerk's window with the same air that she would enter a dry-goods store.

"I would like to look at some stamps, please."

"What denomination do you want?"

"Denomination?"

"Yes. Is it for a letter or a newspaper?"

"Oh, I want to send a letter to my Uncle John; he's just moved to——"

"Then you need a two-cent stamp," said the clerk offering her one of that value.

"I hardly like that color!"

"That is a two-cent stamp, madam. Please stand aside, and let the gentleman behind you come up."

"But haven't you got them in any other color? I never did like that shade of red."

"There is only one color."

"That is strange. I'd think you'd keep them in different shades, so that there'd be some choice. You are sure you have none in a brighter red, or even in a different color—Nile green, or seal brown, or jubilee blue, for instance?"

"You can put two one-cent stamps on your letter if you like."

"Let me see them, please. Ah, that will do. I like that shade so much better. I'll take only one, if you please."

"If it's for a letter you'll need two. These are one-cent stamps and letter postage is two cents per ounce."

"Oh, I don't want to put two stamps on my letter; I don't think they will look well."

"It requires two cents to carry a letter, madam, and you must either put a two-cent stamp on or two ones. It won't go without I must ask you to please hurry, for you are keeping a great many people away from the window."

"That's singular. I don't like the looks of two together. You are sure the other doesn't come in seal-brown, or——"

"No, madam; no!"

"Then I'll have to see if I can suit myself elsewhere."

And she departed.

THE DUTCHMAN'S SERENADE

ANONYMOUS

Vake up, my schveet! Vake up, my lofe!
Der moon dot can't be seen abofe.
Vake oud your eyes, and dough it's late,
I'll make you oud a serenate.

Der shtreet dot's kinder dampy vet,
Und dhere vas no goot blace to set;
My fiddle's getting oud of dune,
So blease get vakey wery soon.

O my lofe! my lofely lofe!
Am you avake up dere abofe,
Feeling sad and nice to hear
Sehneider's fiddle shcrabin' near?

Vell, anyvay, obe loose your ear,
Und try to saw of you kin hear
From dem bedclose vat you'm among,
Der little song I'm going to sung.

Oh, lady, vake! Get vake!
  Und hear der tale I'll tell;
Oh, you vot's schleebin' sound ub dhere,
  I like you pooty vell!

Your plack eyes dhem don't shine
  Ven you'm ashleep—so vake!
(Yes, hurry ub und voke up quick,
  For goodness cracious sake!)

My schveet inbatience, lofe!
  I hobe you vill oxcuse;
I'm singing schveetly (dere, py Jinks!
  Dhere goes a shtring proke loose!)

Oh, putiful, schveet maid!
  Oh, vill she ever voke?
Der moon is mooning—(Jimminy! dhere
  Anoder shtring vent proke!)

Oh, say, old schleeby head!
  (Now I vas gitting mad—
I'll holler now und I don't care
  Uf I vake up her dad!)

I say, you schleeby, vake!
  Vake out! Vake loose! Vake ub!
Fire! Murder! Police! Vatch!
  Oh, cracious! do vake ub!

Dot girl she schleebed—dot rain it rained
Und I looked shtoopid like a geese,
Vhen mit my fiddle I sneaked off
    Dodging der rain und dot bolice!

WIDOW MALONE

BY CHARLES LEVER

Did you hear of the Widow Malone,
                    Ohone!
Who lived in the town of Athlone,
                    Alone!
  Oh, she melted the hearts
  Of the swains in those parts:
So lovely the Widow Malone,
                    Ohone!
So lovely the Widow Malone.

Of lovers she had a full score,
                    Or more,
And fortunes they all had galore;
                    In store;
  From the minister down
  To the clerk of the Crown
All were courting the Widow Malone,
                    Ohone!
All were courting the Widow Malone.

But so modest was Mistress Malone,
　　　　　'Twas known
That no one could see her alone,
　　　　　Ohone!
　Let them ogle and sigh,
　They could ne'er catch her eye,
So bashful the Widow Malone,
　　　　　Ohone!
So bashful the Widow Malone.

Till one Misther O'Brien, from Clare,
　　　　　(How quare!
It's little for blushing they care
　　　　　Down there.)
　Put his arm round her waist,
　Gave ten kisses at laste,
"Oh," says he, "you're my Molly Malone,
　　　　　My own!"
"Oh," says he, "you're my Molly Malone!"

And the widow they all thought so shy,
　　　　　My eye!
Ne'er thought of a simper or sigh,—
　　　　　For why?
　But, "Lucius," says she,
　"Since you've now made so free,
You may marry your Mary Malone,
　　　　　Ohone!
You may marry your Mary Malone."

There's a moral contained in my song,
　　　　　Not wrong;
And one comfort, it's not very long,
　　　　　But strong,—
　If for widows you die,
　Learn to kiss, not to sigh;
For they're all like sweet Mistress Malone,
　　　　　Ohone!
Oh, they're all like sweet Mistress Malone!

HIS LEG SHOT OFF

ANONYMOUS

You have all met him. He is the man with the funny story.
As a listener he would be popular. If he would only keep quiet
and listen to other people tell stories without attempting to emu-
late their ability he would be liked where he is now cordially dis-
liked. But that doesn't suit his temperament. He will buttonhole
you with his forefinger, and with an idiotic smile on his face say.
  "Ha! ha! ha! ha! If I didn't just hear the funniest thing!
Oh, but it was funny! Ha! ha! ha! You don't begin to know
how funny it was! You see it was this way: A long time ago
there was a war,—fighting,—fighting, you know,—between the
North and South. Ha! ha! ha! There was a war, as I was saying, and they got fighting, and this man,—ha! ha! ha!—the funniest thing!—this man, Jim Jones,—you see it was this way,—it
was in the war. you know,—between the North and South,—ha!
ha!—and this man Jim Jones,—ha! ha! ha!—it is too funny for
any thing,—it was too funny! Well, Jim Jones was fighting.
He went into the battle one day, and that is the funny part of
it. Along came a cannon-ball and took off his head! Ha! ha! ha!
(*Laugh here for two minutes; then the face gradually assumes
an air of gravity.*) No, it wasn't his head, it was his leg. It was
funny just the same. Down he went to the ground. It stands
to reason a man with one leg can't walk and go on fighting. So
he just laid down in his tracks. Couldn't do anything else. Just
then along came a battery,—you know that is cannons,—they
have horses to drag them,—men can't pull those big, heavy cannons into battle. Well, you know, this man Jim Jones that had his
leg shot off, he knew this man with the cannons,—ha! ha!—Oh,
but it was funny! And he says to him, 'If you don't carry me
to where a doctor is, my wife's a widow, that's all about it!' He
knew his wife was a widow if he didn't get to where the doctor
was. You know the doctors don't stay up where the soldiers are
fighting in a battle,—they're back, away back, the doctors are.
So this man with his leg shot off, he says, 'You've got to take me

where a doctor is, or my wife's a widow, that's all about it!' Well,
this neighbor of his didn't like to go back on an old friend,—
ha! ha!—with his leg shot off,—this man that had his leg shot
off early in the battle and couldn't go on fighting,—but he says
to him: 'How am I to get you back there?' and he 'lowed he'd
have to carry him. Well, with that he shouldered Jim Jones,—
ha! ha!—threw him over his shoulder just like that, and away
they went! (*Laugh heartily here.*) And that is where the joke
came in,—along came a cannon-ball and took of his head! Not
the man's head, but Jimmy Jones' head! But pshaw, the man
didn't know anything about it. Along he went with Jimmy over
his shoulder. Just then an officer came up. He says: 'Where
are you going with that thing?' Well, the man didn't like to give
a short answer. Soldiers are not allowed to give short answers
to officers. He simply saluted and says: 'Well, it's this way:
This man's an old neighbor of mine. He was coming into battle,
—ha! ha!—and he 'lowed that a cannon-ball came along and
took off his leg. He says if we don't take him to where a doctor
is his wife's a widow and that's all about it,—and so,—ha! ha!—
and so I'm just taking him back to where the doctor is, captain.'
The captain looked at him a moment, and he says: 'Why you
idiot, it isn't his leg, it's his head!' Then the man says,—not
Jimmy Jones,—he had his head off and couldn't say anything,—
'Oh, the confounded rascal, he told me it was his leg!' "

THE STUTTERING UMPIRE

BY THE KHAN

Oh, we had our share of trouble,
　I'll tell you now the source,
The umpire that we sent for,
　Well, he didn't come, of course.
Have you noticed, at the line-up
　When everything's for fair,
The referee, the umpire,
　That should be there, isn't there?

The crowd it grew impatient;
  We heard their angry mutters.
We picked on Johnny Jimson,
  Tho Johnny Jimson stutters;
But, still, he knows the game all right—
  Indeed, he knows it all—
So in his place he hollered:
  "Pup-pup-pup-play bub-ball!"

Jake Mingus was first batter,
  Our county's favorite son;
He hit an' missed. Johnny yelled:
  "Stuh-stuh-stuh-strike wu-one!"
Another ball went o'er the plate,
  And Jakey's bat went whoo!
Then all the crowd heard Johnny shout:
  "Tut-tut-tut-tut-tut-two!"

The next one was a daisy,
  It made the audience howl;
Jakey tapped it, Johnny yelled:
  "Fow-ow-ow-ow-oul!"
And so the game went gaily,
  A game a body likes,
Till Jack had called three balls on Jake
  And also called two strikes.

The breathless crowd was anxious,
  For this will tell the tale;
The pitcher tied himself in knots,
  The catcher did not quail.
Whizz! went the ball—the rabble waits
  The umpire's verdict, but
All that Johnny Jimson said
  Was "Tut-tut-tut——"

Did he mean to say, "Tut-tut-take your base,"
  Or else, "Tut-tut-three strikes?"
Just fix it up to suit yourself
  As anybody likes,
It busted up our little game,
  It was too utterly utter.
Don't try to be an umpire if
  You stut-tut-tut-tutter.

THE MAN WHO WILL MAKE A SPEECH

ANONYMOUS

A man wearing passably good clothes and a look of mental anxiety entered a fashionable drug-store, and said to the clerk:

"Are you pretty well posted on big words?"

"Yes," said the clerk, "I know quite a large number of big words."

"Well, then," said the stranger, "here's the situation: Out where I live I am a pretty big gun, and when anything is going on they call on me for a speech. I made one on election day, another the same evening, and another the next morning, and now I'm laying the sleepers for a speech to eclipse them all."

"What sort of a speech?" asked the clerk.

"Political, of course. My other speeches were political, but were very plain. This time I want to get in some regular old twisters. For one thing I would declare this country in a state of—what do you call it?"

"Peace!"

"No, sir; I mean confusion, excitement, and so on. There's a word to signify it, but I can't speak it."

"Abject terrorism?"

"No—no. Its archany, or something of the kind."

"I guess you mean anarchy, don't you?"

"I do—I do! Bless me if I haven't been trying for a whole hour to get that word! That's the very thing. When called out

I want to lead off with: 'Fellow citizens, the peace has flown, and arnica reigns supreme!' I guess that will knock them."

"You don't mean arnica—you mean anarchy."

"That's what I mean, of course, but every time I think anarchy I get it arnica, and I don't know but I will have to give up the speech."

"Why don't you write it down?"

The man took up a pen and wrote: "A-r-k-a-n-y." Then he said: "Peace has fled and arkany reigns in the land."

"I told you it was anarchy."

"That's so—that's so. This suspense is telling on my memory like a fit of illness. Now, then, a-n-a-r-k-y, anarky, and don't you forget it. You needn't say anything about my calling in here."

"Oh, that's all right. Over seven-eighths of the best speakers in town come to me for big words."

"Many thanks; and now, 'Fellow citizens, peace has fled far, far away, and arkany reigns——' Hold on, is that the right word?"

He halted at the door to examine the slip of paper, and after repeating the right word over several times he went on:

"A state of anchovy is upon us, and where will it end?"

As he walked up the street he was overheard to say:

"Arnica! Arnica! where will it end?"

CARLOTTA MIA

BY T. A. DALY

Giuseppe, da Barber, ees great for "mash,"
He gotta da bigga, da blacka mustache,
Good clo'es an' good styla an' playnta good cash.

W'enever Giuseppe ees walk on da street,
Da people dey talka "How nobby! How neat!
How softa da handa, haw smalla da feet."

He raisa hees hat, an' he shaka hees curls,
An' smila weeth teetha so shiny like pearls;
Oh, many da heart of da silly young girls
   He gotta,
   Yes playnta he gotta—
   But notta—
   Carlotta!

Giuseppe, da Barber, he maka da eye,
An' lika da steam-engine puffa an' sigh
For catcha Carlotta w'en she ees go by.

Carlotta she walka weeth her nose in da air,
An' look through Giuseppe weeth far-away stare,
As eef she no see dere ees som'body dere.

Giuseppe, da Barber, he gotta da cash,
He gotta da clo'es an' da bigga mustache,
He gotta da silly young girls for da "mash."
   But notta—
   You bat my life, notta—
   Carlotta;
   I gotta!

THE VASSAR GIRL

BY WALLACE IRWIN

"Oh, Martha's back from Vassar,"
Said farmer James McCassar:
"O Martha, come into the house and mix
  a batch of bread."
 But Martha's accents fluttered
 As she murmured, as she stuttered,
 "I have studied the satanic
 Ways of bacilli organic,
And it throws me in a panic, pa, to mix
 a batch of bread."

Chorus

At Vassar-oh, at Vassar-oh,
  That's what we learn at Vassar!
We love our Alma Mater so
  We do not like to sass 'er.
We have a superstition
  There's nothing like the damsel with
    the dear old Vassar V.

"Oh, Martha's back from Vassar,"
Said farmer James McCassar:
"O Martha, go out to the barn and milk
  the brindle cow."
  But Martha cried: "Oh, bother!"
  As she faced her poor old father,
  "With golf I love to tussle
  And with basket-ball to hustle—
But I haven't got the muscle to subdue
  the brindle cow."

Chorus

At Vassar-oh, at Vassar-oh,
  That's what we learn at Vassar!
We love our Alma Mater so
  We do not like to sass 'er.
We have a superstition
  There's nothing like the damsel with
    the dear old Vassar V.

"Oh, Martha's home from Vassar!"
Cried the angry James McCassar:
"O Martha, take yer study-books and
  don't come home no more!"
  So the maiden in contrition
  Got a typist-girl's position,
  Wed a millionaire named Harris
  Who, lest poverty embarrass,
Made his wife a millionairess. And she's
  ne'er been heard of more.

Chorus

At Vassar-oh, at Vassar-oh,
  That's what we learn at Vassar!
We love our Alma Mater so
  We do not like to sass 'er.
Learning's road is rough and stony;
But for golden matrimony
  There's nothing like the maiden with
    the dear old Vassar V.

From " Shame of the Colleges," Outing Publishing Co., by permission.

A SHORT SERMON

ANONYMOUS

(*Delivered in usual singsong style of the conventional curate.*)
I am going to preach to you this morning, my friends, upon
the young man who was sick of the palsy. Now, this young man
was sick of the palsy. The palsy, as you are all aware, is a very
terrible disease, a wasting scourge. And this young man was
sick of the palsy. And the palsy, as you know, is strongly
hereditary. It had been in his family. His father had been sick
of the palsy, and his mother had been sick of the palsy, and they
had *all* of them, in fact, been sick of the palsy. And this young
man had been sick of the palsy. Yes, my dear friends, he had had
it for years and years, and—*he was sick of it.*

A LANCASHIRE DIALECTIC SKETCH

(Tummy and Meary)

ANONYMOUS

Tummy and Meary wor barn to be wed, tha knaws. And th' neet afoor they were to be wed, Tummy he goes to Meary, and he says, "Meary, lass," he says, "I'se noonan barn to wed tha." "Oo isn't?" hoo says. "Nooa," says Tummy, "I isn't. I'se chaanged my mind." "Why, tha greeat thick-heead," hoo says, "tha's allus a-chaangin' thy mind." "Ah, weel," say Tummy, "I *ha'* chaanged my mind, and that's enough for *thee.*" Weel, tha knaws Meary didn't want for to loose Tummy, for she didn't knaw where she'd pick up another as good. Soa she tried all sooarts of waays for keepin' him on. First hood tried carneyin' an' cooaxin' of him, and when she found as cooaxin' weren't o' noa use hoo tried bully-raggin' him, and when she found as bully-raggin' weren't o' noa use, she tried *stratagem*—and that's a woman's last resource!

"Tummy," hoo says, "tho tha's a' love for me, I still ha' a gradely liking for thee, lad. And, tha sees, if tha gies me up, folks 'll lay a' blame upo' thee. Noo, I'll tell tha what tha mun do. Tha mun gooa to th' church wi' me i' th' mornin', and when the parson says to thee, 'Wilt tha ha' Meary for to be thy wedded wife?' tha mun say, 'Yes, I will.' And when th' parson says to me, 'Meary, lass, will tha ha' Tummy for to be thy wedded husband?' I'll say, 'Noa, I weean't.' And then tha'll get off scot-free, tha seeas, and th' folk'll lay a' th' blame upo' me." Weel, Tummy, he were a coward at heart, and he didn't want Meary for to gooa aboot sayin' nasty things aboot him, and so he went—*poor lad!* And when they'd getten to' th' church i' th' mornin', parson he says to Tummy, "Tummy," he says, "wilt thou have Meary for to be thy wedded wife?" And Tummy, he speaks oot bold-like, "Aw! Ah will!" And soona then th' parson he turns to Meary, and he says, "Meary, lass, wilt thou have Tummy for to be thy wedded husband?" And Meary shoo up and shoo says, "Aw!

Ah will!" Tummy says, "Nay, nay; that winnot dew. Tha was to say as tha wouldn't." "Aye, but," says Meary, "there's others can chaange their minds, Tummy, as weel as thee!" Sooa hoo gat him!

HIS BLACKSTONIAN CIRCUMLOCUTION

ANONYMOUS

"I received, this afternoon," said the bright-eyed, common-sense girl, the while a slight blush of maidenly coyness tinted her peach-hued cheeks, "a written proposal of marriage from Horace J. Pokelong, the rising young attorney, and——"

"Huh! that petrified dub!" jealously ejaculated the young dry-goods dealer, who had been hanging back because of his timidity and excessive adoration.

"He says," proceeded the maiden, gently ignoring the interruption, and reading aloud from the interesting document, " 'I have carefully and comprehensively analyzed my feelings toward you, and the result is substantially as follows, to wit: I respect, admire, adore and love you, and hereby give, grant and convey to you my heart and all my interest, right and title in and to the same, together with all my possessions and emoluments, either won, inherited or in any other manner acquired, gained, anticipated or expected, with full and complete power to use, expend, utilize, give away, bestow or otherwise make use of the same, anything heretofore stated, exprest, implied or understood, in or by my previous condition, standing, walk, attitude or actions, to the contrary notwithstanding; and I furthermore——' "

"I—I——!" fairly shouted the listener, springing to his feet, and extending his arms. "Miss Brisk—Maud—I love you! Will you marry me?"

"Yes, I will!" promptly answered the lass, as she contentedly snuggled up in his encircling embrace. "And I'll reply to the ponderous appeal of that pedantic procrastinator with the one expressive slangism, 'Twenty-three!' I am yours, Clarence!"

KATRINA LIKES ME POODY VELL

ANONYMOUS

Somedimes ven I'm a-feeling bad,
  Cause dings dey don'd go righd,
I gid so kinder awful sick,
  Und lose my abbedide.
Und ven I go me to der house,
  Und by dot daple sit,
Dot widdles makes me feel gwide bale,
  Und I don'd kin ead a bit.

My head dot shbind arount unt rount,
  Und my eyes dem look so vild,
Dot of my mudder she was dere,
  She voodn't know her shild.
Dot is der dime Katrina comes,
  Und nice vords she does dell,
Mit her heart a-busding oud mit loaf,
  For she likes me poody vell.

She gifes me efery kind of dings
  Dot she dinks will done me goot;
She cooks me shblendid sassage mead,
  Und oder kinds of foot;
She ties vet rags arount my head
  When dot begins to shvell,
Und soaks my feet mit Brandred's bills,
  For she likes me poody vell.

She sings me nice und poody songs,
  Mit a woice dot's shweed und glear,
Und says, "Dot of I vas to die
  She voodn't leef a year."
Of dot aind so, or if id is,
  I don'd vas going to dell;
But dis much I am villing to shwore—
  She likes me poody vell.

AT THE RESTAURANT

ANONYMOUS

Waiter—"Well, ladies, what will it be?"

Mrs. Etamine—"I don't know what you girls are going to take, but I can't eat a thing—unless it's ice-cream."

Miss De Beige—"I'm sure I don't want anything except cream. I never *can* eat in this hot weather."

Miss Satine—"I'd like some ice-cream, if they've got any *real* pistache."

Miss Foulard—"Oh, I wouldn't trust them to give me pistache *here!* I don't believe they know what pistache is. I'm going to take chocolate."

Mrs. E.—"I'd take chocolate, too, only it's so heavy all by it-self."

Miss De B.—"Why don't you take it with strawberry?"

Mrs. E.—"Oh, I don't think strawberry and chocolate go well together! The contrast is too striking, don't you think?"

Miss De B.—"Well, perhaps it *is* a little—loud."

Miss F.—"Lemon and chocolate are awfully nice."

Miss S.—"But there's something about pistache, don't you know, so delicate."

Miss F.—"I'm sure lemon is delicate. You can't taste any flavor at all, the way they make it at most places."

Miss S.—"But pistache is so *refined,* don't you know."

Mrs. E.—"Dear me, here's this man standing by waiting—it's perfectly horrid to have him looming over us like a ghost or something. Do let's give our orders and get him away!"

Miss De B.—"Well, what are you going to order?"

Mrs. E.—"Why, I told you—chocolate and lemon."

Miss F.—"No; that was what I ordered, wasn't it?"

Mrs. E.—"Why, so it was! Chocolate and strawberry I meant. Some people think that's too heavy—too cloying, you know—but I think it's about as good as anything."

Miss De B.—"Well, I think I'll take that, too. I don't know, tho. Lemon is awfully good. I know a lady up in the Catskills —she had the loveliest little boy, just six years old, with curly hair

By permission of *Puck*, New York

that hung ever so far down his back, and he used to come to me every morning and ask for candy in the prettiest way—just like a little dog, and he learned it all himself—his mother told me nobody taught him—tho I've always believed that that child never *could* have originated the idea all by himself——"

Mrs. E.—"Excuse me, Clara, but the man is waiting."

Miss De B.—"As I was *saying,* she was poisoned by eating lemon ice-cream; but I believe they found out afterward that some one put the rat-poison in the freezer by mistake—I beg your pardon, Mrs. Etamine; I didn't know you were speaking—oh, yes—strawberry ice-cream, waiter, and a fork, if you please—don't bring me a spoon—I don't want it."

Miss S.—"Well, if I can't have pistache——"

Miss F.—"You can't—I'm sure they haven't got it here. I'll take—let me see—some chocolate, I guess. Is your chocolate good, waiter?"

Miss S.—"Oh, it's sure to be good—they never give you bad chocolate. Well, I *did* want pistache; but I think I'll take lemon. Some lemon ice-cream, waiter—lemon flavor—and don't bring it in half melted."

Mrs. E. (*impressively*)—"Some chocolate and strawberry ice-cream, waiter, mixed. And a spoon. Do you understand me, waiter? A spoon. *Not* a fork."

Miss F.—"Chocolate ice-cream—don't forget!"

Miss S.—"Lemon ice-cream!"

Miss De B.—"Strawberry—and a fork!"

Mrs. E.—"Chocolate and strawberry—spoon, of course, waiter. I suppose you know *that.*"

Waiter—"Ice-cream? Yes, ma'am. We ain't got nothin' only verniller, ma'am. Yaas'm—all out of everythin' only verniller. What'll it be, ladies?"

A-FEARED OF A GAL

ANONYMOUS

Oh, darn it all! a-feared of her,
    And such a mite of a gal;
Why, two of her size rolled into one
    Won't ditto Sister Sal!
Her voice is sweet as the whippoorwill's,
    And the sunshine's in her hair;
But I'd rather face a redskin's knife,
    Or the grip of a grizzly bear.
Yet Sal says: "Why, she's such a dear,
    She's just the one for you."
Oh, darn it all! a-feared of a gal,
    And me just six feet two!

Tho she ain't any size, while I'm
    Considerable tall,
I'm nowhere when she speaks to me,
    She makes me feel so small.
My face grows red, my tongue gets hitched,
    The plagued thing won't go;
It riles me, 'cause it makes her think
    I'm most tarnation slow.
And tho folks say she's sweet on me,
    I guess it can't be true.
Oh, darn it all! a-feared of a gal,
    And me just six feet two!

My sakes! just s'pose if what the folks
    Is saying should be so!
Go, Cousin Jane, and speak to her,
    Find out and let me know;
Tell her the gals should court the men,
    For isn't this leap-year?

That's why I'm kind of bashful like,
  A-waiting for her here.
And should she hear I'm scared of her,
  You'll swear it can't be true.
Oh, darn it all, a-feared of a gal,
  And me just six feet two!

LEAVING OUT THE JOKE

ANONYMOUS

Some people are bright enough to enjoy a good joke, but do not have retentive memories, so as to be able to repeat it to others. Failures of this kind are sometimes very ludicrous. We give some good specimens.

The most famous of this class was the college professor, who, on parting with a student that had called on him, noticed that he had a new coat, and remarked that it was too short.

The student, with an air of resignation, replied: "It will be long enough before I get another."

The professor enjoyed the joke heartily, and going to a meeting of the college faculty just afterward, he entered the room in great glee and said:

"Young Sharp got off such a joke just now. He called on me a little while ago, and as he was leaving, I noticed his new coat, and told him it was too short, and he said: "It will be a long time before I get another."

No one laughed, and the professor sobering down, remarked: "It doesn't seem so funny as when he said it."

A red-haired woman who was ambitious of literary distinction found but poor sale for her book. A gentleman, in speaking of her disappointment, said: "Her hair is red (read) if her book is not." An auditor, in attempting to relate the joke elsewhere, said: "She has red hair if her book hasn't."

The most unfortunate attempt at reproducing another's wit was made by an Englishman who didn't understand the pun, but judged from the applause with which it was greeted that it must be excellent. During a dinner at which he was a guest a waiter let a boiled tongue slip off the plate on which he was bearing it, and it fell on the table.

The host at once apologized for the mishap as a *lapsus linguæ* (slip of the tongue). The joke was the best thing at the dinner, and our friend concluded to bring it up at his own table.

He accordingly invited his company and instructed his servant to let fall a roast of beef as he was bringing it to the table.

When the "accident" occurred, he exclaimed: "That's a *lapsus linguæ*."

Nobody laughed, and he said again, "I say that's a *lapsus linguæ*," and still no one laughed.

A screw was loose somewhere; so he told about the tongue falling, and they did laugh.

"Why is this," said a waiter, holding up a common kitchen utensil, "more remarkable than Napoleon Bonaparte? Because Napoleon was a great man, but this is a grater." When the funny man reproduced it in his circle, he asked the question right, but answered it, "Because Napoleon was a great man, but this is a nutmeg-grater."

THE CYCLOPEEDY

BY EUGENE FIELD

Havin' lived next door to the Hobart place f'r goin' on thirty years, I calc'late that I know jest about ez much about the case ez anybody else now on airth, exceptin' perhaps it's ol' Jedge Baker, and he's so plaguey old 'nd so powerful feeble that *he* don't know nothin'.

It seems that in the spring uv '47—the year that Cy Watson's oldest boy wuz drownded in West River—there come along a book agent sellin' volyumes 'nd tracks f'r the diffusion uv knowledge, 'nd havin' got the recommend of the minister 'nd uv the select-men, he done an all-fired big business in our part uv the county. His name wuz Lemuel Higgins, 'nd he wuz ez likely a talker ez I ever heerd, barrin' Lawyer Conkey, 'nd everybody allowed that when Conkey wuz round he talked so fast that the town pump ud have to be greased every twenty minutes.

One of the first uv our folks that this Lemuel Higgins struck wuz Leander Hobart. Leander had jest marr'd one uv the Peasley girls, 'nd had moved into the old homestead on the Plainville road, —old Deacon Hobart havin' give up the place to him, the other boys havin' moved out West (like a lot o' darned fools that they wuz!). Leander wuz feelin' his oats jest about this time, 'nd nuthin' wuz too good f'r him.

"Hattie," sez he, "I guess I'll have to lay in a few books f'r readin' in the winter time, 'nd I've half a notion to subscribe f'r a cyclopeedy. Mr. Higgins here says they're invalerable in a family, and that we orter have 'em, bein' as how we're likely to have the fam'ly bime by."

"Lor's sakes, Leander, how you talk!" sez Hattie, blushin' all over, ez brides allers does to heern tell uv sich things.

Waal, to make a long story short, Leander bargained with Mr. Higgins for a set uv them cyclopeedies, 'nd he signed his name to a long printed paper that showed how he agreed to take a cyclopeedy oncet in so often, which wuz to be ez often ez a new one uv the volyumes wuz printed. A cyclopeedy isn't printed all at oncet, because that would make it cost too much; consekently the man that gets it up has it strung along fur apart, so as to hit folks once every year or two, and gin'rally about harvest time. So Leander kind uv liked the idee, and he signed the printed paper 'nd made his affidavit to it afore Jedge Warner.

The fust volyume of the cyclopeedy stood on a shelf in the old seckertary in the settin'-room about four months before they had any use f'r it. One night 'Squire Tuner's son come over to visit Leander 'nd Hattie, and they got to talkin' about apples, 'nd the sort uv apples that wuz the best. Leander allowed that the Rhode Island greenin' wuz the best, but Hattie and the Turner boy stuck up f'r the Roxbury russet, until at last a happy idee struck Leander, and sez he: "We'll leave it to the cyclopeedy, b'gosh! Whichever one the cyclopeedy sez is the best will settle it."

"But you can't find out nothin' 'bout Roxbury russets nor Rhode Island greenin's in *our* cyclopeedy," sez Hattie.

"Why not, I'd like to know?" sez Leander, kind uv indignant like.

" 'Cause ours hain't got down to the R yet," sez Hattie. "All ours tells about is things beginnin' with A."

"Well, ain't we talkin' about Apples?" sez Leander. "You aggervate me terrible, Hattie, by insistin' on knowin' what you don't know nothin' 'bout."

Leander went to the seckertary 'nd took down the cyclopeedy 'nd hunted all through it f'r Apples, but all he could find wuz "Apple—See Pomology."

"How in the thunder kin I see Pomology," sez Leander, "when there ain't no Pomology to see? Gol durn a cyclopeedy, any-how!"

And he put the volyume back onto the shelf 'nd never sot eyes into it agin.

That's the way the thing run f'r years 'nd years. Leander would've gin up the plaguey bargain, but he couldn't; he had signed a printed paper 'nd had swore to it before a justice of the peace. Higgins would have had the law on him if he had throwed up the trade.

The most aggervatin' feature uv it all wuz that a new one uv them cussid cyclopeedies wuz allus sure to show up at the wrong time,—when Leander wuz hard up or had jest been afflicted some way or other. His barn burnt down two nights afore the volyume containin' the letter B arrived, and Leander needed all his chink to pay f'r lumber, but Higgins sot back on that affidavit and de-fied the life out uv him.

"Never mind, Leander," sez his wife, soothin' like, "it's a good book to have in the house, anyhow, now that we've got a baby."

"That's so," sez Leander, "babies does begin with B, don't it?"

You see their fust baby had been born; they named him Peas-ley,—Peasley Hobart,—after Hattie's folks. So, seein' as how he wuz payin' f'r a book that told about babies, Leander didn't begredge that five dollars so very much after all.

"Leander," sez Hattie, "that B cyclopeedy ain't no account. There ain't nothin' in it about babies except 'See Maternity'!"

"Waal, I'll be gosh durned!" sez Leander. That wuz all he said, and he couldn't do nothin' at all, f'r that book agent, Lem-uel Higgins, had the dead-wood on him,—the mean, sneakin' critter!

So the years passed on, one of the cyclopeedies showin' up now 'nd then,—sometimes every two years 'nd sometimes every four, but allus at a time when Leander found it pesky hard to give up a fiver. It warn't no use cussin' Higgins; Higgins jest laffed when Leander allowed that the cyclopeedy wuz no good 'nd that he wuz bein' robbed. Meantime Leander's family wuz increasin' and growin'. Little Sarey had the hoopin'-cough dreadful one winter, but the cyclopeedy didn't help out at all, 'cause all it said wuz: "Hoopin' Cough—See Whoopin' Cough"—and uv course, there warn't no Whoopin' Cough to see, bein' as how the W hadn't come yet.

Oncet when Hiram wanted to dreen the home pasture, he went to the cyclopeedy to find out about it, but all he diskivered wuz: "Drain—See Tile." This wuz in 1859, and the cyclopeedy had only got down to G.

The cow wuz sick with lung fever one spell, and Leander laid her dyin' to that cussid cyclopeedy, 'cause when he went to readin' 'bout cows it told him to "See Zoology."

But what's the use uv harrowin' up one's feelin's talkin' 'nd thinkin' about these things? Leander got so after a while that the cyclopeedy didn't worry him at all: he grew to look at it ez one uv the crosses that human critters has to bear without complainin' through this vale uv tears. The only thing that bothered him wuz the fear that mebbe he wouldn't live to see the last volyume,—to tell the truth, this kind uv got to be his hobby, and I've heern him talk 'bout it many a time settin' round the stove at the tavern 'nd squirtin' tobacco juice at the sawdust box. His wife, Hattie, passed away with the yaller janders the winter W come, and all that seemed to reconcile Leander to survivin' her wuz the prospect uv seein' the last volyume uv that cyclopeedy. Lemuel Higgins, the book agent, had gone to his everlastin' punishment; but his son, Hiram, had succeeded to his father's business 'nd continued to visit the folks his old man had roped in. By this time Leander's children had growed up; all on 'em wuz marr'd, and there wuz numeris grandchildren to amuse the ol' gentleman. But Leander wuzn't to be satisfied with the common things uv airth; he didn't seem to take no pleasure in his grandchildren like most men do; his mind wuz allers sot on somethin' else,—for hours 'nd hours, yes, all day long, he'd set out on the front stoop lookin' wistfully up the road for that book agent to come along with a cyclopeedy. He didn't want to die till he'd got all the cyclopeedies his contract called for; he wanted to have everything straightened out before he passed away.

When—oh, how well I recollect it—when Y come along he wuz so overcome that he fell over in a fit uv paralysis, 'nd the old gentleman never got over it. For the next three years he drooped 'nd pined and seemed like he couldn't hold out much longer. Finally he had to take to his bed,—he was so old 'nd feeble,—but he made 'em move the bed up ag'inst the window so he could watch for that last volyume of the cyclopeedy.

The end come one balmy day in the spring uv '87. His life wuz a-ebbin' powerful fast; the minister wuz there, 'nd me, 'nd Dock Wilson, 'nd Jedge Baker, 'nd most uv the fam'ly. Lovin' hands smoothed the wrinkled forehead 'nd breshed back the long, scant, white hair, but the eyes of the dyin' man wuz sot upon that piece uv road over which the cyclopeedy man allus come.

All to oncet a bright 'nd joyful look come into them eyes, 'nd ol' Leander riz up in bed 'nd sez: "It's come!"

"What is it, father?" asked his daughter Sarey, sobbin' like.

"Hush," sez the minister, solemnly; "he sees the shinin' gates uv the Noo Jerusalem."

"No, no," cried the aged man; "it is the cyclopeedy—the letter Z—it's comin'!"

And, sure enough! the door opened, and in walked Higgins. He tottered rather than walked, f'r he had growed old 'nd feeble in his wicked perfession.

"Here's the Z cyclopeedy, Mr. Hobart," says Higgins.

Leander clutched it; he hugged it to his pantin' bosom; then stealin' one pale hand under the pillar he drew out a faded banknote 'nd gave it to Higgins.

"I thank Thee for this boon," sez Leander, rollin' his eyes up devoutly; then he gave a deep sigh.

"Hold on," cried Higgins, excitedly, "you've made a mistake—it isn't the last——"

But Leander didn't hear him—his soul hed fled from its mortal tenement 'nd hed soared rejoicin' to realms uv everlastin' bliss.

"He is no more," sez Dock Wilson, metaphorically.

"Then who are his heirs?" asked that mean critter Higgins.

"We be," sez the fam'ly.

"Do you conjointly and severally acknowledge and assume the obligation of deceased to me?" he asked 'em.

"What obligation?" asked Peasley Hobart, stern like.

"Deceased died owin' me f'r a cyclopeedy!" sez Higgins.

"That's a lie!" sez Peasley. "We seen him pay you for the Z!"

"But there's another one to come," sez Higgins.

"Another?" they all asked.

"Yes, the index," sez he. So there wuz.

Reprinted by permission of the author.

ECHO

BY JOHN G. SAXE

I asked of Echo, t'other day
  (Whose words are often few and funny),
What to a novice she could say
  Of courtship, love, and matrimony.
    Quoth Echo plainly,—"Matter-o'-money!"

Whom should I marry? Should it be
  A dashing damsel, gay and pert,
A pattern of inconstancy;
  Or selfish, mercenary flirt?
    Quoth Echo, sharply,—"Nary flirt!"

What if, aweary of the strife
  That long has lured the dear deceiver,
She promise to amend her life,
  And sin no more; can I believe her?
    Quoth Echo, very promptly,—"Leave her!"

But if some maiden with a heart
  On me should venture to bestow it,
Pray, should I act the wiser part
  To take the treasure or forego it?
    Quoth Echo, with decision,—"Go it!"

But what if, seemingly afraid
  To bind her fate in Hymen's fetter,
She vow she means to die a maid,
  In answer to my loving letter?
  Quoth Echo, rather coolly,—"Let her!"

What if, in spite of her disdain
  I find my heart entwined about
With Cupid's dear delicious chain
  So closely that I can't get out?
  Quoth Echo, laughingly,—"Get out!"

But if some maid with beauty blest,
  As pure and fair as Heaven can make her,
Will share my labor and my rest
  Till envious Death shall overtake her?
  Quoth Echo (sotto voce),—"Take her!"

Reprinted by permission of Houghton, Mifflin & Company.

OUR RAILROADS

ANONYMOUS

He stood in the station, she at his side—
She is a fair, young, blushing bride.
On their honeymoon they're starting now;
It always follows the marriage vow.
He looks at the flaring railroad maps,
At the train of cars and his baggage traps,
And whispered: "Pettie, how shall we go,—
By the Kankakee or the Kokomo?

"These railroad maps confuse the eye,
There's the C. B. Q. and the R. N. Y.
And this one says your life's at stake
On any road but the Sky Blue Lake.
The N. E. R. L. P. Q. J.
Have sleepers on the entire way;
But I've heard these trains are much more slow
Than the Kankakee or the Kokomo."

She murmured: "Sweetie, I've heard pa say
What a fine old road is the P. G. K.;
But mamma seemed to disagree,
And prefers the X. S. H. O. P.
This chart says, dearie, the views are fine
On the Texas-Cowboy-Mustang line;
But still, perhaps, we'd better go
On the Kankakee or the Kokomo."

A conductor chanced to pass them by
And the bridegroom caught his gentle eye;
He said: "O man, with the cap of blue,
Inform me quick, inform me true,
Which road is best for a blushing, pure,
Young, timid bride on her wedding tour?
And tell us quickly what you know
Of the Kankakee or the Kokomo?"

The conductor's eyes gave a savage gleam;
These words rolled out in a limpid stream:
"There's the A. B. J. D. V. R. Z.
Connects with the Flip-Flap-Biff-Bang-B,
You can change on the Leg-off-Sueville-Grand,
And go through on the Pan-cake-ace-Full-Hand.
That road you named is blocked by snow,
The Kankakee and the Kokomo.

"The Pennsylvania, Pittsburg Through,
Connects with the Oshkosh Kalamazoo,
With a smoking car all the afternoon;
Just the thing for a honeymoon;
And the Central-Scalp-Tooth-Bungville-switch
Goes through a vine-land country rich.
Of the road you named I nothing know,
The Kankakee and the Kokomo."

The bride said: "Honey, 'tis best, by far,
Like the dollar, we return to pa
(That's a pun I heard while on a train
On the U. R. N. G. Jersey main)."
The conductor smiled; his eye-teeth showed;
He had spoiled the trade of a rival road.
He knew in his heart there was no snow
On the Kankakee or the Kokomo.

And the bride and groom returned to pa,
Who heard it all and then said: "Pshaw!
If you found you couldn't go that way,
Why didn't you go on the Cross-eyed Bay?"
The bridegroom gave a howl of pain;
The railroad names had turned his brain.
He raves, insane, forevermore;
In a madhouse, chained unto the floor,
He gibbers: "Tootsie, shall we go
By the Kankakee or the Kokomo?"

WAKIN' THE YOUNG 'UNS

(The old man from the foot of the stairs—5 a. m.)

BY JOHN C. BOSS

Bee-ull! Bee-ull! O Bee-ull! my gracious,
    Air you still sleepin'?
    Th' hour-hand's creepin'
        Nearder five.
(Wal, durned ef this 'ere ain't vexatious!)
    Don't ye hyar them cattle callin'?
An' th' ole red steer a-bawlin'?
        Come, look alive!
            Git up! Git up!

Mar'ann! Mar'ann! (Jist hyar her snorin'!)
 Mar'ann! it's behoovin'
 Thet you be a-moovin'!
  Brisk, I say!
Hyar the kitchen stove a-roarin'?
 The kittle's a-spilin'
 Ter git hisse'f bilin'.
  It's comin' day.
   Git up! Git up!

Jule! O Jule! Now whut is ailin'?
 You want ter rest?
 Wal' I'll be blest!
  S'pose them cows
'Ll give down milk 'ithout you pailin'?
 You mus' be goin crazy;
 Er' more like, gittin' lazy.
  Come, now, rouse.
   Git up! Git up!

Jake, you lazy varmint! Jake! Hey Jake!
 Whut you layin' theer fur?
 You know the stock's ter keer fur;
  So, hop out!
(Thet boy is wusser'n a rock ter wake!)
 Don't stop to shiver,
 But jist unkiver,
  An' pop out!
   Git up! Git up!

Young 'uns! Bee-ull! Jake! Mar'ann! Jule!
 (Wal' durn my orn'ry skin!
 They've gone ter sleep agin,
  Fur all my tellin'!)
See hyar, I hain't no time ter fool!
 It's the las' warnin'
 I'll give this mornin'.
  I'm done yellin'!
   Git up! Git up!

Solus

Wal, whut's th' odds—an hour, more or less?
  B'lieve it makes 'em stronger
  Ter sleep a leetle longer
    Thar in bed.
The time is comin' fas' enough, I guess,
  When I'll wish, an' wish 'ith weepin'
  They was back up yender sleepin',
    Overhead,
        Ter git up.

PAT'S REASON

ANONYMOUS

One day I observed in a crowded horse-car,
A lady was standing. She had ridden quite far,
And seemed much disposed to indulge in a frown,
As nobody offered to let her sit down.
And many there sat who, to judge by their dress,
Might a gentleman's natural instincts possess,
But who, judged by their acts, make us firmly believe
That appearances often will sadly deceive.
There were some most intently devouring the news,
And some thro' the windows enjoying the views;
And others indulged in a make-believe nap,
While the lady still stood holding on by the strap.
At last a young Irishman, fresh from the "sod,"
Arose with a smile and most comical nod,
Which said quite as plain as in words could be stated
That the lady should sit in the place he'd vacated.
"Excuse me," said Pat, "that I caused you to wait
So long before offerin' to give you a sate,
But in troth I was only just waitin' to see
If there wasn't more gintlemin here beside me."

QUIT YOUR FOOLIN'

ANONYMOUS

Girls is queer! I used to think
    Emmy didn't care for me,
For, whenever I would try
    Any lovin' arts, to see
How she'd take 'em—sweet or sour—
    Always saucy-like says she:
        "Quit your foolin'!"

Once a-goin' home from church,
    Jest to find if it would work,
Round her waist I slipt my arm—
    My! you'd ought 'o seen her jerk,
Spunky? well, she acted so—
    And she snapt me up as perk—
        "Quit your foolin'!"

Every time 'twas just the same,
    Till one night I says, says I—
Chokin' some I must admit,
    Tremblin' some I don't deny—
"Emmy, seein' as I don't suit,
    Guess I'd better say good-by
        An' quit foolin'."

Girls is queer! She only laughed—
    Cheeks all dimplin'; "John," says she,
"Foolin' men that never gits
    Real in earnest, ain't for me."
Wan't that cute? I took the hint,
    An' a chair, an' staid, an' we
        Quit our foolin'.

SHE WOULD BE A MASON

BY JAMES L. LAUGHTON

The funniest thing I ever heard,
The funniest thing that ever occurred,
Is the story of Mrs. Mehitable Byrde,
    Who wanted to be a Mason.

Her husband, Tom Byrde, a Mason true—
As good a Mason as any of you;
He is tyler of Lodge Cerulean Blue,
And tyles and delivers the summons due—
And she wanted to be a Mason, too,
    This ridiculous Mrs. Byrde.

She followed round, this inquisitive wife,
And nagged him and teased him half out of his life;
So to terminate this unhallowed strife,
    He consented at last to admit her.
And first, to disguise her from bonnet and shoon,
This ridiculous lady agreed to put on
His breech—ah! forgive me—I meant pantaloons;
    And miraculously did they fit her.

The lodge was at work on the Master's degree,
The light was ablaze on the letter C;
High soared the pillars J and B.
The officers sat like Solomon, wise;
The brimstone burned amid horrible cries;
The goat roamed wildly through the room;
The candidate begged to let him go home;
And the devil himself stood up at the east,
As broad as an alderman at a feast,
    When in came Mrs. Byrde.

O horrible sounds! O horrible sight!
Can it be that Masons take delight
In spending thus the hours of night?
Ah! could their wives and daughters know
The unutterable things they say and do,
Their feminine hearts would burst with wo!
    But this is not all my story.
Those Masons joined in a hideous ring,
The candidate howling like everything,
And thus in tones of death they sing
    (The candidate's name was Morey):
"Double, double, toil and trouble,
Fire burn and cauldron bubble;
Blood to drink and bones to crack,
Skulls to smash and lives to take,
Hearts to crush and souls to burn;
Give old Morey another turn!"

The brimstone gleamed in lurid flame,
Just like a place we will not name;
Good angels, that inquiring came
From blissful courts, looked on with shame
    And tearful melancholy.
Again they dance, but twice as bad,
They jump and sing like demons mad;
    The tune is far from jolly:
"Double, double, toil and trouble,
Fire burn and cauldron bubble;
Blood to drink and bones to crack,
Skulls to smash and lives to take,
Hearts to crush and souls to burn;
Give old Morey another turn!"

Trembling with horror stood Mrs. Byrde,
Unable to speak a single word.
She staggered and fell in the nearest chair,
On the left of the junior warden there,
And scarcely noticed, so loud the groans,

That the chair was made of human bones.
Of human bones! On grinning skulls
That ghastly throne of horror rolls;
Those skulls, the skulls that Morgan bore;
Those bones, the bones that Morgan wore.
His scalp across the top was flung,
His teeth around the arms were strung.
Never in all romance was known
Such uses made of human bone.

There came a pause—a pair of paws
Reached through the floor, up sliding-doors,
And grabbed the unhappy candidate!
How can I, without tears, relate
The lost and ruined Morey's fate?
She saw him sink in a fiery hole,
She heard him scream, "My soul! My soul!"
While roars of fiendish laughter roll,
    And drown the yells for mercy:
"Double, double, toil and trouble,
Fire burn and cauldron bubble;
Blood to drink and bones to crack,
Skulls to smash and lives to take,
Hearts to crush and souls to burn;
Give old Morey another turn!"

The ridiculous woman could stand no more,
She fainted and fell on the checkered floor,
'Midst all the diabolical roar.
What then, you ask me, did befall
Mehitable Byrde? Why, nothing at all—
She dreamed she had been in a Mason's hall.

HENRY THE FIFTH'S WOOING

BY SHAKESPEARE

K. Henry. Fair Katharine, and most fair,
Will you vouchsafe to teach a soldier terms
Such as will enter at a lady's ear
And plead his love-suit to her gentle heart?

Katharine. Your majesty shall mock at me; I can not speak your England.

K. Hen. O fair Katharine, if you will love me soundly with your French heart, I will be glad to hear you confess it brokenly with your English tongue. Do you like me, Kate?

Kath. Pardonnez-moi, I can not tell vat is "like me."

K. Hen. An angel is like you, Kate, and you are like an angel.

Kath. Que dit-il? que je suis semblable à les anges?

Alice. Oui, vraiment, sauf votre grace, ainsi dit-il.

K. Hen. I said so, dear Katharine; and I must not blush to affirm it.

Kath. O les langues des hommes sont pleines des tromperies.

K. Hen. What says she, fair one? that the tongues of men are full of deceits?

Alice. Oui, dat de tongues of de mans is be full of deceits: dat is de princess.

K. Hen. The princess is the better Englishwoman. I' faith, Kate, my wooing is fit for thy understanding; I am glad thou canst speak no better English; for, if thou couldst, thou wouldst find me such a plain king that thou wouldst think I had sold my farm to buy my crown. I know no ways to mince it in love, but directly to say, "I love you": then if you urge me further than to say, "Do you in faith?" I wear out my suit. Give me your answer; i' faith, do: and so clap hands and a bargain: how say you, lady?

Kath. Sauf votre honneur, me understand vell.

K. Hen. Marry, if you would put me to verses or to dance for your sake, Kate, why you undid me: for the one I have neither words nor measures, and for the other, I have no strength in measure, yet a reasonable measure in strength. If I could win a lady at leap-frog, or by vaulting into my saddle with my armor on my back, under the correction of bragging be it spoken, I should quickly leap into a wife. Or if I buffet for my love, or bound my horse for her favors, I could lay on like a butcher and sit like a jackanapes, never off. But, Kate, I can not look greenly nor gasp out my eloquence, nor I have no cunning in protestation: only downright oaths, which I never use till urged, nor never break for urging. If thou canst love a fellow of this temper, Kate, whose face is not worth sun-burning, that never looks in his glass for love of anything he sees there, let thine eye be thy cook. I speak to thee plain soldier: if thou canst love me for this, take me: if not, to say to thee that I shall die, is true; but for thy love, no; yet I love thee, too. And while thou livest, dear Kate, take a fellow of plain and uncoined constancy; for he perforce must do thee right, because he hath not the gift to woo in other places: for these fellows of infinite tongue, that can rhyme themselves into ladies' favors, they do always reason themselves out again. What! a speaker is but a prater; a rhyme is but a ballad. A good leg will fall; a straight back will stoop; a black beard will turn white; a curled pate will grow bald; a fair face will wither; a full eye will wax hollow: but a good heart, Kate, is the sun and the moon; or rather the sun and not the moon, for it shines bright and never changes, but keeps his course truly. If thou would have such a one, take me; and take me, take a soldier; take a soldier, take a king. And what sayest thou then to my love? speak, my fair, and fairly, I pray thee.

Kath. Is it possible dat I should love de enemy of France?

K. Hen. No; it is not possible you should love the enemy of France, Kate: but, in loving me, you should love the friend of France; for I love France so well that I will not part with a village of it; I will have it all mine; and, Kate, when France is mine and I am yours, then yours is France and you are mine.

Kath. I can not tell vat is dat.

K. Hen. No, Kate? I will tell thee in French; which I am sure will hang upon my tongue like a new-married wife about her husband's neck, hardly to be shook off. Quand j'ay la possession de France, et quand vous avez la possession de moi,—let me see,

what then? Saint Denis be my speed!—donc votre est France
et vous êtes mienne. It is as easy for me, Kate, to conquer the
kingdom as to speak so much more French; I shall never move
thee in French, unless it be to laugh at me.

Kath. Sauf votre honneur, le François que vous parlez, est
meilleur que l'Anglois lequel je parle.

K. Hen. No, faith, is't not, Kate; but thy speaking of my
tongue, and I thine, most truly-falsely, must needs be granted to
be much at one. But, Kate, dost thou understand thus much English, canst thou love me?

Kath. I can not tell.

K. Hen. Can any of your neighbors tell Kate. I'll ask them.
Come, I know thou lovest me; and at night, when you come into
your closet, you'll question this gentlewoman about me; and I
know, Kate, you will to her dispraise those parts in me that you
love with your heart; but, good Kate, mock me mercifully; the
rather, gentle princess, because I love thee cruelly. How answer
you, la plus belle Katharine du monde, mon très chère et divine
déesse?

Kath. Your majestee ave faussee French enough to deceive
de most sage demoiselle dat is en France.

K. Hen. Now, fie upon my false French! By mine honor, in
true English, I love thee, Kate; by which honor I dare not swear
thou lovest me; yet my blood begins to flatter me that thou dost,
notwithstanding the poor and untempering effect of my visage.
I was created with a stubborn outside, with an aspect of iron,
that, when I come to woo ladies, I fright them. But, in faith
Kate, the elder I wax, the better I shall appear; my comfort is,
that old age, that ill layer up of beauty, can do no more spoil upon
my face: thou hast me, if thou hast me, at the worst; and thou
shalt wear me, if thou wear me, better and better: and therefore,
tell me, most fair Katharine, will you have me? Put off your
maiden blushes; avouch the thoughts of your heart with the looks
of an empress; take me by the hand, and say, "Harry of England,
I am thine"; which word thou shalt no sooner bless mine ear
withal, but I will tell thee aloud, "England is thine, Ireland is
thine, France is thine, and Henry Plantagenet is thine"; who,
tho I speak it before his face, if he be not fellow with the best

king, thou shalt find the best king of good fellows. Come, your answer in broken music; for thy voice is music and thy English broken; therefore, queen of all, Katharine, break thy mind to me in broken English; wilt thou have me?

Kath. Dat is as it sall please de Roi mon père.

K. Hen. Nay, it will please him well, Kate; it shall please him, Kate.

Kath. Den it sall also content me.

K. Hen. Upon that I kiss your hand, and I call you my queen.

Kath. Laissez, mon seigneur, laissez, laissez.

K. Hen. Then I will kiss your lips, Kate.

Kath. Il n'est pas la coutume de France.

K. Hen. Madam my interpreter, what says she?

Alice. Dat it is not be de fashion pour les ladies of France— I can not tell vat is *baiser* en Anglish.

K. Hen. To kiss.

Alice. Your majesty entendre bettre que moi.

K. Hen. It is not the fashion for the maids in France to kiss before they are married, would you say?

Alice. Oui, vraiment.

K. Hen. O Kate, nice customs curtsy to great kings. Dear Kate, you and I can not be confined within the weak list of a country's fashion: we are the makers of manners, Kate; and the liberty that follows our places stops the mouth of all find-faults; as I will do yours, for upholding the nice fashion of your country in denying me a kiss; therefore, patiently and yielding. (*Kisses her.*) You have witchcraft in your lips, Kate; there is more eloquence in a sugar touch of them than in the tongues of the French council; and they should sooner persuade Harry of England than a general petition of monarchs.

SCENE FROM "THE RIVALS"

BY RICHARD BRINSLEY SHERIDAN

Mrs. M. There, Sir Anthony, there stands the deliberate simpleton who wants to disgrace her family and lavish herself on a fellow not worth a shilling.

Lyd. Madam, I thought you once——

Mrs. M. You thought, miss! I don't know any business you have to think at all. Thought does not become a young woman. But the point we would request of you is, that you will promise to forget this fellow—to illiterate him, I say, from your memory.

Lyd. Ah, madam! our memories are independent of our wills. It is not so easy to forget.

Mrs. M. But I say it is, miss! There is nothing on earth so easy as to forget, if a person chooses to set about it. I'm sure I have as much forgot your poor, dear uncle as if he had never existed, and I thought it my duty to do so; and let me tell you, Lydia, these violent memories don't become a young woman.

Sir A. Surely, the young woman does not pretend to remember what she is ordered to forget! Ah, this comes of her reading.

Lyd. What crime, madam, have I committed, to be treated thus?

Mrs. M. Now don't attempt to extirpate yourself from the matter; you know I have proof controvertible of it. But tell me, will you promise me to do as you are bid? Will you take a husband of your friends' choosing?

Lyd. Madam, I must tell you plainly that, had I no preference for any one else, the choice you have made would be my aversion.

Mrs. M. What business have you, miss, with preference and aversion? They don't become a young woman; and you ought to know that, as both always wear off, 'tis safest, in matrimony, to begin with a little aversion. I am sure I hated your poor dear uncle before marriage as if he'd been a blackamoor, and yet, miss, you are sensible what a wife I made; and, when it pleased heaven to release me from him, 'tis unknown what tears I shed!

Sir A. He-e-m!

Mrs. M. But, suppose we were going to give you another choice, will you promise us to give up this Beverley?

Lyd. Could I belie my thoughts so far as to give that promise, my actions would certainly as far belie my words.

Mrs. M. Take yourself to your room! You are fit company for nothing but your own ill humors.

Lyd. Willingly, ma'am; I can not change for the worse. [*Exit.*

Mrs. M. There's a little intricate hussy for you!

Sir. A. It is not to be wondered at, ma'am; all that is the natural consequence of teaching girls to read. In my way hither, Mrs. Malaprop, I observed your niece's maid coming forth from a circulating library; she had a book in each hand—they were half-bound volumes, with marble covers. From that moment, I guessed how full of duty I should see her mistress!

Mrs. M. Those are vile places, indeed!

Sir A. Madam, a circulating library in a town is as an evergreen tree of diabolical knowledge! It blossoms through the year! And, depend upon it, Mrs. Malaprop, that they who are so fond of handling the leaves, will long for the fruit at last.

Mrs. M. Fie, fie, Sir Anthony; you surely speak laconically. (*Sir Anthony places a chair for her and another for himself, bows to her respectfully and waits till she is seated.*)

Sir A. Why, Mrs. Malaprop, in moderation, now, what would you have a woman know?

Mrs. M. Observe me, Sir Anthony—I would by no means wish a daughter of mine to be a progeny of learning. I don't think so much learning becomes a young woman. For instance—I would never let her meddle with Greek, or Hebrew, or algebra, or simony, or Fluxions, or paradoxes, or such inflammatory branches of learning; nor will it be necessary for her to handle any of your mathematical, astronomical, diabolical instruments; but, Sir Anthony, I would send her, at nine years old, to a boarding-school, in order to learn a little ingenuity and artifice. Then, sir, she should have a supercilious knowledge in accounts; and, as she grew up, I would have her instructed in geometry, that she might know something of the contagious countries; above all, she should be a perfect mistress of orthodoxy—that is, she should not mispronounce and misspell words as our young women of the present day constantly do. This, Sir Anthony, is what I would have a woman know; and I don't think there is a superstitious article in it.

Sir A. Well, well, Mrs. Malaprop, I will dispute the point no further with you, tho I must confess that you are a truly moderate and polite arguer, for almost every third word you say is on my side of the question. But to the more important point in debate—you say you have no objection to my proposal?

Mrs. M. None, I assure you. I am under no positive engagement with Mr. Acres; and as Lydia is so obstinate against him, perhaps your son may have better success.

Sir A. Well, madam, I will write for the boy directly. He knows not a syllable of this yet, tho I have for some time had the proposal in my head. He is at present with his regiment.

Mrs. M. We have never seen your son, Sir Anthony; but I hope no objection on his side.

Sir A. Objection! Let him object, if he dare! No, no, Mrs. Malaprop; Jack knows that the least demur puts me in a frenzy directly. My process was always very simple. In his younger days 'twas—"Jack, do this." If he demurred, I knocked him down; and if he grumbled at that, I always sent him out of the room.

Mrs. M. Ay, and the properest way, o' my conscience! Nothing is so conciliating to young people as severity. (*Both rise.*) Well, Sir Anthony, I shall give Mr. Acres his discharge, and prepare Lydia to receive your son's invocations; and I hope you will represent her to the captain as an object not altogether illegible.

Sir A. Madam, I will handle the subject prudently. I must leave you. Good morning, Mrs. Malaprop. (*Both bow profoundly; Sir Anthony steps back as if to go out, then returns to say:*) And let me beg you, Mrs. Malaprop, to enforce this matter roundly to the girl—take my advice, keep a tight hand. Good-morning, Mrs. Malaprop. If she rejects this proposal, clap her under lock and key. Good-morning, Mrs. Malaprop. And if you were just to let the servants forget to bring her dinner for three or four days, you can't conceive how she'd come about. Good-morning, Mrs. Malaprop.

SCENES FROM "RIP VAN WINKLE"

AS RECITED BY THE LATE A. P. BURBANK

CHARACTERS: *Rip Van Winkle; Derrick Von Beekman, the villain of the play, who endeavors to get Rip drunk in order to have him sign away his property to Von Beekman; Nick Vedder, the village innkeeper.*

SCENE I: *The village inn. Von Beekman, alone. Enter Rip, laughing like a child himself, and shaking off the children.*

Rip (*to the children outside*). Hey! You let my dog Schneider alone dere; you hear dat, Sock der Jacob, der bist eine fordonner spitspoo—yah——Why, hullo, Derrick! how you was? Did you hear dem liddle fellers just now? Dey most plague me crazy. Ha, ha, ha! I like to laugh my outsides in every time I tink about it. Just now, as we was comin' through the willage— Schneider und me—Schneider's my dog; I don't know whether you know him? Well, dem liddle fellers, dey took Schneider und —ha, ha, ha!—dey—ha, ha!—*dey tied a tin-kettle mit Schneider's tail!* Ha, ha, ha! My, how he did run den, mit the kettle banging about! My, how scared he was! Well, I didn't hi him comin'. He run betwixt me und my legs und spilt me und all dem children in the mud,—yah, dat's a fact. Ha, ha, ha!

Derrick. Ah, yes, that's all right, Rip, very funny, very funny; but what do you say to a glass of liquor, Rip?

Rip. What do I generally say to a glass? I generally say it's a fine thing—when dere's plenty in it—und I say more to what is *in* it than to the glass.

Derrick. Certainly, certainly. Say, hello there! Nick Vedder, bring out a bottle of your best.

Rip. Dat's right—fill 'em up. You wouldn't believe it, Derrick, dat's the first one I've had to-day. I guess, maybe, the reason is, I couldn't got it before. Ah, Derrick, my score is too big! Well, here is your good health und your family's, und may dey all live long und prosper! Ah, you may well go "Ah" und smack your chops over dat. You don't give me such schnapps when I come. Where you got dat?

Nick. That's high Dutch, Rip,—high Dutch, and ten years in bottle.

Rip. Well, come on, fill 'em up again. Git out mit dat vater, Nick Vedder; I don't want no vater in my liquor. Good liquor und vater, Derrick, is just like man und wife—*dey don't agree well togedder!* Dat's me und *my* wife, anyway. Well, come on again. Here is your good health und your family's, und may dey all live long und prosper!

Nick. That's right, Rip; drink away, and "drown your sorrows in the flowing bowl."

Rip. Drown my sorrows? Yah, but *she* won't drown. My wife is my sorrow und you cannick drown her. She tried it once, but she couldn't do it. Didn't you know dat Gretchen like to get drown? No? Dat's the funniest thing of the whole of it. It's the same day I got married; she was comin' across dat Hudson River dere in the ferry-boat to get married mit me.

Derrick. Yes.

Rip. Well, the boat she was comin' in got upsetted.

Derrick. Ah!

Rip. Well, but she wasn't in it.

Nick. Oh!

Rip. No, dat's what I say; if she had been in the boat what got upsetted, maybe she might have got drowned. She got left behind somehow or odder. Women is always behind dat way—always.

Derrick. But surely, Rip, you would have risked your life to save her.

Rip (incredulously). You mean I would yump in und pull Gretchen out? Oh, would I? Oh, you mean den—yes, I believe I would den. But it would be a good deal more my duty now as it was den. When a feller gets married a good many years mit his wife, he gets very much attached to her. But if Mrs. Van Winkle was a-drownin' in the water now, und should say to me, "Rip, come und save your wife!" I would say, "Mrs. Van Winkle, I will yust go home und tink about it!" Oh, no, Derrick, if ever Gretchen tumbles in the water now, she's got to swim; I told you dat—ha, ha, ha, ha! Hullo! dat's her a-comin' now; I guess it's better I go oud!   [*Exit Rip.*

SCENE II: *Rip's home. Shortly after his conversation with Von Beekman, Rip's wife found him carousing and dancing upon the village green with the pretty girls. She drove him away in no very gentle fashion. Returning home after nightfall in a decidedly muddled condition, he puts his head through the open window at the rear, not observing his irate wife, who stands in ambush behind the clothes-press, with her ever-ready broomstick, to give him a warm reception; but seeing only his little daughter Meenie, of whom he is very fond, Rip says:*

Rip. Meenie! Meenie, my darlin'!

Meenie. Hush-sh-h. (*Shakes finger to indicate the presence of her mother.*)

Rip. Eh! what's the matter? I don't see nothing, my darlin'. Meenie, is the old wildcat home? Oh, say, is dot you, Gretchen? My darlin', my angel, don't do dat,—let go my head, won't you? Well, den, hold on to it so long what you like. For what you do dat, eh? You must want a bald-headed husband, I reckon.

Gretchen. Who was that you called a wildcat?

Rip. Who was dat I call a wildcat? Well, now, let me see, who was dat I called a wildcat? Dat must have been the time I came in the window dere, wasn't it? Yes, I know, it was the same time. Well, now, let me see. (*Suddenly.*) It was de dog Schneider dat I call it.

Gretchen. The dog Schneider? That's a likely story.

Rip. Of course it is likely,—he's my dog. I'll call him a wildcat much as I please. (*Gretchen begins to weep.*) Oh, well; dere, now, don't you cry, don't you cry, Gretchen; you hear what I said? Listen now. If you don't cry, I nefer drink anoder drop of liquor in my life.

Gretchen. O Rip, you have said so so many, many times, and you never kept your word yet.

Rip. Well, I say it dis time, und I mean it.

Gretchen. O Rip! if I could only trust you.

Rip. You mustn't *suspect* me. Can't you see **repentance** in my eye?

Gretchen. Rip, if you will only keep your word, I shall be the happiest woman in the world.

Rip. You can believe it. I nefer drink anoder drop so long what I live, if you don't cry.

Gretchen. O Rip, how happy we shall be! And you'll get back all the village, Rip, just as you used to have it; and you'll fix up our little house so nicely; and you and I, and our darling little Meenie here—how happy we shall be!

Rip. Dere, dere, now! you can be just so happy what you like. Go in de odder room, go along mit you; I come in dere pooty quick. (*Exit Gretchen and Meenie.*) My! I swore off from drinking so many, many times, und I never kept my word yet. (*Taking out bottle.*) I don't believe dere is more as one good drink in dat bottle, anyway. It's a pity to waste it! You goin' to drink dat? Well, now, if you do, it is de last one, remember dat, old feller. Well, here is your good health, und——

(*Enter Gretchen, suddenly, who snatches the bottle from him.*)

Gretchen. Oh, you paltry thief!

Rip. What you doin'? You'll spill the liquor.

Gretchen. Yes, I *will* spill it. *That's the last drop you drink under my roof!*

Rip. Eh! What?

Gretchen. Out, I say! you drink no more here.

Rip. Why, Gretchen, are you goin' to turn me oud like a dog? Well, maybe you are right. I have got no home. I will go. But mind, Gretchen, after what you say to me to-night, I can nefer darken your door again—nefer; I will go.

Meenie. Not into the storm, father. Hark, how it thunders!

Rip. Yah, my child; but not as bad to me as the storm in my home. I will go. God bless you, my child! Don't you nefer forget your father.

Gretchen (*relenting*). No, Rip,—I——

Rip. No; you have driven me from your house. You have opened the door for me to go. You may nefer open it for me to come back. I wipe the disgrace from your door. Good-by, Gretchen, good-by! [*Rip exits into the storm.*

PART III
SERIOUS HITS

IF WE HAD THE TIME

BY RICHARD BURTON

If I had the time to find a place
And sit me down full face to face
    With my better self, that can not show
    In my daily life that rushes so:
It might be then I would see my soul
Was stumbling toward the shining goal,
    I might be nerved by the thought sublime,—
        If I had the time!

If I had the time to let my heart
Speak out and take in my life apart,
    To look about and to stretch a hand
    To a comrade quartered in no-luck land;
Ah, God! If I might but just sit still
And hear the note of the whippoorwill,
    I think that my wish with God's would rhyme,—
        If I had the time!

If I had the time to learn from you
How much comfort my word could do;
    And I told you then of my sudden will
    To kiss your feet when I did you ill;
If the tears aback of the coldness feigned
Could flow, and the wrong be quite explained,—
    Brothers, the souls of us all would chime,
        If we had the time!

THE FOOL'S PRAYER

BY EDWARD ROWLAND SILL

The royal feast was done; the king
  Sought some new sport to banish care,
And to his jester cried: "Sir Fool,
  Kneel now, and make for us a prayer!"

The jester doffed his cap and bells,
  And stood the mocking court before:
They could not see the bitter smile
  Behind the patient grin he wore.

He bowed his head, and bent his knee
  Upon the monarch's silken stool;
His pleading voice arose, "O Lord,
  Be merciful to me, a fool!

"No pity, Lord, could change the heart
  From red with wrong to white as wool;
The rod must heal the sin; but, Lord,
  Be merciful to me, a fool!

" 'Tis not by guilt the onward sweep
  Of truth and right, O Lord, we stay;
'Tis by our follies that so long
  We hold the earth from heaven away.

"These clumsy feet still in the mire,
  Go crushing blossoms without end;
These hard, well-meaning hands we thrust
  Among the heartstrings of a friend.

"The ill-timed truth we might have kept,—
  Who knows how sharp it pierced and stung?
The word we had not sense to say,—
  Who knows how grandly it had rung?

"Our faults no tenderness should ask,
    The chastening stripe must cleanse them all;
But for our blunders,—oh, in shame
    Before the eyes of heaven we fall.

"Earth bears no balsam for mistakes;
    Men crown the knave, and scourge the tool
That did his will; but Thou, O Lord,
    Be merciful to me, a fool!"

The room was hushed; in silence rose
    The king, and sought his garden cool,
And walked apart, and murmured low:
    "Be merciful to me, a fool!"

THE EVE OF WATERLOO

BY LORD BYRON

There was a sound of revelry by night,
And Belgium's capital had gathered then
Her beauty and her chivalry, and bright
The lamps shone o'er fair women and brave men;
A thousand hearts beat happily; and when
Music arose with its voluptuous swell,
Soft eyes looked love to eyes which spake again,
And all went merry as a marriage-bell;—
But hush! hark! a deep sound strikes like a rising knell!

Did ye not hear it?—No; 'twas but the wind,
Or a car rattling o'er the stony street;
On with the dance! let joy be unconfined;
No sleep till morn, when youth and pleasure meet
To chase the glowing hours with flying feet—
But hark!—that heavy sound breaks in once more,
As if the clouds its echo would repeat;
And nearer, clearer, deadlier than before!
Arm! arm! it is—it is the cannon's opening roar!

Ah! then and there was hurrying to and fro,
And gathering tears, and tremblings of distress,
And cheeks all pale, which but an hour ago
Blushed at the praise of their own loveliness;
And there were sudden partings, such as press
The life from out young hearts, and choking sighs
Which ne'er might be repeated: who could guess
If ever more should meet those mutual eyes,
Since upon night so sweet such awful morn could rise?

And there was mounting in hot haste: the steed,
The mustering squadron, and the clattering car,
Went pouring forward with impetuous speed,
And swiftly forming in the ranks of war;
And the deep thunder peal on peal afar,
And near, the beat of the alarming drum
Roused up the soldier ere the morning star;
While thronged the citizens with terror dumb,
Or whispering, with white lips, "The foe! They come! they come!"

And Ardennes waves above them her green leaves,
Dewy with Nature's tear-drops, as they pass,
Grieving, if aught inanimate e'er grieves,
Over the unreturning brave,—alas!
Ere evening to be trodden like the grass,
Which now beneath them, but above shall grow
In its next verdure, when this fiery mass
Of living valor, rolling on the foe
And burning with high hope, shall molder cold and low.

Last noon beheld them full of lusty life,
Last eve in Beauty's circle proudly gay,
The midnight brought the signal-sound of strife,
The morn, the marshaling in arms,—the day,
Battle's magnificently stern array!
The thunder-clouds close o'er it, which when rent,
The earth is covered thick with other clay,
Which her own clay shall cover, heaped and pent,
Rider and horse, friend, foe, in one red burial blent.

THE WRECK OF THE JULIE PLANTE

BY WILLIAM HENRY DRUMMOND

On wan dark night on Lac St. Pierre,
  De win' she blow, blow, blow,
An' de crew of de wood scow Julie Plante
  Got scar't an' run below—
For de win' she blow lak hurricane;
  Bimeby she blow some more,
An' de scow bus' up on Lac St. Pierre
  Wan arpent from de shore.

De captinne walk on de fronte deck,
  An' walk de hin' deck, too—
He call de crew from up de hole;
  He call de cook also.
De cook she's name was Rosie,
  She come from Montreal,
Was chambre maid on lumber barge,
  On de Grande Lachine Canal.

De win' she blow from nor'—eas'—wes',
  De sout' win' she blow, too,
W'en Rosie cry, "Mon cher captinne,
  Mon cher, w'at shall I do?"
Den de captinne t'row de big ankerre,
  But still the scow she dreef,
De crew he can't pass on de shore,
  Becos' he los' hees skeef.

De night was dark lak wan black cat,
  De wave run high an' fas',
W'en de captinne tak de Rosie girl
  An' tie her to de mas'.
Den he also tak de life preserve
  An' jump off on de lak'
An' say, "Good-by, ma Rosie, dear,
  I go drown for your sak."

Nex' morning very early
  'Bout ha'f-pas' two—t'ree—four—
De captinne—scow—an' de poor Rosie
  Was corpses on de shore.
For de win' she blow lak hurricane;
  Bimeby she blow some more,
An' de scow bus' up on Lac St. Pierre
  Wan arpent from de shore.

Now, all good wood scow sailor man
  Tak' warning by dat storm
An' go an' marry some nice French girl
  An' leev on wan beeg farm.
De win' can blow lak' hurricane
  An s'pose she blow some more,
You can't get drown on Lac St. Pierre
  So long you stay on shore.

From "The Habitant," by permission of the publishers, G. P. Putnam's Sons, New York and London.

FATHER'S WAY

BY EUGENE FIELD

My father was no pessimist; he loved the things of earth,—
Its cheerfulness and sunshine, its music and its mirth.
He never sighed or moped around whenever things went wrong,—
I warrant me he'd mocked at fate with some defiant song;
But, being he warn't much on tune, when times looked sort o' blue,
He'd whistle softly to himself this only tune he knew,—

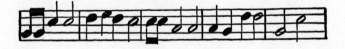

Now mother, when she heard that tune which father whistled so,
Would say, "There's something wrong to-day with Ephraim, I
    know;
He never tries to make believe he's happy that 'ere way
But that I'm certain as can be there's somethin' wrong to pay."
And so betimes, quite natural-like, to us observant youth
There seemed suggestion in that tune of deep, pathetic truth.

When Brother William joined the war, a lot of us went down
To see the gallant soldier boys right gayly out of town.
A-comin' home, poor mother cried as if her heart would break,
And all us children, too,—for *hers,* and *not* for *William's* sake!
But father, trudgin' on ahead, his hands behind him so,
Kept whistlin' to himself, so sort of solemn-like and low.

And when my oldest sister, Sue, was married and went West,
Seemed like it took the tuck right out of mother and the rest.
She was the sunlight in our home,—why, father used to say
It wouldn't seem like home at all if Sue should go away;
But when she went, a-leavin' us all sorrer and all tears,
Poor father whistled lonesome-like—and went to feed the steers.

When crops were bad, and other ills befell our homely lot,
He'd set of nights and try to act as if he minded not;
And when came death and bore away the one he worshiped so,
How vainly did his lips belie the heart benumbed with wo!
You see the telltale whistle told a mood he'd not admit,—
He'd always stopt his whistlin' when he thought we noticed it.

I'd like to see that stooping form and hoary head again,—
To see the honest, hearty smile that cheered his fellow men.
Oh, could I kiss the kindly lips that spake no creature wrong,
And share the rapture of the heart that overflowed with song!
Oh, could I hear the little tune he whistled long ago,
When he did battle with the griefs he would not have *us* know!

I AM CONTENT

TRANSLATED BY CARMEN SYLVA

A spindle of hazelwood had I;
Into the mill-stream it fell one day—
The water has brought it me back no more.

As he lay a-dying, the soldier spake:
          "I am content!
Let my mother be told in the village there,
   And my bride in the hut be told,
      That they must pray with folded hands,
         With folded hands for me."
The soldier is dead—and with folded hands,
      His bride and his mother pray.
On the field of battle they dug his grave,
And red with his life-blood the earth was dyed,
      The earth they laid him in.
The sun looked down on him there and spake:
          "I am content."

And flowers bloomed thickly upon his grave,
      And were glad they blossomed there.
And when the wind in the tree-tops roared,
The soldier asked from the deep, dark grave:
      "Did the banner flutter then?"
"Not so, my hero," the wind replied,
"The fight is done, but the banner won,
Thy comrades of old have borne it hence,
      Have borne it in triumph hence."
Then the soldier spake from the deep, dark grave:
          "I am content."

And again he hears the shepherds pass,
   And the flocks go wand'ring by,
And the soldier asked: "Is the sound I hear,
   The sound of the battle's roar?"
  And they replied: "My hero, nay!
  Thou art dead and the fight is o'er,
Our country joyful and free."
Then the soldier spake from the deep, dark grave:
     "I am content."

Then he heareth the lovers, laughing, pass,
   And the soldier asks once more:
"Are these not the voices of them that love,
   That love—and remember me?"
"Not so, my hero," the lovers say,
"We are those that remember not;
For the spring has come and the earth has smiled,
   And the dead must be forgot."
Then the soldier spake from the deep, dark grave:
     "I am content."

A spindle of hazelwood had I;
Into the mill-stream it fell one day—
The water has brought it me back no more.

THE EAGLE'S SONG

BY RICHARD MANSFIELD

The lioness whelped, and the sturdy cub
Was seized by an eagle and carried up
And homed for a while in an eagle's nest,
And slept for a while on an eagle's breast,
And the eagle taught it the eagle's song:
"To be staunch and valiant and free and strong!"

The lion whelp sprang from the eerie nest,
From the lofty crag where the queen birds rest;
He fought the king on the spreading plain,
And drove him back o'er the foaming main.

He held the land as a thrifty chief,
And reared his cattle and reaped his sheaf,
Nor sought the help of a foreign hand,
Yet welcomed all to his own free land!

Two were the sons that the country bore
To the Northern lakes and the Southern shore,
And Chivalry dwelt with the Southern son,
And Industry lived with the Northern one.
Tears for the time when they broke and fought!
Tears was the price of the union wrought!
And the land was red in a sea of blood,
Where brother for brother had swelled the flood!

And now that the two are one again,
Behold on their shield the word "Refrain!"
And the lion cubs twain sing the eagle's song,
"To be staunch and valiant and free and strong!"
For the eagle's beak and the lion's paw,
And the lion's fangs and the eagle's claw,
And the eagle's swoop and the lion's might,
And the lion's leap and the eagle's sight,
Shall guard the flag with the word "Refrain!"
Now that the two are one again!
Here's to a cheer for the Yankee ships!
And "Well done, Sam," from the mother's lips!

BREAK, BREAK, BREAK

BY ALFRED, LORD TENNYSON

Break, break, break,
  On thy cold gray stones, O sea!
And I would that my tongue could utter
  The thoughts that arise in me.

O well for the fisherman's boy,
  That he shouts with his sister at play!
O well for the sailor lad,
  That he sings in his boat on the bay!

And the stately ships go on
  To their haven under the hill;
But O for the touch of a vanish'd hand,
  And the sound of a voice that is still!

Break, break, break,
  At the foot of thy crags, O sea!
But the tender grace of a day that is dead
  Will never come back to me.

VIRGINIUS

BY MACAULAY

Straightway Virginius led the maid a little space aside,
To where the reeking shambles stood, piled up with horn and hide.
Hard by, a butcher on a block had laid his whittle down,—
Virginius caught the whittle up, and hid it in his gown.
And then his eyes grew very dim, and his throat began to swell,
And in a hoarse, changed voice he spake, "Farewell, sweet child,
    farewell!
The house that was the happiest within the Roman walls,—
The house that envied not the wealth of Capua's marble halls,
Now, for the brightness of thy smile, must have eternal gloom,
And for the music of thy voice, the silence of the tomb.

"The time is come. The tyrant points his eager hand this way;
See how his eyes gloat on thy grief, like a kite's upon the prey;
With all his wit he little deems that spurned, betrayed, bereft,
Thy father hath, in his despair, one fearful refuge left;
He little deems that, in my hand, I clutch what still can save
Thy gentle youth from taunts and blows, the portion of the slave;
Yea, and from nameless evil, that passeth taunt and blow,—
Foul outrage, which thou knowest not,—which thou shalt never
     know.
Then clasp me round the neck once more, and give me one more
     kiss;
And now, mine own dear little girl, there is no way but this!"
With that he lifted high the steel, and smote her in the side,
And in her blood she sank to earth, and with one sob she died.
Then, for a little moment, all the people held their breath;
And through the crowded forum was stillness as of death;
And in another moment broke forth from one and all
A cry as if the Volscians were coming o'er the wall;
Till, with white lips and bloodshot eyes, Virginius tottered nigh,
And stood before the judgment seat, and held the knife on high:
"O dwellers in the nether gloom, avengers of the slain,
By this dear blood I cry to you, do right between us twain;
And e'en as Appius Claudius has dealt by me and mine,
Deal you by Appius Claudius and all the Claudian line!"
So spake the slayer of his child; then where the body lay,
Pausing, he cast one haggard glance, and turned and went his way.
Then up sprang Appius Claudius: "Stop him, alive or dead!
Ten pounds of copper to the man who brings his head!"
He looked upon his clients, but none would work his will;
He looked upon his lictors, but they trembled and stood still.
And as Virginius through the press his way in silence cleft,
Ever the mighty multitude fell back to right and left;
And he hath passed in safety unto his woful home,
And there ta'en horse, to tell the camp what deeds are done in
     Rome.

THE WOMEN OF MUMBLES HEAD

BY CLEMENT SCOTT

Bring, novelist, your note-book! bring, dramatist, your pen!
And I'll tell you a simple story of what women do for men.
It's only a tale of a life-boat, of the dying and the dead,
Of the terrible storm and shipwreck that happened off Mumbles
Head!
Maybe you have traveled in Wales, sir, and know it north and
south;
Maybe you are friends with the "natives" that dwell at Oyster-
mouth;
It happens, no doubt, that from Bristol you've crossed in a casual
way,
And have sailed your yacht in the summer in the blue of Swansea
Bay.

Well! it isn't like that in the winter, when the lighthouse stands
alone,
In the teeth of Atlantic breakers that foam on its face of stone;
It wasn't like that when the hurricane blew, and the storm-bell
tolled, or when
There was news of a wreck, and the lifeboat launched, and a
desperate cry for men.
When in the world did the coxswain shirk? a brave old salt was
he!
Proud to the bone of as four strong lads as ever had tasted the
sea,
Welshmen all to the lungs and loins, who, about that coast, 'twas
said,
Had saved some hundred lives apiece—at a shilling or so a head!

So the father launched the life-boat, in the teeth of the tempest's
roar,
And he stood like a man at the rudder, with an eye on his boys
at the oar.
Out to the wreck went the father! out to the wreck went the sons!
Leaving the weeping women, and booming of signal guns;

Leaving the mother who loved them, and the girls that the sailors
love;
Going to death for duty, and trusting to God above!
Do you murmur a prayer, my brothers, when cozy and safe in
bed,
For men like these, who are ready to die for a wreck off Mumbles Head?

It didn't go well with the life-boat! 'twas a terrible storm that
blew!
And it snapped the rope in a second that was flung to the drown-
ing crew;
And then the anchor parted—'twas a tussle to keep afloat!
But the father stuck to the rudder, and the boys to the brave old
boat.
Then at last on the poor doomed life-boat a wave broke moun-
tains high!
"God help us now!" said the father. "It's over, my lads! Good-by!"
Half of the crew swam shoreward, half to the sheltered caves,
But the father and sons were fighting death in the foam of the
angry waves.

Up at the lighthouse window two women beheld the storm,
And saw in the boiling breakers a figure,—a fighting form;
It might be a gray-haired father, then the women held their
breath;
It might be a fair-haired brother, who was having a round with
death;
It might be a lover, a husband, whose kisses were on the lips
Of the women whose love is the life of men going down to the sea
in ships.
They had seen the launch of the life-boat, they had seen the worst,
and more,
Then, kissing each other, these women went down from the light-
house, straight to shore.

There by the rocks on the breakers these sisters, hand in hand,
Beheld once more that desperate man who struggled to reach the
land.

'Twas only aid he wanted to help him across the wave,
But what are a couple of women with only a man to save?
What are a couple of women? well, more than three craven men
Who stood by the shore with chattering teeth, refusing to stir—
    and then
Off went the women's shawls, sir; in a second they're torn and
    rent,
Then knotting them into a rope of love, straight into the sea they
    went!

"Come back!" cried the lighthouse-keeper. "For God's sake, girls,
    come back!"
As they caught the waves on their foreheads, resisting the fierce
    attack.
"Come back!" moaned the gray-haired mother, as she stood by the
    angry sea,
"If the waves take you, my darlings, there's nobody left to me!"
"Come back!" said the three strong soldiers, who still stood faint
    and pale,
"You will drown if you face the breakers! you will fall if you
    brave the gale!"
"*Come back?*" said the girls, "we will not! go tell it to all the
    town.
We'll lose our lives, God willing, before that man shall drown!"

"Give one more knot to the shawls, Bess! give one strong clutch
    of your hand!
Just follow me, brave, to the shingle, and we'll bring him safe
    to land!
Wait for the next wave, darling! only a minute more,
And I'll have him safe in my arms, dear, and we'll drag him to
    the shore."
Up to the arms in the water, fighting it breast to breast,
They caught and saved a brother alive. God bless them! you know
    the rest—
Well, many a heart beat stronger, and many a tear was shed,
And many a glass was tossed right off to "The Women of Mumbles
    Head!"

WILLIAM TELL AND HIS BOY

BY WILLIAM BAINE

"Place there the boy," the tyrant said;
"Fix me the apple on his head.
        Ha! rebel, now!
There's a fair mark for your shaft;
To yonder shining apple waft
An arrow."   And the tyrant laughed.
        With quivering brow.
Bold Tell looked there; his cheek turned pale;
His proud lips throbbed as if would fail
        Their quivering breath.
"Ha! doth he blanch?" fierce Gesler cried,
"I've conquered, slave, thy soul of pride."
No voice to that stern taunt replied,
        All mute as death.

"And what the meed?" at length Tell asked.
"Bold fool, when slaves like thee are tasked,
        It is my will.
But that thine eye may keener be,
And nerved to such nice archery,
If thou cleav'st yon, thou goest free.
        What! pause you still?
Give him a bow and arrow there
One shaft—but one." Gleams of despair
Rush for a moment o'er the Switzer's face:
Then passed away each stormy trace,
And high resolve came in their place,
        Unmoved, yet flushed,
"I take thy terms," he muttered low,
Grasped eagerly the proffered bow—
        The quiver searched,
Sought out an arrow keen and long,
Fit for a sinewy arm, and strong,
And placed it on the sounding thong
        The tough yew arched.

He drew the bow, whilst all around
That thronging crowd there was no sound,
  No step, no word, no breath.
All gazed with an unerring eye,
To see the fearful arrow fly;
The light wind dies into a sigh,
  And scarcely stirred.
Afar the boy stood, firm and mute;
He saw the strong bow curved to shoot,
  But never moved.
He knew the daring coolness of that hand
He knew it was a father scanned
  The boy he loved.

The Switzer gazed—the arrow hung
"My only boy!" sobbed on his tongue;
  He could not shoot.
"Ha!" cried the tyrant, "doth he quail?
Mark how his haughty brow grows pale!"
But a deep voice rung on the gale—
  "Shoot in God's name!"
Again the drooping shaft he took,
And turned to Heaven one burning look,
  Of all doubts reft.
"Be firm, my boy!" was all he said.
The apple's left the stripling's head.
  Ha! Ha! 'tis cleft!
And so it was, and Tell was free.
Quick the brave boy was at his knee
  With rosy cheek.

His loving arms his boy embrace;
But again that tyrant cried in haste,
"An arrow in thy belt is placed;
  What means it? Speak";
The Switzer raised his clenched hand high,
Whilst lightning flashed across his eye
  Incessantly.

"To smite thee, tyrant, to the heart,
Had Heaven willed it that my dart
    Had touched my boy."
"Rebellion! Treason! chain the slave!"
A hundred swords around him wave,
Whilst hate to Gesler's features gave
    Infuriate joy.

But that one arrow found its goal
Hid with revenge in Gesler's soul;
    And Lucerne's lake
Heard his dastard soul outmoan
When Freedom's call abroad was blown,
And Switzerland, a giant grown,
    Her fetters brake.
From hill to hill the mandate flew,
From lake to lake the tempest grew,
    With wakening swell,
Till proud oppression crouched for shame,
And Austria's haughtiness grew tame
And Freedom's watchword was the name of
    William Tell.

LASCA

BY F. DESPREZ

I want free life and I want fresh air;
And I sigh for the canter after the cattle,
The crack of the whips like shots in battle,
The mellay of horns, and hoofs, and heads
That wars, and wrangles, and scatters, and spreads;
The green beneath and the blue above,
And dash and danger and life and love.
And Lasca! Lasca used to ride
On a mouse-gray mustang, close to my side,
With blue *serape* and bright-belled spur;
I laughed with joy as I looked at her!

Little knew she of books or creeds;
An *Ave Maria* sufficed her needs;
Little she cared, save to be by my side,
To ride with me, and ever to ride,
From San Saba's shore to Lavaca's tide.
She was as bold as the billows that beat,
She was as wild as the breezes that blow;
From her little head to her little feet
She was swayed, in her suppleness, to and fro
By each gust of passion; a sapling pine,
That grows on the edge of a Kansas bluff,
And wars with the wind when the weather is rough,
Is like this Lasca, this love of mine.
She would hunger that I might eat,
Would take the bitter and leave me the sweet;
But once, when I made her jealous for fun,
At something I'd whispered, or looked, or done,
One Sunday, in San Antonio,
To a glorious girl on the Alamo,
She drew from her garter a dear little dagger,
And—sting of a wasp!—it made me stagger!
An inch to the left or an inch to the right,
And I shouldn't be maundering here to-night;
But she sobbed, and, sobbing, so swiftly bound
Her torn *reboso* about the wound
That I quite forgave her. Scratches don't count
    In Texas, down by the Rio Grande.

Her eye was brown,—a deep, deep brown;
Her hair was darker than her eye;
And something in her smile and frown,
Curled crimson lip, and instep high,
Showed that there ran in each blue vein,
Mixed with the milder Aztec strain,
The vigorous vintage of old Spain.
The air was heavy, the night was hot,
I sat by her side, and forgot—forgot;
Forgot the herd that were taking their rest;

Forgot that the air was close opprest,
That the Texas norther comes sudden and soon,
In the dead of night or the blaze of noon;
That once let the herd at its breath take fright,
That nothing on earth can stop the flight;
And wo to the rider, and wo to the steed,
Who falls in front of their mad stampede!
Was that thunder? No, by the Lord!
I spring to my saddle without a word.
One foot on mine, and she clung behind.
Away! on a hot chase down the wind!
But never was fox-hunt half so hard,
And never was steed so little spared.
For we rode for our lives. You shall hear how we fared
      In Texas, down by the Rio Grande.

The mustang flew, and we urged him on;
There was one chance left, and you have but one—
Halt, jump to the ground, and shoot your horse;
Crouch under his carcass, and take your chance;
And if the steers, in their frantic course,
Don't batter you both to pieces at once,
You may thank your star; if not, good-by
To the quickening kiss and the long-drawn sigh,
And the open air and the open sky,
      In Texas, down by the Rio Grande.

The cattle gained on just as I felt
For my old six-shooter, behind in my belt,
Down came the mustang, and down came we,
Clinging together, and—what was the rest?
A body that spread itself on my breast,
Two arms that shielded my dizzy head,
Two lips that hard on my lips were prest;
Then came thunder in my ears
As over us surged the sea of steers,
Blows that beat blood into my eyes,
And when I could rise
Lasca was dead!

I gouged out a grave a few feet deep,
And there in earth's arms I laid her to sleep;
And there she is lying, and no one knows,
And the summer shines and the winter snows;
For many a day the flowers have spread
A pall of petals over her head;
And the little gray hawk that hangs aloft in the air;
And the sly coyote trots here and there,
And the black snake glides, and glitters, and slides
Into the rift in a cotton-wood tree;
And the buzzard sails on,
And comes and is gone,
Stately and still like a ship at sea;
And I wonder why I do not care
For the things that are like the things that were.
Does half my heart lie buried there
    In Texas, down by the Rio Grande?

THE VOLUNTEER ORGANIST

BY S. W. FOSS

The gret big church wuz crowded full uv broadcloth an' uv silk,
An' satins rich as cream thet grows on our ol' brindle's milk;
Shined boots, biled shirts, stiff dickeys an' stovepipe hats were
    there,
An' doods 'ith trouserloons so tight they couldn't kneel down in
    prayer.

The elder in his poolpit high, said, as he slowly riz:
"Our organist is kep' to hum, laid up 'ith roomatiz,
An' as we hev no substitoot, as Brother Moore aint here,
Will some 'un in the congregation be so kind's to volunteer?"

An' then a red-nosed, drunken tramp, of low-toned, rowdy style,
Give an interductory hiccup, an' then staggered up the aisle.
Then through thet holy atmosphere there crep' a sense er sin,
An' through thet air of sanctity the odor uv old gin.

Then Deacon Purington he yelled, his teeth all set on edge:
"This man profanes the house of God! W'y this is sacrilege!"
The tramp didn't hear a word he said, but slouched 'ith stumblin'
    feet,
An' sprawled an' staggered up the steps, an' gained the organ
    seat.

He then went pawin' through the keys, an' soon there rose a strain
Thet seemed to jest bulge out the heart an' 'lectrify the brain;
An' then he slapped down on the thing 'ith hands an' head an'
    knees,
He slam-dashed his hull body down kerflop upon the keys.

The organ roared, the music flood went sweepin' high an' dry;
It swelled into the rafters an' bulged out into the sky,
The ol' church shook an' staggered an' seemed to reel an' sway,
An' the elder shouted "Glory!" an' I yelled out "Hooray!"

An then he tried a tender strain thet melted in our ears,
Thet brought up blessed memories and drenched 'em down 'ith
    tears;
An' we dreamed uv ol' time kitchens 'ith Tabby on the mat,
Uv home an' luv an' baby-days an' mother an' all that!

An' then he struck a streak uv hope—a song from souls forgiven—
Thet burst from prison-bars uv sin an' stormed the gates uv
    heaven;
The morning stars they sung together—no soul wuz left alone—
We felt the universe wuz safe an' God wuz on His throne!

An' then a wail uv deep despair an' darkness come again,
An' long, black crape hung on the doors uv all the homes uv men;
No luv, no light, no joy, no hope, no songs of glad delight,
An' then—the tramp, he staggered down an' reeled into the night!

But we knew he'd tol' his story, tho he never spoke a word,
An' it was the saddest story thet our ears had ever heard;
He hed tol' his own life history an' no eye was dry the day,
W'en the elder rose an' simply said: "My brethren, let us pray."

By permission of *The Blade*, Toledo, Ohio.

LIFE COMPARED TO A GAME OF CARDS

ANONYMOUS

Life is like a game of cards
  Which each one has to learn.
Each shuffles, cuts and deals a pack,
  And each a trump does turn.

Some turn a high card at the top,
  While others turn a low.
Some hold a hand quite flushed with trumps,
  While others none can show.

When hearts are trumps we play for love
  And pleasure decks the hour.
No thought of danger ever comes
  In roses' lovely bower.

When diamonds chance to turn the pack
  'Tis then men play for gold,
And heavy sums are won and lost
  By gamblers young and old.

When clubs are trumps beware of war
  On ocean and on land,
For fearful things have come to pass
  When clubs were in the hand.

But last of all is when the spade is turned by the hand of time,
And finishes up the game in every land and clime;
No matter how much a man may make or how much a man may
    save,
You'll find the spade turns up at last to dig each player's
    grave.

OLD DADDY TURNER

ANONYMOUS

This was the picture in front of "Old Daddy Turner's" cabin in the Kaintuck" quarter the other afternoon: Two colored men sitting on a wash-bench, silent and sorrowful; an old dog, sleeping in the sun at their feet, and a colored woman calling to a boy who was on the fence: "Now, Jeems Henry, you git right down from dat! Doan you know day Daddy Turner am jist on de p'int of dyin' and gwine up to hebben?"

Here was the picture inside: The poor old, white-headed man lying on his dying bed, flesh wasted away and strength departed. Near him sat his faithful old wife, rocking to and fro and moaning and grieving. Farther away was a colored man and woman, solemn-faced and sad-hearted, shaking their heads as they cast glances toward the bed. For a long time the old man lay quiet and speechless, but at length he signed to be propped up. A sun as warm as springtime poured into the room. He took notice of it, and a change came to his face as his eyes rested upon his grieving wife.

"Ize bin gwine back in my mind!" he whispered, as he reached out his thin hand for her to clasp. "Fur ober fo'ty y'ars we's trabbled 'long the same path. We sung de same songs—we prayed de same prayers—we had hold of han's when we 'listed in de Gospel ranks an' sot our faces to'rds de golden gates of hebben. Ole woman, Ize gwine to part wid you! Yes, Ize gwine ter leave yer all alone!"

"O Daddy! Daddy!" she wailed as she leaned over him.

"Doan't take on so, chile! It's de Lawd's doin's, not mine. To-morrow de sun may be as bright an' warm, but de ole man won't be heah. All de arternoon Ize had glimpses of a shady path leadin' down to de shor' of a big broad ribber. Ize seen people gwine down dar to cross ober, an' in a leetle time I'll be wid 'em."

She put her wrinkled face on the pillow beside his and sobbed, and he placed his hand on her head and said:

"It's de Lawd, chile—de bressed Lawd! Chile, Ize tried to be good to yer. You has been good to me. We am nuffin but

ole cull'd folk, po' in eberyting, but tryin' to do right by ebery-
body. When dey tole me I'd got to die, I wasn't sartin if de
Lawd wanted a po' ole black man like me up dar. Yes, chile, He
will! Dis mawnin' I heard de harps playin', de rustle of wings,
an' a cloud sorter lifted up an' I got a cl'ar view right frew
de pearly gates. I saw ole slaves an' nayburs dar, an' dey was
jist as white as anybody, an' a hundred han's beckoned me to
come right up dar 'mong 'em."

"O Daddy! I'll be all alone—all alone!" she wailed.

"Hush, chile! Ize gwine to be lookin' down on ye! Ize gwine
to put my han' on yer head an' kiss ye when yer heart am big
wid sorrow; an' when night shuts down an' you pray to de Lawd,
I'll be kneelin' long side of ye. Ye won't see me, but I'll be wid ye.
You's old an' gray. It won't be long before ye'll git de summons.
In a little time de cloud will lif' fur ye, an' I'll be right dar by
de pearly gates to take ye in my arms."

"But I can't let you go—I will hold you down heah wid me!"

"Chile! Ize sorry for ye, but Ize drawin' nigh dat shady path!
Hark! I kin h'ah de footsteps of de mighty parade of speerits
marchin' down to de 'broad ribber! Dey will dig a grave an' lay
my ole bones dar, an' in a week all de world but you will forgit
me. But doan' grieve, chile. De Lawd isn't gwine to shet de
gates on me 'cause I'm ole an' po' an' black. I kin see dem
shinin' way up dar—see our boy at the gate—h'ah de sweetest
music dat angels kin play!—Light de lamp, chile, 'cause de
night has come!"

"Oh! he's gwine—he's gwine!" she wailed, as her tears fell
upon his face.

"Chile! hold my han'! Ober heah am de path! I kin see men
an' women an' chil'en marchin' 'long! Furder down am de sunlight. It shines on de great ribber! Ober de ribber am—de—
gates—of——"

Of heaven! On earth, old and poor and low—beyond the gates,
an angel with the rest.

THE TRAMP

ANONYMOUS

Now, is that any way for to treat a poor man?
  I just asked for a penny or two;
Don't get your back up, and call me a "bum,"
  Because I have nothing to do.

Once I was strong and handsome,
  Had plenty of money and clothes:
That was afore I tippled,
  And whisky had painted my nose.

Down in the Lehigh Valley
  Me and my people grew.
Gentlemen, I was a farmer,
  And a very good farmer, too.

Me and my wife, and Nellie,—
  Nellie was just sixteen;
And she was the prettiest creature
  That ever that valley had seen.

Beaux? Why, she had a dozen;
  They come from near and fur:
But they was mostly farmers,
  And that didn't quite suit her.

But one of 'em was a New Yorker,
  Stylish and handsome and tall.
Hang him! If I had him I'd—
  Well, just let me catch him, that's all.

Well, he was the fellow for Nellie,—
  She didn't know no ill.
Her mother tried to prevent it;
  But you know a young girl's will.

Well, it's the same old story,
  Common enough, you'll say:
He was a smooth-tongued villain,
  And he got her to run away.

About a month or so after,
  We heard from the poor young thing:
He had gone away, and left her
  Without any wedding-ring.

Back to our home we brought her,—
  Back to her mother's side,
Filled with a raging fever;
  And she fell at our feet, and died.

Frantic with grief and sorrow,
  Her mother began to sink:
Dead! in less than a fortnight.
  That's when I took to drink.

And all I want is a penny or two,
  Just to help me on my way;
And I'll tramp till I find that hell-hound.
  If it takes till the judgment-day.

THE DANDY FIFTH

BY F. H. GASSAWAY

'Twas the time of the workingmen's great strike, when all the land
    stood still
At the sudden roar from the hungry mouths that labor could
    not fill;
When the thunder of the railroad ceased, and startled towns
    could spy
A hundred blazing factories painting each midnight sky;
Through Philadelphia's surging streets marched the brown ranks
    of toil,
The grimy legions of the shops, the tillers of the soil.

White-faced militiamen looked on, while women shrank with
    dread;
'Twas muscle against money then, 'twas riches against bread.
Once, as the mighty mob tramped on, a carriage stopt the way,
Upon the silken seat of which a young patrician lay;
And as, with haughty glance, he swept along the jeering crowd,
A white-haired blacksmith in the ranks took off his cap and bowed.
That night the Labor League was met, and soon the chairman said,
"There hides a Judas in our midst, one man who bows the head,
Who bends the coward's servile knee when capital rolls by."
"Down with him!" "Kill the traitor cur!" rang out the savage
    cry.
Up rose the blacksmith, then, and held erect his head of gray:
"I am no traitor, tho I bowed to a rich man's son to-day;
And, tho you kill me as I stand, as like you mean to do,—
I want to tell you a story short, and I ask you'll hear me through.
I was one of those who enlisted first, the old flag to defend;
With Pope and Halleck, with 'Mac' and Grant, I followed to the
    end.
'Twas somewhere down on the Rapidan, when the Union cause
    looked drear,
That a regiment of rich young bloods came down to us from here.
Their uniforms were by tailors cut; they brought hampers of good
    wine;
And every squad had a servant, too, to keep their boots in shine;
They'd naught to say to us dusty 'vets,' and, through the whole
    brigade
We called them the kid-gloved Dandy Fifth, when we passed
    them on parade.
Well, they were sent to hold a fort that Rebs tried hard to take,
'Twas the key of all our line, which naught while it held out
    could break.
But a fearful fight we lost just then, the reserve came up too
    late,
And on that fort, and the Dandy Fifth, hung the whole division's
    fate.
Three times we tried to take them aid, and each time back we fell,
Tho once we could hear the fort's far guns boom like a funeral
    knell;

Till at length Joe Hooker's corps came up, and then straight
    through we broke;
How we cheered as we saw those dandy coats still back of the
    drifting smoke!
With bands all front and our colors spread we swarmed up the
    parapet,
But the sight that silenced our welcome shout I shall never in
    life forget.
Four days before had their water gone,—they had dreaded that
    the most,—
The next, their last scant ration went, and each man looked a
    ghost
As he stood gaunt-eyed, behind his gun, like a crippled stag at
    bay,
And watched starvation, not defeat, draw nearer every day.
Of all the Fifth, not fourscore men could in their places stand,
And their white lips told a fearful tale, as we grasped each blood-
    less hand.
The rest in the stupor of famine lay, save here and there a few
In death sat rigid against the guns, grim sentinels in blue;
And their colonel could not speak or stir, but we saw his proud
    eye thrill
As he simply glanced to the shot-scarred staff where the old flag
    floated still!
Now, I hate the tyrants who grind us down, while the wolf snarls
    at our door,
And the men who've risen from us, to laugh at the misery of the
    poor;
But I tell you, mates, while this weak old hand I have left the
    strength to lift,
I will touch my cap to the proudest swell who fought in the
    Dandy Fifth!"

ON LINCOLN

BY WALT WHITMAN

O Captain! my Captain! our fearful trip is done;
The ship has weathered every rack, the prize we sought is won;
The port is near, the bells I hear, the people all exulting,
While follow eyes the steady keel, the vessel grim and daring;
But, O heart! heart! heart! O the bleeding drops of red,
Where on the deck my Captain lies, fallen, cold and dead.

O Captain! my Captain! rise up and hear the bells;
Rise up—for you the flag is flung—for you the bugle trills,
For you bouquets and ribbon'd wreaths—for you the shores a-
    crowding;
For you they call, the swaying mass, their eager faces turning;
Here Captain! dear father! this arm beneath your head!
It is some dream, that on the deck you've fallen cold and dead.

My Captain does not answer, his lips are pale and still;
My Captain does not feel my arm, he has no pulse nor will;
The ship is anchor'd safe and sound, its voyage is closed and done;
From fearful trip the victor ship comes in with object won;
Exult, O shores, and ring, O bells! but I with mournful tread
Walk the deck my Captain lies, fallen, cold and dead.

THE LITTLE STOWAWAY

ANONYMOUS

" 'Bout three years ago, afore I got this berth as I'm in now,
I was second engineer aboard a Liverpool steamer bound for New
York. There'd been a lot of extra cargo sent down just at the last
minute, and we'd no end of a job stowin' it away, and that ran
us late o' startin'; so that, altogether, you may think, the cap'n
warn't in the sweetest temper in the world, nor the mate neither.
On the mornin' of the third day out from Liverpool, the chief

engineer cum down to me in a precious hurry, and says he: 'Tom, what d'ye think? Blest if we ain't found a stowaway!'

"I didn't wait to hear no more, but up on deck like a sky-rocket; and there I did see a sight, and no mistake. Every man-Jack o' the crew, and what few passengers we had aboard, was all in a ring on the fo'c'stle, and in the middle was the fust mate, lookin' as black as thunder. Right in front of him, lookin' a reg'lar mite among them big fellers, was a little bit o' a lad not ten year old—ragged as a scarecrow, but with bright, curly hair, and a bonnie little face o' his own, if it hadn't been so woful and pale. The mate was a great, hulkin', black-bearded feller with a look that 'ud ha' frightened a horse, and a voice fit to make one jump through a keyhole; but the young un warn't a bit afeard—he stood straight up, and looked him full in the face with them bright, clear eyes o' his'n, for all the world as if he was Prince Halferd himself. You might ha' heerd a pin drop, as the mate spoke.

" 'Well, you young whelp,' says he, 'what's brought you here?'

" 'It was my stepfather as done it,' says the boy, in a weak little voice, but as steady as he could be. 'Father's dead, and mother's married again, and my new father says as how he won't have no brats about eatin' up his wages; and he stowed me away when nobody warn't lookin', and guv me some grub to keep me goin' for a day or two till I got to sea. He says I'm to go to A nt Jane, at Halifax; and here's her address.'

"We all believed every word on't, even without the paper he held out. But the mate says: 'Look here, my lad; that's all very fine, but it won't do here—some o' these men o' mine are in the secret, and I mean to have it out of 'em. Now, you just point out the man as stowed you away and fed you, this very minute; if you don't, it'll be worse for you!'

"The boy looked up in his bright, fearless way (it did my heart good to look at him, the brave little chap!) and says, quietly, 'I've told you the truth; I ain't got no more to say.'

"The mate says nothin', but looks at him for a minute as if he'd see clean through him; and then he sings out to the crew loud enough to raise the dead: 'Reeve a rope to the yard; smart now!'

" 'Now, my lad, you see that 'ere rope? Well, I'll give you ten minutes to confess; and if you don't tell the truth afore the time's up, I'll hang you like a dog!'

"The crew all stared at one another as if they couldn't believe their ears (I didn't believe mine, I can tell ye), and then a low growl went among 'em, like a wild beast awakin' out of a nap.

" 'Silence there!' shouts the mate, in a voice like the roar of a nor'easter. 'Stan' by to run for'ard!' as he held the noose ready to put it round the boy's neck. The little fellow never flinched a bit; but there was some among the sailors (big strong chaps as could ha' felled an ox) as shook like leaves in the wind. I clutched hold o' a handspike, and held it behind my back, all ready.

" 'Tom,' whispers the chief engineer to me, 'd'ye think he really means to do it?'

" 'I don't know,' says I, through my teeth; 'but if he does, he shall go first, if I swings for it!'

"I've been in many an ugly scrape in my time, but I never felt 'arf as bad as I did then. Every minute seemed as long as a dozen; and the tick o' the mate's watch, reg'lar, pricked my ears like a pin.

" 'Eight minutes,' says the mate, his great, deep voice breakin' in upon the silence like the toll o' a funeral bell. 'If you've got anything to confess, my lad, you'd best out with it, for ye're time's nearly up.'

" 'I've told you the truth,' answers the boy, very pale, but as firm as ever. 'May I say my prayers, please?'

"The mate nodded; and down goes the poor little chap on his knees and put up his poor little hands to pray. I couldn't make out what he said, but I'll be bound God heard every word. Then he ups on his feet again, and puts his hands behind him, and says to the mate quite quietly: 'I'm ready.'

"And then, sir, the mate's hard, grim face broke up all to once, like I've seed the ice in the Baltic. He snatched up the boy in his arms, kissed him, and burst out a-cryin' like a child; and I think there warn't one of us as didn't do the same. I know I did for one.

" 'God bless you, my boy!' says he, smoothin' the child's hair

with his great hard hand. 'You're a true Englishman, every inch
of you; you wouldn't tell a lie to save yer life! Well, if so be as
yer father's cast yer off, I'll be yer father from this day forth;
and if I ever forget you, then may God forget me!'

"And he kep' his word, too. When we got to Halifax, he
found out the little un's aunt, and gev' her a lump o' money to
make him comfortable; and now he goes to see the youngster
every voyage, as reg'lar as can be; and to see the pair on 'em
together—the little chap so fond of him, and not bearin' him
a bit o' grudge—it's 'bout as pretty a sight as ever I seed. And
now, sir, yer parding, it's time for me to be goin' below; so I'll
just wish yer good-night."

SAINT CRISPIAN'S DAY

BY SHAKESPEARE

King Henry. What's he that wishes so?
My cousin Westmoreland?—No, my fair cousin:
If we are marked to die, we are enough
To do our country loss; and if to live,
The fewer men the greater share of honor.
God's will! I pray thee, wish not one man more.
By Jove, I am not covetous for gold;
Nor care I who doth feed upon my cost;
It yers me not if men my garments wear;
Such outward things dwell not in my desires;
But if it be a sin to covet honor
I am the most offending soul alive.
No, 'faith, my coz, wish not a man from England:
God's peace! I would not lose so great an honor,
As one man more, methinks, would share from me,
For the best hope I have. O, do not wish one more.
Rather proclaim it, Westmoreland, through my host,
That he which hath no stomach to this fight,
Let him depart; his passport shall be made,
And crowns for convoy put into his purse:
We would not die in that man's company
That fears his fellowship to die with us.

This day is called—the feast of Crispian:
He that outlives this day, and comes safe home,
Will stand a tiptoe when this day is nam'd,
And rouse him at the name of Crispian.
He that shall live this day, and see old age,
Will yearly on the vigil feast his neighbors,
And say,—*"To-morrow is Saint Crispian"*:
Then will he strip his sleeve, and show his scars,
And say, *"These wounds I had on Crispian's day."*
Old men forget; yet all shall be forgot,
But he'll remember, with advantages,
What feats he did that day: then shall our names,
Familiar in their mouths as household words,—
Harry the king, Bedford and Exeter,
Warwick and Talbot, Salisbury and Gloster,—
Be in their flowing cups freshly remember'd:
This story shall the good man teach his son;
And *Crispin Crispian* shall ne'er go by,
From this day to the ending of the world,
But we in it shall be remember'd:
We few, we happy few, we band of brothers;
For he to-day that sheds his blood with me
Shall be my brother; be he ne'er so vile,
This day shall gentle his condition:
And gentlemen in England now a-bed,
Shall think themselves accurs'd they were not here;
And hold their manhoods cheap, whiles any speaks
That fought with us upon SAINT CRISPIAN'S DAY.

THE C'RRECT CARD

BY GEORGE R. SIMS

"C'rrect card, sir? C'rrect card, sir? What! you've seen my face before? Well I dare say as how you have, sir, and so have many more; but they passes me by without a word—but perhaps it's just as well; a poor crippled chap like me, sir, ain't fit company for a swell. But I've seen the time when they all was proud with me to be talking seen—when I rode for Lord Arthur

Forester, and wore the black and green. How did it happen? I'll tell you, sir. You knew little Fanny Flight—old Farmer Flight's one daughter—always so pretty and bright? You used to joke with her sometimes, sir, and say as, if you she'd marry, you'd set up a 'pub' together, an' pitch your folks to Old Harry. You was just down for the holidays, sir, from Oxford, where you were at school; but *you* only played at being in love, while I . . . . . . was a cursed fool! Well, there were lots of 'm after her, sir, what with her ways and face; but I was in earnest, you see, sir, and rode a waiting race. 'Twas one fine April morning, when she came out to see us train, and just as she stood with her little hand holding on by my horse's mane, I felt as how I could do it, and came with a rush, you see, an' I said to her—all of a tremble, sir,—'Fan, will you marry me?' And she blushed an' smiled, an' whinnied, and after a bit she agreed that as soon as I found the money to pay for our keep and feed, why we'd run in harness together. We'd ha' made a tidyish pair; for I weren't a bad looking colt at the time, and *she*—such a nice little mare! Such a mouth! such a forehead! such action! Ah, well, let 'em say what they may, that's the sort to make running with us, sir, —tho, hang it! they never can *stay*.

"Well, the time went on, and I rode my best, an' they called me a 'cuteish' chap, and Lord Arthur put me up to ride for the Leicestershire Handicap. Lord Arthur, he was a *gentleman*— never was stingy or mean—an' he said, 'I'll give you five hundred, my man, if you win with the black and green.' Well, the horse I rode was Rasper; perhaps you remember him?—Black all but one white foot, sir; *and* a temper!—he'd pull like sin. But jump like a bird if he had a mind—plenty of power and pace—and I knew he had it in him, and I swore I'd win the race. The night before the race came off I went down to Farmer Flight's—they'd got to expect me regular now on Tuesday and Friday nights— and I told her what Lord Arthur said, and how, if I chanced to win, we'd go into double harness on the strength of his lordship's tin. An' she put my colors in her hair, and her arms around my neck, and I felt . . . . . but, hang it! a chap's a fool as can't keep his feelings in check. But then, you sees, sir, I *was* a fool—a big one as ever was seen—but then I was only twenty

when I rode in the black and green. I got up early next morning, an' felt as light as a feather, and I went to start for the
stables; and mother she asked me whether I'd not take my flask
in my pocket, in case it might come in handy; but 'Mother,' I
says, 'when a chap's in love, he don't feel to want any brandy.'
And I thought, as I put on a new pair o' spurs, and a jacket
bran new and clean, that I'd give long odds that I'd pull it off
—ten to one on the black and green. Well, Lord Arthur gave
me my orders, and a leg up on to my horse, and I just had taken
my canter an' was coming back up the course, when who should
I spy but Fanny, in a stylish sort of a trap, talking away like
blazes to a dark, long-whiskered chap; but I hadn't time to think
of more, for we got the word to start, and Rasper gave a thunder-
ing tear that nearly pulled out my heart; an' then I pulled him
together, for mine was a waiting race, and I knew that what was to
win it was Rasper's pluck not pace. Well, I got round all right
the first time; the fences were easy enough—at least to a couple
like *we* were; the only one that was tough was a biggish hedge,
with a post and rails; but the taking-off was fair, and I shouldn't
call it a dangerous jump, as long as you took it with care. And
Rasper! that very morning I said to Lord Arthur, I said, 'I think
as that horse there could jump a *church*, if he took the thing
into his head'; an' that morning he went like a lady and looked as
bright as a bean, and I knew, if it only lasted, I'd win with the
black and green. I was riding Rasper easy, when, just as we
passed the stand, it struck me the carriage that Fanny was in
was somewhere upon my right hand; and I took a pull at Rasper,
and a glance toward that side, and I saw what made me forget
the race and forget the way to ride—only a kiss! An' what's a
kiss to the like of him and her? But I could not help letting
Rasper feel that I wore a long-necked spur; an' tho I set my
teeth to be cool and steadied him with the rein, I knew that the
devil in Rasper was up, and couldn't be laid again; an' the very
next fence, tho I kept him straight, and he went at it after the
rest, I could feel that he meant to do his worst, and I couldn't ride
my best. For, you know, when a man feels desperate-like, he's
no more head than a child, and it's all *up* with a jock, you see, if
he goes at his fences wild. Over the next fence—over the next—

till I thought, as my teeth I set, if I only could keep my head to my work, I might pull through with it yet; and I took a pull at Rasper, an' fell back a bit to the tail, for I'd never forget the one difficult spot—the hedge with the post and rail. How it all comes back! We're in the field—now for a rattling burst; for the race is half won by the horse and man that crosses that fence first. I run up to my horses and pass them—I've given Rasper his head; I can hear, some lengths behind me, the trampling and the tread; and now I send him at it firmly but not too fast— he stops—lays his ears back—REFUSES! *The devil's come out at last!* And I dig in the steel and let him feel the sting of stout whalebone, and I say, 'You shall do it, you devil! if I break your neck and my own.' And the brute gives a squeal, and rushes at the post and rail like mad—no time to rise him at it—not much use if I had; and then . . . well, I feel a crash and a blow, and hear a woman scream, and I seem to be dying by inches in a horrid sort of a dream.

"No, thank ye—I'd rather not, sir. You see they ain't all like you; these gents as has plenty of money don't care who they gives it to; but as for stopping an' saying a word, an' hearing a fellow's tale, they'd rather give him a crown, sir, or stand him a quart of ale. But it brings back old times to be talking to you. Ah! the jolly old times as I've seen, when I rode for Lord Arthur (c'rrect card, sir?) and wore the black and green!"

THE ENGINEER'S STORY

BY ROSA H. THORPE

No, children, my trips are over,
    The engineer needs rest;
My hand is shaky; I'm feeling
    A tugging pain i' my breast;
But here, as the twilight gathers,
    I'll tell you a tale of the road,
That'll ring in my head forever,
    Till it rests beneath the sod.

We were lumbering along in the twilight,
 The night was drooping her shade,
And the "Gladiator" labored,—
 Climbing the top of the grade;
The train was heavily laden,
 So I let my engine rest,
Climbing the grading slowly,
 Till we reached the upland's crest.

I held my watch to the lamplight,—
 Ten minutes behind the time!
Lost in the slackened motion
 Of the up-grade's heavy climb;
But I knew the miles of the prairie
 That stretched a level track,
So I touched the gauge of the boiler,
 And pulled the lever back.

Over the rails a-gleaming,
 Thirty an hour, or so,
The engine leaped like a demon,
 Breathing a fiery glow;
But to me—a-hold of the lever—
 It seemed a child alway,
Trustful and always ready
 My lightest touch to obey.

I was proud, you know, of my engine,
 Holding it steady that night,
And my eye on the track before us,
 Ablaze with the Drummond light.
We neared a well-known cabin,
 Where a child of three or four,
As the up train passed, oft called me,
 A-playing around the door.

My hand was firm on the throttle
  As we swept around the curve,
When something afar in the shadow
  Struck fire through every nerve.
I sounded the brakes, and crashing
  The reverse-lever down in dismay,
Groaning to heaven,—eighty paces
  Ahead was the child at its play!

One instant,—one, awful and only,
  The world flew round in my brain,
And I smote my hand hard on my forehead
  To keep back the terrible pain;
The train I thought flying forever,
  With mad, irresistible roll,
While the cries of the dying, the night-wind
  Swept into my shuddering soul.

Then I stood on the front of the engine—
  How I got there I never could tell—
My feet planted down on the crossbar,
  Where the cow-catcher slopes to the rail,
One hand firmly locked on the coupler,
  And one held out in the night,
While my eye gauged the distance, and measured
  The speed of our slackening flight.

My mind, thank the Lord! it was steady;
  I saw the curls of her hair,
And the face that, turning in wonder,
  Was lit by the deadly glare.
I know little more—but I heard it—
  The groan of the anguished wheels,
And remember thinking—the engine
  In agony trembles and reels.

One rod! To the day of my dying
   I shall think the old engine reared back,
And as it recoiled, with a shudder
   I swept my hand over the track;
Then darkness fell over my eyelids,
   But I heard the surge of the train,
And the poor old engine creaking,
   As racked by a deadly pain.

They found us, they said, on the gravel,
   My fingers enmeshed in her hair,
And she on my bosom a-climbing,
   To nestle securely there.
We are not much given to crying—
   We men that run on the road—
But that night, they said, there were faces
   With tears on them, lifted to God.

For years in the eve and the morning,
   As I neared the cabin again,
My hand on the lever prest downward
   And slackened the speed of the train.
When my engine had blown her a greeting,
   She always would come to the door;
And her look with a fulness of heaven
   Blesses me evermore.

THE FACE UPON THE FLOOR

BY H. ANTOINE D'ARCY

'Twas a balmy summer evening, and a goodly crowd was there,
Which well-nigh filled Joe's barroom on the corner of the square;
And as songs and witty stories came through the open door,
A vagabond crept slowly in and posed upon the floor.

"Where did it come from?" some one said. "The wind has
    blown it in."
"What does it want?" another cried. "Some whisky, rum or gin?"
"Here, Toby, seek him, if your stomach's equal to the work—
I wouldn't touch him with a fork, he's as filthy as a Turk."

This badinage the poor wretch took with stoical good grace;
In fact, he smiled as tho he thought he'd struck the proper place.
"Come, boys, I know there's kindly hearts among so good a
    crowd—
To be in such good company would make a deacon proud.

"Give me a drink—that's what I want—I'm out of funds, you
    know,
When I had the cash to treat the gang, this hand was never slow.
What? You laugh as tho you thought this pocket never held
    a sou,
I once was fixt as well, my boys, as any one of you.

"There, thanks; that's braced me nicely; God bless you one and
    all;
Next time I pass this good saloon, I'll make another call.
Give you a song? No, I can't do that, my singing days are past;
My voice is cracked, my throat's worn out, and my lungs are
    going fast.

"Say! give me another whisky, and I'll tell you what I'll do—
I'll tell you a funny story, and a fact, I promise, too.
That I was ever a decent man, not one of you would think;
But I was, some four or five years back. Say, give me another
    drink.

"Fill her up, Joe, I want to put some life into my frame—
Such little drinks, to a bum like me, are miserably tame;
Five fingers—there, that's the scheme—and corking whisky, too.
Well, here's luck, boys; and landlord, my best regards to you.

"You've treated me pretty kindly, and I'd like to tell you how
I came to be the dirty sot you see before you now.
As I told you, once I was a man, with muscle, frame and health,
And but for a blunder, ought to have made considerable wealth.

"I was a painter—not one that daubed on bricks and wood,
But an artist, and, for my age, was rated pretty good.
I worked hard at my canvas, and was bidding fair to rise,
For gradually I saw the star of fame before my eyes.

"I made a picture perhaps you've seen, 'tis called the 'Chase of
     Fame,'
It brought me fifteen hundred pounds, and added to my name.
And then I met a woman—now comes the funny part—
With eyes that petrified my brain, and sunk into my heart.

"Why don't you laugh? 'Tis funny that the vagabond you see
Could ever love a woman, and expect her love for me;
But 'twas so, and for a month or two her smiles were freely given,
And when her loving lips touched mine it carried me to heaven.

"Did you ever see a woman for whom your soul you'd give,
With a form like the Milo Venus, too beautiful to live;
With eyes that would beat the Koh-i-nor, and a wealth of chestnut
     hair?
If so, 'twas she, for there never was another half so fair.

"I was working on a portrait, one afternoon in May,
Of a fair-haired boy, a friend of mine, who lived across the way;
And Madeline admired it, and, much to my surprize,
Said that she'd like to know the man that had such dreamy eyes.

"It didn't take long to know him, and before a month had flown,
My friend had stolen my darling, and I was left alone;
And ere a year of misery had passed above my head,
The jewel I had treasured so had tarnished, and was dead.

"That's why I took to drink, boys. Why I never saw you smile,
I thought you'd be amused, and laughing all the while.
Why, what's the matter, friend? There's a tear-drop in your
    eye,
Come, laugh like me; 'tis only babes and women that cry.

"Say, boys, if you give me just another whisky, I'll be glad,
And I'll draw right here a picture of the face that drove me mad.
Give me that piece of chalk with which you mark the baseball
    score—
You shall see the lovely Madeline upon the barroom floor."

Another drink, and, with chalk in hand, the vagabond began
To sketch a face that well might buy the soul of any man.
Then as he placed another look upon the shapely head,
With a fearful shriek he leaped and fell across the picture dead.

THE FUNERAL OF THE FLOWERS

BY T. DE WITT TALMAGE

The summer is ended, and we have all been invited to attend
the Funeral of the Flowers. It occurred on a long slope which at
one side dipt into the warm valleys, and on the other side arose
very high into the frosty air, so that on one boundary line lived
cactus and orange-blossom and camellia, and on the other re-
sided balsam-pine and Alpine strawberry, and all kinds of growths
between.

Living midway that steep slope of land there was a rose, that
in common parlance we called "Giant of Battle." It was red and
fiery, looking as if it had stood on fields of carnage where the
blood dashed to the lip. It was a hero among flowers. Many of
the grasses of the field worshiped it as a god, the mignonette
burning incense beneath it, the marigold throwing glittering rays
of beauty before it, the mistletoe crawling at its feet. The fame

of this Giant of Battle was world-wide, and some said that its ancestors on the father's side had stood on the plains of Waterloo, and on its mother's side at Magneta, and drank themselves drunk on human gore. But children are not to blame for what their ancestors do, and this rose, called Giant of Battle, was universally adored.

But the Giant got sick. Whether it was from the poisonous breath of the Nightshade that had insolently kissed him, or from grief at the loss of a Damask-rose that had first won his heart by her blushes, and then died, we know not; but the Giant of Battle was passing rapidly away. There was great excitement up and down the slopes. A consultation of botanical physicians was called, and Doctor Eglantine came and thrust a thorn for a lancet into the Giant's veins, on the principle that he had too much blood and was apoplectic, and Doctor Balm of Gilead attempted to heal the pain by poultices; but still the Giant grew worse and worse. The Primrose called in the evening to see how the dying hero was, and the Morning-glory stopt before breakfast to see if it could do any good. Every flower or grass that called had a prescription for him that would surely cure. Neighbor Horse-sorrel suggested acids, and Honeysuckle proposed sugars, and Myrrh suggested bitters, and Ladies'-slipper, having taken off her shoes, said all the patient wanted was more quiet about the room.

But too much changing of medicine only made the Giant more and more sick, and one afternoon, while sitting up in bed with a cup of honeysuckle to his lips, and with the fan of the south wind fluttering in his face, his head dropt and he died. As the breath went out of him a Clematis that had been overlooking the sad scene, said: "What time is it?" and a cluster of Four-o'clocks answered, "A little past the middle of the afternoon."

The next morning the funeral bells all rang: the Blue-bells and the Canterbury-bells and the Fox-glove-bells and Hare-bells and all the flowerdom came to the obsequies of the Giant of Battle. He was laid out on a trellis, and on a catafalque, such as dead monarchs never had, of dahlia and phlox and magnolia and geranium and gladiola. There was a great audience of flowers. Solemnity came down upon them. Even the Cock's-comb stopt strutting, and Larkspur ceased her fickleness, and Snap-, dragon looked gentle, and Snowdrop seemed to melt, and Bachelor's-button wished it had some one to express its grief to. The Passion-flower came in and threw herself on the pale cheek of the Giant with most ardent demonstration of affection. Amaranth and Hydrangea and Daffodil and Spiderwort and Spiræa having come far from the night and dew, stood around with their eyes full of tears.

The funeral services began. Rose of Sharon and Lily of the Valley took part in them. The Star of Bethlehem sang a hymn to the tune of Bonny Doon. Forget-me-not said a few words of commemoration. Then Heartsease arose for the work of comfort, and read the lesson of the day: "As a flower of the field, so he flourisheth. For the wind passeth over it, and it is gone; and the place thereof shall know it no more." And all the bells, Fox-glove-bells and Blue-bells and Canterbury-bells and Hare-bells, prolonged the strain through all that day, tolling, tolling out, "No more! no more!"

CATO'S SOLILOQUY ON IMMORTALITY

BY JOSEPH ADDISON

It must be so: Plato, thou reasonest well!
Else, whence this pleasing hope, this fond desire,
This longing after immortality?
Or, whence this secret dread and inward horror
Of falling into naught? Why shrinks the soul
Back on herself and startles at destruction?
'Tis the divinity that stirs within us;
'Tis Heaven itself, that points out an hereafter
And intimates eternity to man.
Eternity! thou pleasing, dreadful thought!
Through what variety of untried being,
Through what new scenes and changes must we pass!
The wide, the unbounded prospect lies before me;
But shadows, clouds, and darkness rest upon it.

OPPORTUNITY

BY JOHN J. INGALLS

Master of human destinies am I
Fame, love and fortune, on my footsteps wait.
Cities and fields I walk, I penetrate
Deserts and seas remote—and passing by
Hovel and mart and palace, soon or late,
I knock unbidden once at every gate—
If sleeping, wake, if feasting, rise, before
I turn away. It is the hour of fate
And they who follow me, reach every state

Mortals desire, and conquer every foe
Save death: but those who doubt or hesitate
Condemned to failure, penury and wo,
Seek me in vain and uselessly implore;
I answer not and I return no more.

OPPORTUNITY'S REPLY

BY WALTER MALONE

They do me wrong who say I come no more,
   When once I knock and fail to find you in:
For every day I stand outside your door,
   And bid you wake and rise to fight and win.

Wail not for precious changes passed away;
   Weep not for golden ages on the wane;
Each night I burn the records of the day;
   At sunrise every soul is born again.

Laugh like a boy at splendors that have sped;
   To vanished joys be blind, and deaf and dumb;
My judgments seat the dead past with its dead,
   But never bind a moment yet to come.

THE ERL-KING

BY JOHANN WOLFGANG VON GOETHE

(Translated by Sir Walter Scott)

Oh, who rides by night thro' the woodland so wild?
It is the fond father embracing his child,
And close the boy nestles within his loved arm,
To hold himself fast, and to keep himself warm.

"O father, see yonder! see yonder!" he says;
"My boy, upon what dost thou fearfully gaze?"
"Oh, 'tis the Erl-king with his crown and his shroud."
"No, my son, it is but a dark wreath of the cloud."

"Oh, come and go with me, thou loveliest child;
By many a gay sport shall thy time be beguiled;
My mother keeps for thee full many a fair toy,
And many a fine flower shall she pluck for my boy."

"O father, my father, and did you not hear
The Erl-king whisper so low in my ear?"
"Be still, my heart's darling—my child, be at ease;
It was but the wild blast as it sung thro' the trees."

"Oh, wilt thou go with me, thou loveliest boy?
My daughter shall tend thee with care and with joy;
She shall bear thee so lightly thro' wet and thro' wild,
And press thee, and kiss thee, and sing to my child."

"O father, my father, and saw you not plain,
The Erl-king's pale daughter glide past thro' the rain?"
"Oh, yes, my loved treasure, I knew it full soon;
It was the gray willow that danced to the moon."

"Oh, come and go with me, no longer delay,
Or else, silly child, I will drag thee away."
"O father! O father! now, now keep your hold,
The Erl-king has seized me—his grasp is so cold!"

Sore trembled the father; he spurr'd thro' the wild,
Clasping close to his bosom his shuddering child.
He reaches his dwelling in doubt and in dread,
But, clasp'd to his bosom, the infant was dead!

CARCASSONNE

BY M. E. W. SHERWOOD

How old I am! I'm eighty years. I've worked both hard and
    long,
Yet patient as my life has been, one dearest sight I have not seen,
It almost seems a wrong. A dream I had when life was young.
Alas! our dreams, they come not true.
I thought to see fair Carcassonne,
That lovely city, Carcassonne.

One sees it dimly from the height beyond the mountain blue.
Fain would I walk five weary leagues, I do not mind the road's
    fatigues,
Thro' morn and evening's dew.
But bitter frosts would fall at night, and on the grapes that
    withered blight,
I could not go to Carcassonne,
I never went to Carcassonne.

They say it is as gay all times as holidays at home.
The gentles ride in gay attire, and in the sun each gilded spire
Shoots up like those at Rome.
The bishop the procession leads, the generals curb their prancing
    steeds.
Alas! I saw not Carcassonne.
Alas! I know not Carcassonne.

Our vicar's right. He preaches loud and bids us to beware.
He says, "Oh, guard the weakest part and most the traitor in the
    heart
Against ambition's snare."
Perhaps in autumn I can find two sunny days with gentle wind,
I then could go to Carcassonne,
I still could go to Carcassonne.

My God and Father, pardon me, if this my wish offends.
One sees some hope more high than he in age, as in his infancy
To which his heart ascends.
My wife, my son have seen Narbonne, my grandson went to
    Perpignan,
But I have not seen Carcassonne,
But I have not seen Carcassonne.

Thus sighed a peasant bent with age, half dreaming in his chair.
I said, "My friend, come, go with me to-morrow; thine eyes shall
    see those streets
That seem so fair."
That night there came for passing soul the church-bell's low and
    solemn toll.
He never saw gay Carcassonne.
Who has not known a Carcassonne?

THE MUSICIANS

ANONYMOUS

    The strings of my heart were strung by Pleasure,
      And I laughed when the music fell on my ear,
    For he and Mirth played a joyful measure,
      And they played so loud that I could not hear
    The wailing and mourning of souls a-weary,
      The strains of sorrow that sighed around;
    The notes of my heart sang blithe and cheery,
      And I heard no other sound.
    Mirth and Pleasure, the music brothers,
      Played louder and louder in joyful glee,

But sometimes a discord was heard by others
   Tho only the rhythm was heard by me.
Louder and louder and faster and faster,
   The hands of those brothers played strain on strain,
Till, all of a sudden a mighty master
   Swept them aside, and Pain,
Pain, the Musician, the soul refiner,
   Resting the strings of my quivering heart;
And the air that he played was a plaintive minor,
   So sad that the tear-drops were forced to start.
Each note was an echo of awful anguish,
   As shrill, as solemn, as sad as slow,
And my soul for a season seemed to languish
   And faint with its weight of wo.
With skilful hands that were never weary,
   This master of music played strain on strain;
And between the bars of the Miserere
   He drew up the strings of my heart again.
And I was filled with a vague, strange wonder
   To see that they did not break in two;
They are drawn so tight they will snap asunder
   I thought, but instead they grew
In the hands of the Master, firmer and stronger,
   And I could hear on the stilly air;
Now my ears were deafened by mirth no longer,
   The sounds of sorrow, and grief and despair.
And my soul grew tender and kind to others;
   My nature grew sweeter and my mind grew broad
And I held all men to be my brothers,
   Linked by the chastening rod,
My soul was lifted to God and heaven,
   And when on my heart-strings fell again
The hands of Mirth and Pleasure, even,
   There was no *discord* to mar the strain,
For Pain, the Musician, the soul refiner,
   Attuned the strings with a master hand,
And whether the music be major or minor,
   It is always *sweet* and grand.

ON THE RAPPAHANNOCK

ANONYMOUS

The sun had set, and in the distant west
The last red streaks had faded; night and rest
Fell on the earth; stilled was the cannon's roar;
And many a soldier slept to wake no more.
'Twas early spring—a calm and lovely night—
The moon had flooded all the earth with light.
On either side the Rappahannock lay
The armies; resting till the break of day
Should call them to renew the fight. So near
Together were the camps that each could hear
The other's sentry call. And now appear
The blazing bivouac fires on every hill,
And save the tramp of pickets all is still.
Between those silent hills in beauty flows
The Rappahannock. How its bosom glows!
How all its sparkling waves reflect the light
And add new glories to the starlit night!
But hark! From Northern hill there steal along
The strains of martial music mixed with song:
"Star Spangled Banner, may'st thou ever wave,
Over the land we shed our blood to save!"
And still they sing those words: "Our cause is just.
We'll triumph in the end; in God we trust;
Star Spangled Banner, wave, forever wave,
Over a land united, free and brave!"
Scarce had this died away when along
The river rose another glorious song:
A thousand lusty throats the chorus sing:
With "Rally Round the Flag," the hilltops ring.
And well they sang. Each heart was filled with joy.
From first in rank to little drummer-boy.
The loud huzzas and wildest cheers were given,
That seemed to cleave the air and reach to heaven.
The Union songs, the loud and heartfelt cheers
Fall in the Southern camp on listening ears.

While talking at their scanty evening meal
They pause and grasp their trusty blades of steel.
Fearless they stand and ready for the fray;
Such sounds can startle them, but not dismay.
Alas! Those strains of music which of yore
Could rouse their hearts are felt by them no more.
When the last echo of the song had died
And all was silent on the Northern side,
There came from Southern hill, with gentle swell,
The air of "Dixe," which was loved so well
By every man that wore the coat of gray,
And is revered and cherished to this day.
"In Dixie's Land" they swore to live and die,
That was their watchword, that their battle-cry.
Then rose on high the wild Confederate yell,
Resounding over every hill and dell.
Cheer after cheer went up that starry night
From men as brave as ever saw the light.
Now all is still. Each side has played its part.
How simple songs will fire a soldier's heart!
But hark! O'er Rappahannock's stream there floats
Another tune; but ah! how sweet the notes.
Not such as lash men's passions into foam,
But—richest gem of song—'tis "Home, Sweet Home!"
Played by the band, it reached the very soul,
And down the veteran's cheeks the tear-drops stole.
On either side the stream, from North and South,
Men who would march up to the cannon's mouth
Wept now like children. Tender hearts and true
Were beating 'neath those coats of gray and blue.
The sentry stopt and rested on his gun,
While back to home his thoughts unhindered run.
He thought of loving wife and children there
Deprived of husband's and of father's care.
And stripling lads, scarce strong enough to bear
The weight of saber or of knapsack, tried
To stop their tears with foolish, boyish pride.
They might as well have sought to stop the tide!

Through both those hostile camps the music stole
And stirred each soldier to his inmost soul.
From North and South, in sympathy, there rose
A shout tremendous; forgetting they were foes,
Both armies joined and shouted with one voice
That seemed to make the very heavens rejoice.

Sweet music's power! One chord doth make us wild.
But change the strain, we weep as little child.
Touch yet another, men charge the battery-gun,
And by those martial strains a victory's won!
But there's one strain that friends and foes will win,
One magic touch that makes the whole world kin:
No heart so cold, but will, tho far it roam,
Respond with tender thrill to "Home, Sweet Home!"

COMO

BY JOAQUIN MILLER

The red-clad fishers row and creep
Below the craigs, as half asleep,
Nor even make a single sound.
The walls are steep,
The waves are deep;
And if the dead man should be found
By these same fishers in their round,
Why, who shall say but he was drowned?

The lake lay bright, as bits of broken moon
Just newly set within the cloven earth;
The ripened fields drew round a golden girth
Far up the steppes, and glittered in the noon.
And when the sun fell down, from leafy shore
Fond lovers stole in pairs to ply the oar.
The stars, as large as lilies, flecked the blue;
From out the Alps the moon came wheeling through
The rocky pass the great Napoleon knew.

A gala night it was—the season's prime;
We rode from castled lake to festal town,
To fair Milan—my friend and I; rode down
By night, where grasses waved in rippled rhyme;
And so what theme but love in such a time?
His proud lip curved the while in silent scorn
At thought of love; and then, as one forlorn,
He sighed, then bared his temples, dashed with gray,
Then mocked, as one outworn and well blasé.

A gorgeous tiger-lily, flaming red,
So full of battle, of the trumpets blare,
Of old-time passion, upreared its head.
I galloped past, I leaned, I clutched it there.
From out the long, strong grass I held it high,
And cried, "Lo! this to-night shall deck her hair
Through all the dance. And mark! the man shall die
Who dares assault, for good or ill design,
The citadel where I shall set this sign."

He spoke no spare word all the after while.
That scornful, cold, contemptuous smile of his!
Why, better men have died for less than this.
Then in the hall the same old hateful smile!
Then marvel not that when she graced the floor,
With all the beauties gathered from the four
Far quarters of the world, and she, my fair,
The fairest, wore within her midnight hair
My tiger-lily—marvel not, I say,
That he glared like some wild beast well at bay!

Oh, she shone fairer than the summer star,
Or curled sweet moon in middle destiny.
More fair than sunrise climbing up the sea,
Where all the loves of Ariadne are.

Who loves, who truly loves, will stand aloof,
The noisy tongue makes most unholy proof
Of shallow waters—all the while afar
From out the dance I stood, and watched my star,
My tiger-lily, borne an oriflamme of war.

A thousand beauties flashed at love's advance,
Like bright white mice at moonlight in their play,
Or sunfish shooting in the shining bay,
The swift feet shot and glittered in the dance.
Oh, have you loved, and truly loved, and seen
Aught else the while than your own stately queen?
Her presence, it was majesty—so tall;
Her proud development encompassed—all.
She filled all space. I sought, I saw but her.
I followed as some fervid worshiper.

Adown the dance she moved with matchless pace.
The world—my world—moved with her. Suddenly
I questioned whom her cavalier might be.
'Twas he! His face was leaning to her face!
I clutched my blade; I sprang; I caught my breath,
And so stood leaning still as death.
And they stood still. She blushed, then reached and **tore**
The lily as she passed, and down the floor
She strewed its *heart* like bits of gushing gore.

'Twas he said heads, not hearts, were made to break.
He taught me this that night in splendid scorn.
I learned too well. The dance was done. Ere morn
We mounted—he and I—but no more spake.
And this for woman's love! My lily worn
In her dark hair in pride to be thus torn
And trampled on for this bold stranger's sake!
Two men rode silent back toward the lake.
Two men rode silent down, but only *one*
Rode *up* at *morn* to greet the *rising sun*.

The walls are steep,
The waves are deep;
And if the dead man should be found
By red-clad fishers in their round,
Why, who shall say but he was—drowned?

AUX ITALIENS

BY OWEN MEREDITH

At Paris it was, at the Opera there;
　And she looked like a queen in a book, that night,
With the wreath of pearl in her raven hair,
　And the brooch on her breast, so bright.

Of all the operas that Verdi wrote,
　The best, to my taste, is the Trovatore;
And Mario can soothe with a tenor note
　The souls in purgatory.

The moon on the tower slept soft as snow;
　And who was not thrilled in the strangest way,
As we heard him sing, while the gas burned low,
　"Non ti scordar di me?"

The emperor there, in his box of state,
　Looked grave, as if he had just then seen
The red flag wave from the city-gate,
　Where his eagles in bronze had been.

The empress, too, had a tear in her eye.
　You'd have said that her fancy had gone back again,
For one moment, under the old blue sky,
　To the old glad life in Spain.

Well! there in our front-row box we sat
  Together, my bride-betrothed and I;
My gaze was fixt on my opera-hat,
  And hers on the stage hard by.

And both were silent, and both were sad.
  Like a queen, she leaned on her full white arm,
With that regal, indolent air she had;
  So confident of her charm!

I have not a doubt she was thinking then
  Of her former lord, good soul that he was!
Who died the richest and roundest of men,
  The Marquis of Carabas.

I hope that, to get to the kingdom of heaven,
  Through a needle's eye he had not yet to pass;
I wish him well for the jointure given
  To my lady of Carabas.

Meanwhile I was thinking of my first love,
  As I had not been thinking of aught for years,
Till over my eyes there began to move
  Something that felt like tears.

I thought of the dress that she wore last time,
  When we stood, 'neath the cypress-trees, together,
In that lost land, in that soft clime,
  In the crimson evening weather;

Of that muslin dress (for the eve was hot),
  And her warm, white neck in its golden chain.
And her full, soft hair, just tied in a knot,
  And falling loose again;

And the jasmine-flower in her fair, young breast;
   Oh, the faint, sweet smell of that jasmine-flower,
And the one bird singing alone to his nest,
   And the one star over the tower.

I thought of our little quarrels and strife,
   And the letter that brought me back my ring,
And it all seemed then, in the waste of life,
   Such a very little thing!

For I thought of her grave below the hill,
   Which the sentinel cypress-tree stands over.
And I thought . . . . "were she only living still,
   How I could forgive her and love her."

And I swear, as I thought thus, in that hour,
   And of how, after all, old things were best,
That I smelt the smell of that jasmine-flower,
   Which she used to wear in her breast.

It smelt so faint, and it smelt so sweet,
   It made me creep, and it made me cold!
Like the scent that steals from the crumbling sheet
   When a mummy is half unrolled.

And I turned and looked. She was sitting there
   In a dim box, over the stage; and drest
In that muslin dress, with that full soft hair,
   And that jasmine in her breast!

I was here, and she was there,
   And the glittering horseshoe curved between—
From my bride-betrothed, with her raven hair,
   And her sumptuous, scornful mien.

To my early love, with her eyes downcast,
   And over her primrose face the shade
(In short, from the Future back to the Past),
   There was but one step to be made.

To my early love from my future bride
   One moment I looked. Then I stole to the door,
I traversed the passage; and down at her side
   I was sitting, a moment more.

My thinking of her, or the music's strain,
   Or something which never will be exprest,
Had brought her back from the grave again,
   With the jasmine in her breast.

She is not dead, and she is not wed!
   But she loves me now, and she loved me then!
And the very first word that her sweet lips said,
   My heart grew youthful again.   .

The marchioness there, of Carabas,
   She is wealthy, and young, and handsome still,
And but for her . . . . . well, we'll let that pass—
   She may marry whomever she will.

But I will marry my own first love,
   With her primrose face; for old things are best,
And the flower in her bosom, I prize it above
   The brooch in my lady's breast.

The world is filled with folly and sin,
   And Love must cling where it can, I say;
For Beauty is easy enough to win,
   But one isn't loved every day.

And I think, in the lives of most women and men,
  There's a moment when all would go smooth and even,
If only the dead could find out when
  To come back and be forgiven.

But oh, the smell of that jasmine-flower!
  And oh, that music! and oh, the way
That voice rang out from the donjon tower,
  Non ti scordar di me, non ti scordar di me!

INDEX

INDEX

329

CPSIA information can be obtained at www.ICGtesting.com
Printed in the USA
BVOW07*1752200115

384089BV00006B/53/P